One Fairy Story too Many

One Fairy Story too Many

The Brothers Grimm and Their Tales

John M. Ellis

The University of Chicago Press

Chicago and London

The University of Chicago Press, Chicago 60637
The University of Chicago Press, Ltd., London

Library of Congress Cataloging in Publication Data

Ellis, John M. (John Martin)
  One fairy story too many.

  Bibliography: p.
  Includes index.
  1. Kinder- und Hausmärchen. 2. Grimm, Jacob,
1785–1863—Criticism and interpretation. 3. Grimm,
Wilhelm, 1786–1859—Criticism and interpretation.
I. Title.
PT921.E44 1983   398.2'1'0943   83-1193
ISBN 0-226-20546-0

John M. Ellis is professor of German and dean of
the Graduate Division at the University of California, Santa Cruz. His previous books include *Kleist's
"Prinz Friedrich von Homburg": A Critical Study*
(1970); *The Theory of Literary Criticism: A Logical
Analysis* (1974); *Narration in the German Novelle: Theory and Interpretation* (1974); and *Heinrich von Kleist*
(1978).

Contents

Preface

This book examines the question of what the Grimms' fairy tales really are. The subject is one which has long been, and still remains, in a state of confusion, although virtually all of the evidence necessary for a judgment has been available in published form for a long time—much of it for over half a century. Just how confused opinion remains on the matter can be seen from a remarkable fact: in the last decade, a good deal of the evidence was republished, mostly for the third or fourth time; and because that evidence so obviously conflicted with prevalent opinion, it was welcomed in many quarters as a series of startling new discoveries! Yet there has been no new factual revelation of any real consequence since 1955. What the present situation needs is not new discoveries but a reinterpretation of the entire record of published information of various kinds. The view of the status of the tales which emerged in the nineteenth century was natural enough, given the information available then. But a series of remarkable pieces of information which came to light early in this century were myopically assimilated to that earlier view instead of being allowed to challenge it, and it was therefore not surprising that the recent republication of this material caused such surprise. That the Grimms had not been *completely* justified in their original claims to have faithfully reproduced in their printed text the voice of the German folk story-teller has, therefore, long been obvious; but the degree to which this claim departed from the facts has always been obfuscated by special pleading on the Grimms' behalf.

This study, then, is a work of reinterpretation. Its purpose is to bring together and analyze all of the known evidence and to suggest that it leads to an inescapable conclusion—that the Grimms deliberately, persistently, and completely misrepresented the status of their tales: they made claims for them which they knew to be quite false. Chapter 1 sets out the dimensions of the problem of the tales' status and the historical context of that problem. The second chapter shows how several kinds of misconceptions about the status of the tales originated, and how they developed. Chapter 3 looks at the identities of the individuals who provided texts for the Grimms, and the very strange discrepancies here between the facts, on the one hand, and how they were characterized by the Grimms, on the other. Chapter 4 examines the Grimms' treatment of their sources in preparing the printed text of the first edition of the tales, and contrasts the evidence once more with their own account of what they did. The fifth chapter examines the further activities of the brothers in the preparation of the later editions of the tales, and the sixth contrasts the Grimms' procedures and claims—unfavorably—with those of James Macpherson in the famous Ossian "forgery," in order to form a judgment adequate to the historical context in which the brothers worked. The Conclusion takes a brief look at the strange way in which the Grimms' deceptive statements about the status of the tales have managed and still manage to survive the appearance of evidence which plainly contradicts them. There follow the original texts of three tales (*Frog King; Sleeping Beauty; Hansel and Gretel*) in several different versions—the original manuscript material that the Grimms reworked for their first printed edition, the first edition itself, and versions from two of the six subsequent editions. In order to make this study completely accessible to the English-speaking reader, I have provided English translations of these texts immediately following the German originals. When citing parts of the German originals of these and other stories and statements by the Grimms in the main body of my text, I have also provided a translation immediately following the quotation. Quotation of German scholarship on the Grimms, however, is given in English translation only. In all cases, the translations are my own. It should be noted that these translations are *not* intended for a general use as smooth, idiomatic English versions of the respective tales; they are offered only in relation to the purpose and argument of this book. Since my argument is concerned above all with the Grimms' extensive changes in the texture, tone, and subject matter of their source material, I have tried to make the translated material as faithful as possible to the German texts. The translations incline therefore more to literal readings than would be desirable for other purposes, and are often influenced by the need to bring out in English the difference between successive versions of the same passage. I have also tried to retain qualities such as clumsiness or infelicity when that existed in the German original, instead of resorting to obviously smoother English phraseology. I have, however, violated this principle in one circumstance: in referring to the titles of the Grimms' tales, I have, again for the sake of the English reader's comprehension, used the well-known English titles even when these are far from literal translations; *Dornröschen*, for example, is given in its familiar English title *Sleeping Beauty* rather than *Little Thorn-Rose*.

I must acknowledge various kinds of help in writing this book: first, that of Kenneth Northcott of the University of Chicago, who read the manuscript at an early stage, and made a number of excellent suggestions for its improvement. Siegfried Puknat, Richard Samuel, George Metcalf, and Loisa Nygaard also provided many helpful suggestions. John Kidd carried much of the burden of collating material from the seven different editions, with admirable accuracy; and Joan Hodgson of the University of California, Santa Cruz, library responded cheerfully to my innumerable requests for material that was difficult to find. But most of all, I am indebted to my former student, Cynthia Frank, whose curiosity and enthusiasm first impelled me to look deeper into what seemed a puzzling situation, and who herself noticed some of the oddities that did not seem satisfactorily accounted for in the explanations current in previous scholarship.

1

Introduction:
The Problem of the
Status of the Tales

The Grimms' fairy tales—*Kinder- und Hausmärchen* (*KHM*) constitute one of the best-known and most loved books in the world; translated into dozens of languages, they are read by children and adults everywhere.[1] There are perhaps two different kinds of contexts within which they are read and enjoyed: the first, that of world children's literature, the second that of the folklore and folk literature of Germany in particular and Europe in general. In both contexts, they are thought of as stories told by the simpler German people to their children, and passed on from one generation to the next in this way until recorded for all time by the brothers Grimm. But this widespread view, common to laymen and scholars alike, is in fact based on serious misconceptions, and in this book I want to set out a very different view of the status of the tales.

The first step in this reexamination of the status of the *KHM* must be to turn our attention away from the familiar kinds of present-day context in which we think of them—those of children's books, and German folklore—and back to the context in which they arose, the cultural scene of early nineteenth-century Germany; for the stresses and strains of that original context produced distortions and misconceptions that have been at work ever since.

The first volume of the *KHM* appeared in 1812, in an era extraordinarily rich in the great names of German literature and

1

of German culture generally. The age of German romanticism
had followed so quickly on the heels of German classicism that
the two had overlapped in large measure; in 1812 writers alive
and active included Goethe, Hölderlin, Tieck, Hoffmann, Brentano, Arnim, Eichendorff, the Schlegel brothers, and the Grimms;
Kleist had died only the previous year, Schiller, Novalis, and
Herder a few years previously. Similarly, German philosophy
and music were both at a peak. But this cultural brilliance was
a very recent phenomenon, and in fact the result of a drastic
transformation; only a few decades before, Germany had been
suffering from a cultural poverty which was just as remarkable
as the soon-to-follow richness. So sudden a transformation inevitably brought strains and distortions, and those strains are
very much involved in the outlook of the Grimms and therefore
in the origins of the *KHM*.

Once before, around the year 1200, Germany had had a glorious period when half a dozen of the greatest figures in the
history of German literature were active. But as those great writers died off, a long period of relative cultural poverty set in
which lasted for many centuries; between the years 1200 and 1800
there is scarcely a writer who can stand with even the second
rank of those who were active in these two great eras. While
France, England, and Italy had long since developed brilliant
literatures, the German renaissance had been almost barren. It
is impossible completely to account for this strange phenomenon, but several historical circumstances clearly contributed to
it. To begin with, Germany was unified very late in comparison
to the other great European powers; until late in the nineteenth
century, it remained a hodgepodge of small independent states.
It lacked (and still lacks to this day) a single, dominant cultural
center of the magnitude of Paris or London. Another important
factor was linguistic: no standard language emerged until the
end of the Middle Ages, and so for a long time there was no
linguistic vehicle for the formation of a national literature. In
fact, there was no single dialect with an unbroken literary tradition of any real length; in Old High German times, the leading
literary dialect had been the dialect of the west central area close
to the Rhine, but in the High Middle Ages (circa 1200) preeminence passed to the Upper German dialects of the south, and
in the modern period leadership passed again to the east central
district of Saxony, as a compromise standard language based on

the dialect of that area slowly took hold. In each case, the tradition of former literary dialects was interrupted, and they were relegated to merely regional status. A third major factor was the repeated devastation of Germany during the Thirty Years' War (1618–48)—a crucial period in the development of modern Europe, during which cultural progress in Germany was held up. Almost every European power took part in the Thirty Years' War, but it was fought largely on German soil. The line of battle went up and down Germany and then back again, so that the same area was devastated again and again at intervals of a few years, as one side advanced and then retreated over it. These three decades might have been Germany's renaissance.

Whatever the reasons, however, Germany in the mid-eighteenth century was culturally backward compared to its neighbors, and consequently afflicted by a national cultural inferiority complex—a circumstance that was to shape and to some extent misshape the character of the great revival soon to come. Germany at this time looked enviously at the culture of its neighbors; even so great a German patriot and national hero as Frederick the Great, king of Prussia, despised the German language, spoke and wrote in French, and was so convinced of the great superiority of French literature and culture generally that even when Mozart and Goethe arrived on the scene, he thought little of them.

As the astonishing transformation began to take place between 1770 and 1780, with the appearance of Lessing, Herder, Goethe, Schiller, Haydn, Mozart, and Kant, to be followed by many more great figures in the next few decades, two paths seemed possible for German culture, and from the start there was ambivalence about the choice. The first was to look to European culture: to look, to learn, to some extent to emulate and to borrow, to come up to its standards, and in general to aim to become a worthy member of the family of European cultures. This became the predominant way of the great writers of German classicism. But there was another possibility: to stress the uniqueness of German culture, its specifically German character with its own laws and rules, its own standards and goals.

At the beginning, the resurgence of German culture had seemed to take the second path. The writers of the *Sturm und Drang* ("Storm and Stress") group, which included Herder and the young Goethe, firmly rejected the rather feeble neoclassicism which had prevailed in early eighteenth-century Germany and had advocated a literature based on Aristotle's theories as interpreted by the classic French writers. Instead, the Sturm und Drang took the position that Germany's art should be a reflection of its own culture, and express its own genius in its own unique way. Transcultural standards could not be used to judge any one culture's products; what was really important was the relationship of the whole people to those products. Such was the tenor of the 1773 manifesto of the movement, *Blätter von deutscher Art und Kunst* ("On the German way of life and German art"), to which Goethe contributed an essay on German architecture (praising the Gothic rather than classical style); Justus Möser one on German history, much concerned to argue for Germany as a nation, in spite of its weak and utterly fragmented state in 1773; and Herder essays on Shakespeare—whom he praised as an original and unique genius who broke all the narrow rules of neoclassicism (particularly French neoclassicism)—and on folk poetry, particularly Ossian as an expression of the spirit of an ancient people through its primitive poetry. In this last, it is already possible to see the setting emerge for the later activities of the brothers Grimm.

Yet the Sturm und Drang was soon over; Goethe and Schiller became the leading figures of German classicism, and the emphasis shifted to a broader concern with mankind and literature in general, rather than the narrower preoccupation with the characteristic quality of German culture. By 1795, it might have seemed that the Sturm und Drang had been largely an expression of the national cultural inferiority complex, and that a more mature and confident culture no longer needed to be so concerned to make a case for itself. But just as Germany seemed firmly to have chosen the one path over the other, there came a sudden reversal of direction: in the middle of the last decade of the century, the German romantics appeared on the scene, and the strong nationalism that predominated in this movement made that of the Sturm und Drang seem moderate by comparison. The earlier group was evidently arguing from a position of weakness the case for a culture that was then undeveloped; but the romantics appeared in the middle of a brilliant cultural scene, and their patriotism could hardly be so nervous in character. It was generally quite the reverse—exuberant and confident. To take one example: Möser's essay on German history had been a rational plea for Germany as a nation; but when the romantic Friedrich von Hardenberg wrote (under the pseudonym of Novalis) *his* essay on the history of Germany, *Die Christenheit oder Europa* ("Christendom, or Europe"), it expressed an almost mystic view of the medieval German nation of the Holy Roman Empire as a Christian utopia. Möser and his contemporaries were struggling to put a depressed Germany on the European map; but for Novalis, Germany dominated the European map. With the romantics came a sudden, heady sense of the brilliance of German culture; a nation which had been a poor relation in Europe suddenly reveled not in equality but in preeminence.

Enormously influential and long-lasting attitudes and directions in German culture and scholarship were formed at this time: many of these dominated the nineteenth century and reached into the twentieth. From this period dates the notion that Germany is *the* nation of music. Similarly, the common idea of Germany as the preeminent nation in philosophy arises from the domination of Europe by the philosophy of Hegel until the rise of the analytic movement in the twentieth century. German philological scholarship, initiated at this time, dominated European thinking on the study of language until structuralism began to make an impact toward the middle of the twentieth century. Indeed, German scholars like Jacob Grimm were the founders of the discipline of philology.

The romantics' concern with German culture led in many directions: to an interest in folksongs; to the study of Germanic legends and folklore; to a rediscovery of the national past, including particularly the glorious national literature of the Middle Ages; to the study of the national language and its place in the European family of languages; and so on. But in all of this, German nationalism was a major factor.

Jacob Grimm (1785–1863) and his brother Wilhelm (1786–1859) were very much part of this environment. Enormously active and productive scholars, they made many contributions to the study of German culture apart from their fairy tale collection: notably, a collection of German legends, their famous dictionary of the German language, and Jacob's historical work on the German language. "Grimm's law" is still a landmark in the explanation of how an Indo-European dialect developed into the Germanic group of languages. And all of this was done quite consciously in a spirit of devotion to their fatherland, as countless passages in the brothers' letters make clear.

Such, then, is the general cultural context in which the Grimms' *Kinder- und Hausmärchen* arose. Jacob and Wilhelm presented the *KHM* to their public essentially as a monument of national folklore. In so doing they were making claims about their sources and their treatment of those sources (a reasonably faithful recording of folk material, with little or no editorial contribution on their part) which, as we shall see in later chapters, were fraudulent. But this was not mere idiosyncratic behavior; there were strong contemporary currents moving the Grimms in this direction, and those currents are the ultimate source of the half-truths and untruths which have accompanied the *KHM* from that day to this. Having said this, however, I must add an important caveat: the mood of the times did not determine this situation to the extent that the Grimms innocently followed contemporary ideas without realizing they were themselves distorting the truth; it will become clear that they consciously and deliberately misrepresented what they had done, and deceived their public.

Before it is possible to appreciate what the Grimms really did in publishing their *KHM,* we must first consider what at the time they seemed to be doing, and what since that time they have generally been thought to have done; from this, the central issues and principles involved in the appearance of the *KHM* will emerge.

At the time of the first publication of the *KHM,* the Grimms appeared to be breaking new ground, and that impression has always remained, regardless of changes of emphasis caused by any of the evidence which appeared later on.

Johann Karl August Musäus had published *Volksmärchen der Deutschen* ("Popular fairy tales of the Germans," 1782–87) some thirty years before the brothers Grimm published their fairy tales (1812–15), but a crucial difference between the two seemed immediately visible; while Musäus's tales are simply announced as being by Musäus, the Grimms offered theirs as *Kinder- und Hausmärchen, Gesammelt durch die Brüder Grimm* ("Children's and household fairytales, collected by the Brothers Grimm"). Musäus wrote his tales, but the Grimms apparently collected theirs.

Herder's essay *Ossian und die Lieder alter Völker* ("Ossian and the songs of ancient peoples," 1773)[2] had led the way toward an interest in folk culture in Germany, and in the following decades there was much collecting of folk material: folksongs, legends, folktales, and fairy tales. But while Herder began this movement, its manifestations were not always in the spirit he had intended. His interest was in the direct and natural expression of folk literature as an antidote to the pedantry of neoclassicism, and he therefore valued its unschooled quality and its direct and unreflective language as a vehicle of genuine feeling.

The contrast between the Grimms and Musäus appeared to exemplify a deep difference between those who preserved Herder's attitude to the integrity of the folk material, and those who simply wished to use it for their own purposes. Musäus considered the tales which formed the basis for his text as mere raw material, which had to be reworked by the artist before it achieved real value. In his prefatory essay, he appeals to his reader to decide whether he, Musäus, has been successful in creating from this raw material a real work of art: "whether, then, the author in reworking this raw material has succeeded as his neighbor the sculptor does, who with skillful hand produces, from a clumsy marble cube through the work of his hammer and chisel, now a god, now a demigod or spirit, which sits resplendently in the art galleries, while previously it was only a common piece of masonry."[3] Evidently, Musäus lacked that respect for the inherent eloquence of folk material which made Herder write that "unspoiled children, women, people of good common sense, formed more by activity than by abstract philosophizing—these are, if what I was talking of is eloquence, in that case the sole and best orators of our time."[4] Musäus's use of words like "common" or "clumsy" to refer to folk material would have been unthinkable for Herder.

Achim von Arnim and Clemens Brentano published a folksong collection—*Des Knaben Wunderhorn* ("The boy's magic horn," 1805–8)—and Brentano by himself some volumes of *Märchen,* but their attitudes were much closer to those of Musäus than of Herder. "The credentials of folk-poetry as a source of new poetic vigour lay in its authenticity," writes a recent scholar, "yet Arnim and Brentano freely adapted, polished, archaized, rewrote, and even slipped in poems of their own with faked 'sources' (all to the deep chagrin of the Grimm brothers who were simultaneously collecting German folk-tale and legend . . .)."[5]

The Grimms, indeed, appeared to reach back to Herder for their attitudes. They announced themselves, on the title page of the *KHM*, as collectors rather than writers, and they too wrote disparagingly of the plainness of written language when contrasted with the vigor and color of the folk storyteller's expression. Or so it seemed.

Almost immediately, something happened which was an embarrassment to the position the Grimms had claimed for the *KHM;* in 1819 the preface to the second edition of the *KHM* seemed to retreat from the position taken by those of the two first edition volumes of 1812 and 1815. And, indeed, this proved to be only the first of a long series of similar embarrassments, details of which I shall consider in later chapters. But these embarrassments had remarkably little effect, and even today their importance is not fully grasped either in popular opinion or in the scholarship on the *KHM*. The reason for this is obvious enough. Very soon after their publication, the *KHM* became one of the most loved books in the world. A standard view of the provenance of the tales emerged, which itself became a story as charming and as loved as any of the tales themselves; and, more importantly, it was just as durable, and like any fairy story just as immune to subversion by any consciousness of the facts of the real world. Here is a typical and recent formulation of that tale: the Grimms, we are told, "spent much of their time wandering about the country, gleaning from peasants and the simpler townspeople a rich harvest of legends, which they wrote down as nearly as possible in the words in which they were told."[6]

Now this is, just like the other tales, a fairy story without a word of truth in it—but one with an irresistible appeal both in popular belief and even in scholarly opinion. For what is truly remarkable here is not just that it can be shown to be quite false, but that the evidence of easily available published sources made a large part of this general view dubious more than a hundred and fifty years ago, and all of the rest of it completely untenable more than fifty years ago—long before Heinz Rölleke's republication of some of the most important of this evidence, valuable though Rölleke's editions have been in spreading an awareness that all was not well with the popular view.[7] Yet it survives though all indications have long been to the contrary; and it is possible to see at work a determination that it should survive. When, for example, scholars have come across individual facts that were inconsistent with the popular view, we shall see that they have commonly either ignored them or tried to explain them away and draw the narrowest possible conclusions from them. As a result, many opportunities for a complete reevaluation have been avoided.

There has even been a striking reluctance on the part of those who have known most about the relevant sources either to see the force of any new evidence they brought to light or, at least, to communicate any awareness of possible significance. A particularly striking demonstration of this reluctance could be seen in the years 1970–71, when no less than four full-length biographies of the brothers appeared—by Michaelis-Jena, Gerstner, Peppard, and Denecke.[8] Even at this late date, not one of these scholars offered any serious challenge to the basic outline of the popular view, though mention is made of individual pieces of evidence which should have led in that direction; and often, as we shall see, they resorted to highly implausible ideas in order to avoid the impact of the evidence. Clearly, the general mood of scholarship has been a remarkably inhibited one. Perhaps the most important consequence of this climate was that the discovery of any one discrepancy between the facts and the popular view was able to remain an isolated discovery instead of serving as a warning to scholars that others might also exist. Yet the strangest aspect of all in this situation is that the popular misconception has its origin not in faulty scholarship or careless scholars but, rather, in deception by the Grimms themselves.

It is as well to be aware at the outset of some important corollaries to and extensions of the popular view which show that a good deal is at stake in its being upheld as true, or even more or less true. A number of scholars, for example—justifiably enough, if the facts indeed are as they have assumed them to be—have attributed to the *KHM* and to the Grimms a considerable importance in the general history of folklore studies. And, again, these views continue to be heard today, long after it should be obvious that the facts will not support them. Joseph Campbell is a typical example:

> The special distinction of the work of Jacob and Wilhelm Grimm was its scholarly regard for the sources. Earlier collectors had felt free to manipulate folk materials; the Grimms were concerned to let the speech of the people break directly

into print ... No one before the Grimms had readily acquiesced to the irregularities, the boorishness, the simplicity of the folk tale. Anthologists had arranged, restored, and tempered; poets had built new masterpieces out of the rich raw material. But an essentially ethnographical approach, no one had so much as conceived.[9]

Even as late as 1974, the well-known scholars Iona and Peter Opie concurred in this view: "The Grimms were ... the first to write the tales down in the way ordinary people told them, and not attempt to improve them; and they were the first to realize that everything about the tales was of interest, even including the identity of the person who told the tale."[10] This leads to an important conclusion about the Grimms; they are, if all this is true, the founders of the "scientific study of folklore and folk literature."[11] Ruth Michaelis-Jena, writing recently in the journal *Folklore,* took essentially the same view, seeing the Grimms as "the true begetters of *Märchenforschung* (fairy tale research), pioneers and unique seen in the context of their time"; and she too praised the Grimms' "scientific method," and their "emphasis on the story-teller."[12] To the reader of the most recent published commentary on the Grimms, it must seem that such views are ineradicable, for even writers who have been exposed to and shaken by some of the strong contrary evidence republished during the 1970s continue almost mechanically to express them once more. Linda Dégh, for example, writing in 1979, after expressing surprise at what had recently appeared in print—though nobody who had kept up with the record of what had been in print a quarter of a century earlier should have been surprised—still goes on to tell us, as so many previous writers have done, that the Grimms "established a new discipline: the science of folklore. Their example of collecting oral literature launched general fieldwork."[13]

More indicative still of the continuing currency of this view is an article in the very latest edition of that repository of received opinion, the *Encyclopaedia Britannica.* The author of the article is Ludwig Denecke, former head of the Brothers Grimm Museum in Kassel and author of many books on the Grimms, who maintains that the *KHM* "became and remains a model for the collecting of folktales everywhere," and that it is still "the earliest 'scientific' collection of folktales" having aimed at "a genuine reproduction of the teller's words and ways."[14]

One consequence of the popular view, then, would be a unique importance for the Grimms as folklorists. Another consequence would be a very special status for the tales within German culture. For if it is true, as the best-selling history of German literature puts it, that the Grimms "collected them from the mouth of the common people"[15]—then it would seem also to be true that, as J. G. Robertson says, the tales reflect "the mind of the German Volk,"[16] providing a key to some of its characteristic attitudes and feelings.[17]

Historians of folklore commonly see matters in the same way; Giuseppe Cocchiara, in his *The History of Folklore in Europe,* thinks the *KHM* important because "it preserves the beliefs of ancient Germanic peoples."[18]

It is important to understand why the Grimms' alleged emphasis on the identity and voice of the "storyteller" is so important a part of the basis of these judgments. Many if not most fairy tales are either international in their scope or at least incorporate figures, motifs, or situations which can be found in the tales of many countries. Versions of many of the tales in the *KHM,* for example, can be found in the *Histoire ou Contes du temps passé avec des moralités* (1697) of Charles Perrault and *Il Pentamerone* (1634–36) of Gianbattista Basile.

What is specifically *German* in the character of the *KHM* would have to reside precisely in the *particular* version or flavor of a given tale, and this is why the actual expression of the version told in Germany is so important; it is the specific form, more than the story outline itself, that will be of value for the study of German folklore.

There is much at stake in the popular view, therefore, and this surely gives us another reason for the reluctance of scholars to question it. Even when contrary evidence was becoming well known, and had to be dealt with, it was minimized with formulations such as that of the Opies: "They did not always adhere to the high standards they set themselves"; or Michaelis-Jena: "The brothers had taken it upon themselves to make slight, and what they considered justified, changes."[19] Gerstner brushed the troublesome facts aside with evident impatience. The Grimms, he said, did not want "to change anything essential, or to falsify anything"; nevertheless, "they did not want a slavish reproduction of what they had heard from this or that woman."[20] To question the Grimms' procedure was, for him, simply unreasonable quibbling. To be sure, the odd lapse here or there, or fairly unimportant stylistic changes, need not undermine the general validity of the popular view; we might even, with Kurt Schmidt, excuse it by reminding ourselves of the great difference between modern ethnographic standards and those of the early nineteenth century: "Present-day thinking about the recording of folk traditions is stricter, and it could see the Grimms' conception (actually Wilhelm's) almost as falsification. For the Grimms' era, however, it meant a significant step forwards in the conceptual framework of the discipline."[21] Gerstner developed this point further: "For those born later, it would have been an easy thing to capture the story-telling in shorthand or on tape."[22] If we accept this reassurance, we can go back to enjoying our fairy tale.

Yet the evidence is of far more radical import than this would imply; during the course of this study it will become evident that the changes introduced by the Grimms were far more than mere stylistic matters, and that the facts of their editorial procedure, taken together with the evidence as to their sources, are sufficient completely to undermine any notion that the Grimms' fairy tales are of folk, or peasant, or even German origin. And the facts also show the Grimms' attempts to foster these illusions. I turn in my next chapter to the origin and development of the popular view of the *KHM,* including some ingenious attempts to rescue it from destruction by the facts as they emerged.[23]

2

The Origin
and Development of
Misconceptions
about the Status
of the Tales

From the beginning, the Grimms sought to give the impression that their sources were quintessentially peasant and German in origin, and that they had faithfully transmitted what these sources had given to them. For example, in the preface to the first volume of the first edition, the brothers insisted that they had not added to, altered, or improved the stories at all:

> Wir haben uns bemüht, diese Märchen so rein als möglich war aufzufassen, man wird in vielen die Erzählung von Reimen und Versen unterbrochen finden, die sogar manchmal deutlich alliterieren, beim Erzählen aber niemals gesungen werden, und gerade diese sind die ältesten und besten. Kein Umstand ist hinzugedichtet oder verschönert und abgeändert worden, denn wir hätten uns gescheut, in sich selbst so reiche Sagen mit ihrer eigenen Analogie oder Reminiscenz zu vergrößern, sie sind unerfindlich.[1]

> (We have tried to collect these fairy tales as faithfully as possible; in many cases the narration is interrupted by rhymes and lines of poetry, which sometimes even clearly alliterate, but which are never sung, and precisely these are the oldest and best. No particular has been either added through our own poetic recreation, or improved and altered, because we should have shrunk from augmenting tales that were so rich

in themselves by adding passages analogous to or reminiscent of what was already there, they cannot be fabricated.)

Had the brothers said no more than this, a slight ambiguity might have remained: the word *Umstand* is somewhat vague and might be construed either to refer narrowly to circumstances of plot, or more broadly to the detail of the stories, including words and phrases. But even if *Umstand* is interpreted narrowly, the following word *verschönert* ("improve," or "beautify") still restores to the whole statement much of what it might lose by the more restricted understanding of *Umstand*. Not only is no detail or circumstance invented, but none is changed or improved— suggesting that expression, too, is preserved unaltered. But the Grimms then went on to remove any doubt on this score by praising the actual expression of folktales: "Es ist hier ein Fall, wo alle erlangte Bildung, Feinheit und Kunst der Sprache zu Schanden wird, und wo man fühlt, daß eine geläuterte Schrift-sprache, so gewandt sie in allem andern seyn mag, heller und durchsichtiger aber auch schmackloser geworden, und nicht mehr fest an den Kern sich schließe"[2] ("This is a case where all of the cultivation, refinement, and artistry that our language has reached is to no avail, and where one feels that a purified literary lan-guage, no matter how adroit it is for other purposes, has become clearer and more transparent, but also more insipid and less heart-felt"). Quite clearly, the expression of the tales collected by the brothers was to be regarded by the reader as an integral part of them. To this programmatic statement, the preface to the second volume of the first edition adds the figure of the famous *Märchenfrau* ("fairy tale woman") of Niederzwehren, with all that she implies:

Einer jener guten Zufälle aber war die Bekanntschaft mit einer Bäuerin aus dem nah bei Cassel gelegenen Dorfe Zwehrn, durch welche wir einen ansehnlichen Theil der hier mitge-theilten, darum ächt hessischen, Märchen, so wie mancherlei Nachträge zum ersten Band erhalten haben. Diese Frau, noch rüstig und nicht viel über fünfzig Jahre alt, heißt Viehmännin, hat ein festes und angenehmes Gesicht, blickt hell und scharf aus den Augen, und ist wahrscheinlich in ihrer Jugend schön gewesen. Sie bewahrt diese alten Sagen fest in dem Gedächt-niß, welche Gabe, wie sie sagt, nicht jedem verliehen sey und mancher gar nichts behalten könne; dabei erzählt sie bedäch-tig, sicher und ungemein lebendig mit eigenem Wohlgefallen daran, erst ganz frei, dann, wenn man will, noch einmal langsam, so daß man ihr mit einiger Übung nachschreiben kann. Manches ist auf diese Weise wörtlich beibehalten, und wird in seiner Wahrheit nicht zu verkennen seyn. Wer an leichte Verfälschung der Üeberlieferung, Nachlässigkeit bei Aufbewahrung, und daher an Unmöglichkeit langer Dauer, als Regel glaubt, der müßte hören, wie genau sie immer bei derselben Erzählung bleibt und auf ihre Richtigkeit eifrig ist; niemals änderte sie bei einer Wiederholung etwas in der Sache ab, und bessert ein Versehen, sobald sie es bemerkt, mitten in der Rede gleich selber. Die Anhänglichkeit an das Ueberlieferte ist bei Menschen, die in gleicher Lebensart unabänderlich fortfahren, stärker, als wir, zur Veränderung geneigt, begreifen.[3]

(One of those happy accidents was our acquaintance with a peasant woman from the village of Zwehrn, near Cassel, through whom we received a good part of the fairy tales that we give here, as well as many other additions to the first volume. These can therefore count as genuinely "Hessian" tales. This woman, still robust and not much over fifty years of age, is named Viehmann, she has a firm and pleasant face, with clear, sharp eyes and she was very likely beautiful in her youth. She retains these old legends firmly in her memory, a gift which, as she says, is not given to everyone and many can retain nothing at all. She narrates in a deliberate, assured and uncommonly lively manner, and with personal pleasure in doing so, first of all quite freely and then, if it is wished, again but slowly, so that it is possible, with some practice, to copy down what she says. Much has been retained verbatim in this fashion, and its authenticity is unmistakable. If anyone believes that traditions as a rule are easily corrupted, that their preservation is neglected, and therefore that they cannot long survive, he should hear how exactly she always tells the same story and how zealous she is about correctness; she never changes anything when repeating it, and corrects a mistake in the middle of her recitation as soon as she notices it. The adherence to tradition is greater among people who persevere in the same way of life than we who like change can imagine.)

The emphasis here is even more strongly on word-for-word transmission; such storytellers as the Märchenfrau are, apparently, so accurate in their memory that an oral tradition can be maintained absolutely intact, and those who think that continual slow change in the verbal texture of the stories must eventually erode the tradition are warned to look to her example and see their error.

Here, then, is the ultimate source of the popular view; it was formulated and propagated by the Grimms themselves, and they are responsible for whatever discrepancies are found between that view and the historical facts. It is necessary to stress this point because later writers have always wanted to ignore the Grimms' responsibility. When, finally, evidence began to appear which proved difficult to reconcile with the Grimms' programmatic statements, their critics typically took the attitude, "So we have been mistaken all these years." Thomas Schumann, for example, writes in 1977 that the Grimms' tales are not what they are "commonly assumed to be."[4] Even Heinz Rölleke, most knowledgeable of recent Grimm scholars, when dealing with the recalcitrant material can only bring himself to say: "All these facts show the Grimms' collection of fairy tales in a quite different light than scholarship or commonly accepted traditions have seen them."[5] What both of these writers will not face is the fact that these myths do not result from assumptions commonly made by scholars, or by traditions which somehow arose in some unspecified way; they result from the clear statements of the Grimms.

The earliest evidence that all was not well with this account was provided by the second edition of 1819. For when the 1819 printed text of the *KHM* was compared with its predecessor, it was obvious that there were considerable discrepancies between the two. The tales had obviously been reworked and rewritten for the second edition. This by no means minor alteration of the texts seemed to clash oddly with the assurances given in the two prefaces to the first edition. What had now become of the promises of preserving the tradition *wörtlich* ("verbatim"), of resisting the improper urge to alter anything, of allowing nothing to be improved or made more attractive? While the account of the Märchenfrau was still included in the preface to this new edition, the main programmatic statement of the first volume of the first edition was dropped, and it never appeared in any of the subsequent editions. In its place, an uneasy, defensive statement was now presented:

> Was die Weise betrifft in der wir gesammelt, so ist es uns zuerst auf Treue und Wahrheit angekommen. Wir haben nämlich aus eigenen Mitteln nichts hinzugesetzt, keinen Umstand und

Zug der Sage selbst verschönert, sondern ihren Inhalt so wiedergegeben, wie wir ihn empfangen; daß der Ausdruck großentheils von uns herrührt, versteht sich von selbst, doch haben wir jede Eigentümlichkeit, die wir bemerkten, zu erhalten gesucht, um auch in dieser Hinsicht der Sammlung die Mannigfaltigkeit der Natur zu lassen. Jeder, der sich mit ähnlicher Arbeit befaßt, wird es übrigens begreifen, daß dies kein sorgloses und unachtsames Auffassen kann genannt werden, im Gegentheil ist Aufmerksamkeit und ein Takt nöthig, der sich erst mit der Zeit erwirbt, um das Einfachere, Reinere und doch in sich Vollkommnere, von dem Verfälschten zu unterscheiden. Verschiedene Erzählungen haben wir, sobald sie sich ergänzten, und zu ihrer Vereinigung keine Widersprüche wegzuschneiden waren, als eine mitgetheilt, wenn sie aber abwichen, wo dann jede gewöhnlich ihre eigentümlichen Züge hatte, der besten den Vorzug gegeben und die andern für die Anmerkungen aufbewahrt.[6]

(As far as the manner of our collecting is concerned, what mattered most to us was fidelity and truth. That is to say, we have added nothing of our own, have improved no circumstance or trait of the story itself, but have given its content just as we received it; that the expression largely originates with us is self-evident, but we have tried to retain each characteristic feature that we saw, in order to have the collection retain in this respect too the diversity of nature. Anyone who is concerned with similar work will in any case grasp the fact that this cannot be called a thoughtless and heedless collecting, on the contrary a care and discretion is necessary to distinguish the simpler, more pure, yet more integral and complete from what is corrupted, and this ability only comes with time. We have given many tales as one insofar as they complemented each other and no inconsistencies had to be excised in order to unite them; but if they diverged from each other, in which case each usually had its own characteristic features, we preferred the better of the tales, and kept the others for the notes.)

No matter how the Grimms tried here to persuade their readers that all of this was obvious and unproblematic, it was of course a radical retreat from the principle announced in the first edition. The authenticity of the tales was now to be found in their *content* but not in their *expression,* which derived largely from the Grimms themselves rather than their folk informants. And that, as we have seen, is so important a change that it throws an entirely different light on the status of the *KHM*. Yet curiously enough, this admission seemed to have little impact on the public of the *KHM;* the popular view of the tales' status continued as before. No one asked how the writers of the first preface could now write a second which flatly contradicted the first. And while the prefaces to the first edition were the origin of that popular view, the preface to the second became not the source of its refutation, as might have been expected, but on the contrary a source of ways of explaining away discrepancies between the programmatic statement with which the Grimms launched the first edition *KHM* and the emerging evidence of what they in fact did; in other words, the second edition preface was actually used to rescue the popular view (based on the first preface) from destruction as the facts emerged which should have destroyed it.

This strange reversal occurred because scholars refused to accept what the brothers had plainly told them in the preface to the second edition—that the expression was largely their own, only the content being authentic, and instead behaved as if they had been told merely that the claim of the first edition (i.e. that the expression of the original had also been preserved, and nothing *at all* had been altered) should not be taken absolutely and literally to apply all the time and in every case. Thus, much stress was later given to the notion that it was necessary for the Grimms to combine different stories which complemented each other, or that it was necessary for them to use an editor's judgment to rephrase what seemed likely to be a corrupt reading.[7] But scholars who focused exclusively on these points were really clinging to a modified version of the first edition preface, and simply avoiding the bald assertion in the second edition that the expression was the Grimms' own—not on occasion, not just where necessary in particular unavoidable circumstances, but as a general rule.

However, the major source of solace for the scholar who was reluctant to abandon the popular notion was found not in these details of the preface to the second edition but in an inference from the circumstances of its publication. Jacob, it is known, was becoming more immersed in his philological work as time went on, and the responsibility for the *KHM* was resting more and more with Wilhelm. The prefaces to the two editions appeared to represent two different attitudes: what if the first represented the attitude of one, and the second that of the other? This supposition would effectively defend the integrity of the first edition, however much the later edition departed from the original text. And gradually it became commonplace to assume that it was true. The broadly accepted scholarly (as opposed to popular) view was soon that the claims of the first edition preface for the first edition text were not literally and invariably true, for reasons given in the second edition preface (the need for editorial discretion and judgment in combining different versions and separating genuine from corrupt material), but that they were broadly true, and that the only considerable departures from that standard were in the later editions, where they were the responsibility of Wilhelm, whose attitude was significantly different from Jacob's. Thus scholars attempted to deal with the embarrassing conflict of the two prefaces.

As we shall see, none of this modified account can withstand serious scrutiny in the light of the evidence that was available even fifty years ago—though it has continued to thrive until the present day. But even in 1819 there was here much that was dubious. To begin with, a careful reading of that second edition preface might well have provoked more skepticism.

The problem with which the 1819 preface has to deal is the large discrepancy between the much-altered text of the second edition, on the one hand, and the programmatic statements of the first edition preface, on the other; and it is this problem that evidently caused the new preface to be written. Yet, looked at more closely, the 1819 preface did not deal with *this* discrepancy at all; it simply substitutes a radically different programmatic statement for that of 1812–15.[8] What remains unexplained is why the original programmatic statement was written, if it is now implicitly conceded to be a misdescription of what the brothers actually did in preparing the tales for print.

Even stranger is the claim that the second programmatic statement is "self-evident"; and the brothers' awareness that this was a troubling and unconvincing statement which was far from self-evident is shown by the fact that they reformulated it once more in the later editions, adding another important qualification: "That the expression *and the execution of the individual tale* largely originates with us, is self-evident" ("*und die Ausführung des einzelnen*" [my italics]). Yet they still attempted to bury the problem by claiming that the point is too obvious to be argued over. It would not be difficult to advance arguments against this position, but it would be unnecessary to do so. Whatever the arguments that may be made against the "self-evidence" of the new pro-grammatic statement, the one thing that is incontrovertible is that it was very far from being self-evident to the writers of the first prefaces; it is precisely the reader of these prefaces who will be armed with arguments against the later view. At first the Grimms had argued for authenticity of expression, and now they argued that it was not necessary. What was needed was an ar-gument and explanation to justify the change of position, not the lame assertion that none was necessary and that the new stance was self-evident.

The 1819 preface has in fact the character not of a frank and well-intentioned attempt to discuss the brothers' methods, but instead a reluctant but necessary attempt to deal with an em-barrassing subject. Its purpose is evidently not to reveal all, but to conceal as much as possible and to deal with the subject only to the extent that the text of the second edition makes it necessary to do so.

Similarly, the explanations which were offered of typical sit-uations which would justify an editor's imposing his own expres-sion upon the folk material seemed peculiarly inappropriate to the available evidence of the Grimms' reworking of their material—namely, the rewriting which could be observed when the second edition's text was compared to that of the first. For the Grimms made only some very specific assertions, which met only a few specific situations: e.g., that an editor had to choose between different versions of a tale, or combine fragments of different versions, or be careful to identify corrupt passages in order to amend them. It is certainly possible to question the inherent logic of these arguments. How, for example, would it be possible to identify what is corrupt and separate it from what is pure in the absence of a correct original to measure both against? And how could the need to choose between different versions of a tale require the editor to substitute his own expres-sion for that of *either* version? Even combining different frag-ments will only require some intervention to achieve consistency, not the imposition of a new expression for the tale by the editor. But in any case, none of this seems to have any relevance to the considerable changes introduced into the text of the second edi-tion. For what was obviously involved here was not the result of the specific conditions mentioned by the brothers, but instead a great deal of rephrasing and recasting to achieve a smoother, more fluent text spread over the whole *KHM;* in other words, a general, all-pervasive rewriting which seems best described by that despised phrase from the first edition preface—an "approximation to a literary language." Nevertheless, the Grimms' much more specific examples were accepted as adequately covering what they had done, and that acceptance has continued up to the present day.[9] The need to believe was, and has remained, stronger than the evidence.

The juxtaposition of the texts and prefaces of the two editions, therefore, should have provided ample reasons for a much more fundamental skepticism; but there were similarly many good reasons to be skeptical about the theory that the problem lay in a discrepancy between the two brothers—the purist Jacob having exercised scrupulous control over the first edition, with subsequent editions having been tampered with by the more poetically inclined Wilhelm. This theory has had a very considerable currency, and it is not difficult to see why; it offers its adherents a good deal. It is able to explain the constantly changing form of the later editions, while protecting the integrity of the first edition as a genuine folkloric work. Carsch, for example, explains that "while the older brother intended to keep the tales intact, the younger brother seems to have won his point in time for publilcation of the second edition in 1819."[10] Another representative scholar is Wilhelm Schoof: "In contrast to Jacob who was in favor of a literal reproduction of the tradition, but left the further reworking after the year 1812 to his brother, Wilhelm gave the tales the artistic form which he created in order to make them chiefly suitable for chidren."[11] And similar remarks are made by countless other scholars.[12]

But several decisive arguments can be leveled against this theory, some available from the very beginning, and all based on evidence which has been available for at least half a century. The first is that *both* relevant prefaces were written by Wilhelm. That of the first edition is reprinted in his collection of *Kleinere Schriften* ("Shorter Writings"), not that of Jacob.[13] A handwritten note in the Grimms' own copy of the first edition of the *KHM* confirms the point that Wilhelm wrote the preface. We might, of course, be tempted to speculate that Jacob could have suggested, perhaps as an addition to Wilhelm's draft essay, some wording which Wilhelm would not have used if left to himself; but the text of a personal letter from Wilhelm to Goethe on August 1, 1816, makes this highly unlikely, for here Wilhelm used a key phrase from the 1812 preface to explain his procedure: "Wir haben sie [the tales] . . . so rein als möglich aufgefaßt" ("We have collected the tales as faithfully as possible"). Wilhelm could continue to use this language in 1816 because the publication of the second edition of 1819 had not yet made it necessary to change the story to be told. And so the 1819 preface must be Wilhelm's awkward revision of his *own* earlier position, not just his brother's. A second objection is that the 1812 edition was largely Wilhelm's work anyway; while the collecting had been done equally by both, the printed texts of 1812 were with very few exceptions (only a handful out of sixty) all prepared by Wilhelm. Once more the hand-written notes in the margins of the Grimms' own copy of the first edition are helpful here; they note that only four, or possibly five, were "von Jacob erzählt" ("told by Jacob"). This is certainly an intriguing use of the word "erzählt," suggesting that the storyteller—the "voice" of the stories—is Jacob, which in turn implies that only the basic material came from the informants. This note is Wilhelm's; but Jacob too could lapse into the same kind of formulation. In a letter to Arnim (January 28, 1813), answering Arnim's objection that some of the tales do not seem suitable for children, Jacob retorts: "Das Märchenbuch ist mir daher gar nicht für Kinder geschrieben, aber es kommt ihnen recht erwünscht und das freut mich sehr" ("The book of fairy tales is therefore not written for children at all, but it is just what they like, and that pleases me"). Here Jacob does not say that the tales were not collected or put together for children, but instead that they were not written for children. Both brothers, then, casually used language which implied that *they* had written the *KHM*.

And so, even if the brothers had been at odds over their procedures, and even if Jacob might have acted differently on his own, that would do little to save the authenticity of the first edition, which was *already* largely Wilhelm's work. But the third and most telling objection is that the changes occurring *after* the publication of the first edition were far less in scope than those which occurred in the preparation of the original manuscripts for the first edition. The evidence for this statement will be presented later, along with an analysis of what the Grimms really did in preparing the first edition for publication in 1812–15.

But for the moment it suffices to note that *if* we assume that the first edition, but not subsequent editions, was influenced by Jacob, we should have to judge the situation in a manner diametrically opposed to that which has been usual: Jacob would then seem to have been influential when the *greatest* changes were made, and less influential when much less was changed. For Jacob had, by 1812, been a party to considerably more tampering than that for which Wilhelm is usually held responsible in the later editions.

However, the theory of different brothers for different editions should not have looked plausible even at the outset. What has always been clear is that both brothers cared a great deal about the project, that so great a divergence of views as that which has been hypothesized is scarcely conceivable given their closeness and their mutual commitment to it, and that *both* defended the authenticity of the project in similar terms at the early stages. That being so, it is highly unlikely that Jacob would have stood by without making any protest if Wilhelm had indeed perverted a project that was so dear to him. There are some facts to support this common-sense assumption; for example, after his brother's death, Jacob wrote, in a letter to Franz Pfeiffer (February 19, 1860): "Die späteren Auflagen, weil ich in Grammatik versenkt war, ließ ich Wilhelm redigieren und einleiten, ohne daß meine Sorgfalt für sammeln und erklären je nachgelassen hatte. Wie sollte es auch anders sein können" ("I left the later editions to Wilhelm to edit and introduce, because I was immersed in my work on grammar, but without ever abandoning my concern for collecting and elucidating. How could it be otherwise"). While Jacob may have left the editing to Wilhelm, it is almost inconceivable that he would not have continued to be concerned with the rationale for and character of the collection. Yet though this theory should have seemed implausible at the outset, it survived completely intact until a part of it was questioned in 1963 by Gunhild Ginschel;[14] but even she limited her challenge in curious ways which had the effect both of keeping well clear of any reflection on the authenticity of the tales or the integrity of the brothers' statements about them, and this limitation meant that her account contained an element of implausibility which may well have restricted its impact and its acceptability to other scholars.[15]

Ginschel argued that Jacob's attitudes to collecting fairy tales were just like his brother's. She used one strong and even unassailable argument: that Jacob acted exactly as his brother did when he prepared fairy tale material for publication. His reworking of the material produced the same results as Wilhelm's. So far, Ginschel's argument is on solid ground. But at this point there is an uncomfortable issue to face: if Jacob and Wilhelm both rewrote the tales in a very uninhibited fashion, the discrepancy between what they did and what they said can no longer be regarded as a discrepancy only between the attitudes of the two brothers. How, then, is this discrepancy to be dealt with? Ginschel does her best to produce an explanation which does not involve deception on the brothers' part. Focusing exclusively upon Jacob, she argues that his programmatic statements have been misinterpreted: they do not really mean what everyone thinks they mean. Jacob's strong and often repeated views on the need for faithful transmission of traditional or literary materials do not, she argues, apply to fairy tales but only to other categories of such material; and if Jacob sometimes seemed to be arguing this way about fairy tales, it was because he had a tendency to make issues too sharply polarized when in an argument and with his polemical instincts aroused.

It is unfortunate that Ginschel, in supporting her position with this argument, in effect discredited it; for it requires a great effort of faith to believe that Jacob did not really mean what he appeared to mean where fairy tales were concerned, but did with all other kinds of traditional material. Ginschel's argument became implausible because she would not consider another explanation of the discrepancy between Jacob's words and his deeds: Jacob was deceiving his public. And so, as Ginschel first saw, Jacob's attitudes were like those of Wilhelm; but, as she did not see, that removed any possibility that the first edition preface was an honest statement, or that the first edition of the tales had the status asserted there of an authentic work of folklore.

So much, then, for the origin and development of the popular and scholarly views of the status of the *KHM*. I want now to turn to the actual evidence of that status. It is in two parts: evidence as to the character of the Grimms' informants, and evidence as to the character of their treatment of the texts.

3

The Character of
the Grimms' Sources

In their prefaces, the Grimms wrote of the material they
offered the public in terms which suggested that it was of
folk origin. In explaining the universal occurrence of such
tales, for example, the brothers suggest that they flourish in the
context of a simple life: "Weil diese Poesie dem ersten und ein-
fachsten Leben so nah liegt, so sehen wir darin den Grund ihrer
allgemeinen Verbreitung, denn es giebt wohl kein Volk, welches
sie ganz entbehrt"[1] ("Because this poetry is so close to the primal,
simplest way of life, we see in this the reason for its universal
dissemination, for there is likely no people which does not have
it to some extent"). The preface to the second volume gave more
precise content to this idea, in that an ideal type of folk storyteller
is introduced—the Märchenfrau of Niederzwehren, a peasant
woman. Here, too, the word *Volk* occurs repeatedly, and the description of the Märchenfrau as a peasant places her securely
among the *Volk*. Her specifically Germanic folk status is also
stressed when the stories which emanate from her are described
as *ächt hessisch* ("authentically Hessian"). And the brothers stressed
the Germanic character of their tales even more by going on to
say: "In diesen Volks-Märchen liegt lauter urdeutscher Mythus"
("In these folk fairy tales there is pure Germanic myth"). From
all of this one gets the impression—though it is not explicitly
stated—that the middle-class Grimms had to go among the common people to search out and collect their material. But this is

a false picture, both in general and in the particular case of Dorothea Viehmann (the Märchenfrau). The evidence of its falsity has long been available but not taken seriously; and even the few recent scholars who have seen that it was inaccurate have shied away from the fact that deliberate deception on the Grimms' part is indicated. In what follows I shall give only a brief outline of the known facts, together with an interpretation of them.

With the single exception of Dorothea Viehmann, the Grimms gave very little information about their informants in any of the editions of the *KHM*. They supplied neither names nor dates, but only at most the region of origin of the text. There is a folkish air in this practice of naming the region, a suggestion that the tale sprang from a particular area of the soil of Germany. Otherwise, all information which would have allowed any judgment of the age, literacy, class or national origin of the informants is withheld. Only the peasant woman Dorothea Viehmann is named, and she is held up as an exemplary storyteller; we are surely meant to assume that she is the type which was sought out by the brothers.

But over eighty years ago some important information came to light which should even then have caused some radical rethinking about the nature of the informants. Just before the turn of the century, Herman Grimm (Wilhelm's son) made available to the scholar Johannes Bolte the brothers' own copies of the first printed texts. Marginal handwritten notes in the first volume of the first edition assigned names to the texts, and these names should immediately have made it obvious why they had been withheld from the public; they represented almost exclusively the brothers' close friends and their families. Members of the families Wild and Hassenpflug are very prominent among the names, for example,[2] and from those families came the future spouses of both Wilhelm and his sister Lotte.

There are many reasons why it would have been embarrassing to make this information public: first, these are all thoroughly middle-class, literate sources. That would have undermined the notion of the folk origin of the tales, and of the untutored, natural quality of their transmission by word of mouth, without benefit of literacy and education. Literacy involved the risk of contamination by printed stories, which might be of foreign origin, or at least have nothing to do with the people of a particular region. Second, it would have been embarrassing for the brothers to have to admit that far from diligently seeking out folk sources, they had done no more than collect from close friends and family. That would suggest a procedure both lazier and much less scientifically conscientious, and one much less able to claim a representative and universal significance. Third, the Hassenpflugs were of Huguenot origin, and the everyday language of their household was still French; their involvement would undermine the notion that the collection had a characteristically German quality, since contamination from French sources would be possible and even likely. And fourth, these were mainly young people—far from the preferred type of the old peasant woman, the skilled and experienced storyteller whose memory reaches back toward ancient times and produces ancient folktale material.

Once the reader has absorbed the information contained in the marginalia to the Grimms' copy of the *KHM,* it is possible to look at the place attributions in their published *Notes* to, for example, *Läuschen und Flöhchen (The Louse and the Flea),* "from Cassel," and *Vom treuen Gevatter Sperling (The Dog and the Sparrow),* "from Hessen," and to see that this is a pretentious and deceptive way of referring to the same household; the former is from Dorothea Wild, future wife of Wilhelm Grimm, the latter her sister Gretchen Wild. The variety of terminology is evidently designed deliberately to create a misleading impression of diversity and variety where there is really none. The overwhelming predominance of references to the Hessen district (where the brothers lived) as the source of the tales might by itself have raised doubts as to their seriousness as folklorists; but here, too, scholars have shown that persistent reluctance to entertain any thoughts which might be injurious to the Grimms, or to the status of the *KHM.* Peppard, for example, thought it "a strange quirk of fate that just one Hessian city, Cassel, should produce so many of the world's most famous fairy tales."[3] A quirk of *fate?* It did not occur to Peppard to see this as it so obviously is: a quirk of the brothers, who would surely have collected outside their home town had they been seriously concerned to assemble an authentic collection. Even the occasional mention of "Hanau" or the "River Main district" in the Grimms' notes turns out to be only a misleading reference to the Hassenpflug family, which had originated from Hanau, on the Main, but now lived in Cassel. To be sure, that might indicate some greater variety of place of origin for the material, but shows still less variety in the places in which the brothers collected.

Bolte had this information in 1899, and published it in 1912 in the first volume of his and Polivka's expanded and updated version of the Grimms' *Notes* to the tales; these notes became a much used source in the years since their publication, referred to over and over again in the scholarship on the Grimms. Yet when Heinz Rölleke, in his 1975 edition of the earliest versions of the tales, set out the same information already given by Bolte, it seemed startling; Thomas Schumann talked of "sensational discoveries" by Rölleke,[4] and hailed this as newly published material previously neglected by Grimm scholarship. In one sense, this is an error on Schumann's part—Rölleke had *not* discovered the material. But in another sense Schumann's perception was accurate: from the standpoint of notions about the authenticity of the Grimms' tales which were still prevalent, this information was indeed shocking. From Bolte onward, in fact, one Grimm scholar after another had managed not to face its import. Perhaps it took a person like Schumann, who was not in general a student of the Grimms, to get a clear sight of the discrepancy from which others wished to hide. For, most astonishing of all, even Rölleke himself tried to explain away the troublesome material. In a 1975 article he tried to supply a harmless explanation for the brothers' silence about the identities of their informants, explaining that what they had wanted was to "give the impression that the collective origin of the fairy-tales (especially according to Jacob Grimm's theory) required as it were a collective tradition, and could only be understood in this way."[5] But this is a highly unconvincing argument; it might have some point only if all of the sources were really folk sources, in which case a failure to tell us who they were might relate simply to this alleged desire to stress the collective rather than the individual. What Rölleke's argument cannot deal with is the fact that these are *not* folk sources at all, and that the obvious reason for the Grimms' silence was to conceal that fact. Nor does Rölleke's feeble apology for the Grimms explain the deception apparent in the attempt to create variety, not uniformity in their attribution of place now to "Hessen," now to "Cassel," where the same house was the real reference. But the most devastating counterargument here is that, far from avoiding individual names in order to give an impression of collective transmission, the brothers themselves introduced the particular figure of Dorothea Viehmann in the second volume of the first edition. And so, though better informed than any previous scholar, Rölleke shied away from the far more obvious explanation: the Grimms concealed facts which would have been highly embarrassing and plainly at variance with all of the claims they had made for the significance of their collection.

To be sure, one figure seemed for some time to be an exception to the general impression gained from the marginalia: "die alte Marie" ("old Marie"), an old servant woman in the Wild household, in which Wilhelm's wife grew up. One of the names among those noted in the margins of the Grimms' copy of the first edition was "Marie." Since others were Dortchen, Gretchen, Jeanette, etc., i.e., Dorothea Wild, Gretchen Wild, and Jeanette Hassenpflug, it would have seemed natural to assume that "Marie" was Marie Hassenpflug, just another of the young people identified in this way. But Herman Grimm, the son of Dorothea Wild and Wilhelm Grimm, identified "Marie" in a retrospective essay about his father and uncle published in 1895[6] as the figure who has since become celebrated as "die alte Marie"—a storyteller of the best kind for the Grimms' purposes. Marie Müller was an old woman in 1810, and as a servant would be uncontaminated by book learning and thus could be considered an unspoiled member of the German *Volk*. In his essay, Herman Grimm elaborated on her powers as storyteller. Not only did this protect the folk status of the tales labeled "Marie"; the other tales from the younger members of the Wild household might also then be assumed to have originated from "die alte Marie," who would have related them to Dorothea and her sisters. "One feels immediately," says Herman Grimm, "that Dortchen and Gretchen probably only passed on what had been planted in their minds by old Marie."

A moment's thought should, once more, have made this seem rather improbable. Why would the brothers have taken down stories from Dorothea, for example, at second hand, when the authentic source was available to them in the same house? Would the brothers have referred to Marie Müller in the same way that they referred to their friends, by a first name only, without differentiating her from the others? And if Marie was so important for the collection, why did the prefaces not name her in the same way that Dorothea Viehmann was named? But Herman Grimm's account was unquestioned until very recently. Even the biographies of 1970–71 accepted it completely. Michaelis-Jena actually elaborated this story, declaring Marie to be "the Wilds' old nanny" and "the source of them [the tales from the Wild household] all."[7] In fact, her function in the household was not that of a nanny but of a housekeeper; by making her a nanny, Michaelis-Jena immediately conjures up an image of old Marie telling fairy stories to her charges at their bedtime. Peppard declared her "an ideal source, she represents just the type one would expect to know fairy tales," and in his enthusiasm then greatly overstated Marie's (whether Müller or Hassenpflug) contribution to the collection by saying that "in addition to the daughters in the family, the most significant source was "Old Marie," the house-keeper, who seems to have been the informant for nearly a fourth of the tales included in the first volume." In fact, Marie contributed only less than one eighth of that volume.[8] Gerstner elaborated in a different way: "Distinguished by a good memory, she willingly passed her treasure on to the Grimm brothers."[9] Here we are offered a description of old Marie's excellent memory—though there is no mention of that quality in any written account of her—and of her willingness to pass on her treasure of stories to the brothers Grimm—though the brothers never once mention her giving them stories willingly or unwillingly; in fact, they never mention her as a storyteller at all—or any other of her qualities, for that matter.

All of these scholars were clearly being drawn toward an image of an ideal storyteller, on the one hand ignoring obtrusive facts which militated against that image, and on the other making up their own facts in order to round out that image and give it fuller shape. This image-making is also visible in Gerstner's characterization of the informants: "And so it was predominantly old people to whom the Grimm brothers listened, because these stories were more likely to live on in their memories."[10] Gerstner's reasoning as to why they might have or should have done so sounds reasonable enough; but a priori thinking here negates the facts, which point above all to *young* people, not old.

At last, in 1975, Heinz Rölleke argued that the notation "Marie" must refer to Marie Hassenpflug; and his proof is exceedingly clear and convincing.[11] The details of the dating of the texts (those from "Marie" coincide chronologically with other contributions from the Hassenpflugs) and their place of origin (some

are attributed to the "River Main region," where the Hassenpflugs had lived before moving to Cassel) leave no other possible
conclusion, and there are many other points of detail which are
equally forceful in Rölleke's demonstration.

It is startling to see just how easily Rölleke proves his case; for
all of the facts which so obviously point to his conclusion were
known to previous scholars. In addition to the biographers of
Grimm which I have mentioned, Bolte, Polivka, and Schoof evidently knew these facts as well, and all three were exceptionally
thorough students in matters relating to the Grimms.

One might argue that the authority of Herman Grimm, the
son and nephew of the brothers, was what induced a belief in
what would otherwise not have seemed believable. But, as Rölleke points out, Herman Grimm was born in 1828, while Marie
Müller left the Wild household in 1812 and died in 1826; and
his essay, written in 1895, contained many obvious errors of
fact.[12] There was no need to feel that his testimony was com-
pelling, for it was all too clear that his memory was by that time
highly unreliable.

But was it only a bad memory which produced Herman's mistaken identification of Marie? For Marie is never mentioned as
a source by the brothers, and one wonders how Herman could
have wrongly identified Marie as a woman who left his mother's
household sixteen years before he was born, instead of as his
aunt's sister-in-law, whom he would have known quite well. It is
clear that the brothers themselves deliberately concealed the true
nature of their informants; however, the available evidence allows the possibility that Herman knew this and was himself trying
to invent a more credible story on their behalf.

At all events, "die alte Marie" as Märchenfrau is certainly pure
fiction, and thus Dorothea Viehmann from Niederzwehren would
be the sole remaining support for the notion that the tales are
of folk origin—would be, that is, if the Grimms' account of her
were true; but that, too, represents a deliberate piece of deception on their part.

There are several ironies in the date and manner of the emer-
gence of the real facts of Dorothea Viehmann's life, but they are
ironies typical of the history of the *KHM*. The first lies in the
fact that it was a celebration of the famous Märchenfrau's bi-
centenary on November 8, 1955, which resulted in the revelation
of the fraudulence of the brothers' description of her; a com-

memorative pamphlet containing a biographical essay by Georg Textor set out the astonishing facts.[13] The second is that in that same year there appeared a study (by Rolf Hagen) of French influence in the *KHM,* the conclusion of which was that such influence was only slight and unimportant *(gering).*[14] Just as Hagen's words appeared in print, something else was appearing which would make his conclusion seem sadly mistaken. The Grimms, it will be remembered, said in their preface that Dorothea Viehmann was the ideal storyteller, a German peasant who told from her memory ancient tales from the folk tradition of the Hessen region—"from the heart of the German-speaking area," as Gerstner later put it.[15] But the facts were shockingly different: Dorothea Viehmann's first language was French, not German, and she was a member of the large community of Huguenots who had settled in the area, in which the language of church and school was still French. She was not a peasant but a thoroughly middle-class woman; she was not an untutored transmitter of folk tradition but, on the contrary, a literate woman who knew her Perrault; she was not a German but of French stock. The discrepancy between the Grimms' account of her and the real facts is astonishing, but what is just as astonishing is the way in which scholars have alluded to some of those facts without seeming to notice the way in which they made nonsense of what the Grimms had said. Already in 1959, Schoof reported: "She was the daughter of the innkeeper Johann Isaak Pierson and came from an old Huguenot family . . . Frau Viehmann, whose source was Perrault, just like the Hassenpflugs."[16] Incredibly, Schoof did not comment on the significance of this information, but instead went on to talk of the Grimms' confidence in her as a storyteller, in the process citing the very description of her by the brothers which was so patently contradicted by the facts he had just given. Peppard, too, acknowledged that "many of the tales of the Grimms' most celebrated informant, Frau Viehmann of Zwehren, are her versions of stories by Perrault,"[17] without allowing this remarkable fact to influence the rest of his account. Others of the Grimms' recent biographers, like Denecke and Michaelis-Jena, list works which give this information in their bibliographies—Denecke even includes Textor's biographical essay issued in 1955 on the two-hundredth anniversary of the birth of the Märchenfrau—without allowing it to appear or be reflected in their narratives at all. But if Grimm scholars failed to respond to the enormity of what Textor published for them, that may well have occurred because Textor himself seemed not to understand what he had done.[18] The biographical facts he presented established that Dorothea Viehmann was from a family that was quite well-to-do. Her great-grandfather, after all, had actually been the mayor of Schöneburg; her father was the owner of a prosperous inn, and must have had a place of considerable respect in the community because in the church register only he and another relative—probably his brother—had their names always preceded by *Monsieur* or *Herr*. And yet Textor, it seems, cannot stop himself lapsing into the language of the Grimms' legend about Dorothea Viehmann, and begins his essay with a sentimental reference to the Grimms' visits to her *ärmliche Hütte* ("wretched cottage"). There is no doubt that she, as opposed to the imaginary character the Grimms created, never lived in such a place in her life. Again, Textor assures us that our Märchenfrau never read a book of fairy tales in her childhood. How he could possibly have known this, given the scanty evidence of church register and other similar records from which he worked, would have to remain a mystery but for the fact that it is obviously part of the Grimms' legend. But not only did Textor have no facts to support this claim: his essay gives us other facts that made it absurd. Given her family's economic well-being and her membership in the French community, she would certainly have read Perrault.

It was Ingeborg Weber-Kellermann who first wrote as if it *mattered* that the Märchenfrau was not what the Grimms had said she was: "If this information is taken together with the references to the Hassenpflug sisters (and much besides), the characterization of the *KHM* as Germanic mythology becomes rather shaky."[19] But this did not occur until 1970, fifteen years after the information was first published. And, even then, Weber-Kellermann did not quite grasp the full force of what she was saying. Her reference to the Hassenpflugs concerns the further piece of bad news that they too were a Huguenot family; another major source for the Grimms' tales, they too were contaminated by Perrault and French culture generally as well as by literateness and hence, conceivably, books from any foreign source. But what Weber-Kellermann did not know was that the "'Marie" of the *KHM* sources was Marie Hassenpflug; she still assumed that this was "die alte Marie." What she was in fact pointing to, without knowing it, was that not one but *both* of the legendary *KHM* storytellers thought previously to be old German peasant women were of Huguenot French stock! It might be noted that Weber-Kellermann published her article in the anthropological proceedings of the Hungarian Academy of Sciences—perhaps a reflection on the general unwillingness of German scholars to question so prized a part of the German national heritage.

But Weber-Kellermann's nerve eventually failed too; for she went no further than the conclusion that the Germanic provenance of the Grimms' tales is questionable, after which, evidently concerned to reintroduce a sense of piety and respect for the Grimms and the *KHM*, she ended with a hymn of praise for the brothers: "Side by side with our doubts about the Germanic or 'Hessian-to-the-core' character of the collection, there must be admiration for the inspired personalities of the brothers, who were able to forge a harmony and integrity for the KHM from fortuitous and heterogeneous traditional material."[20] She thus avoided the most critical questions raised by her report: Why was the Grimms' description of Dorothea Viehmann so flagrantly wrong? How could they not have known the true facts of her life? Questions like these should, in turn, have been linked with those suggested by the brothers' failure to mention the identity of their other sources, and their concealing the involvement of the Wilds and Hassenpflugs. Indeed, the Grimms cannot have failed to know the truth about Dorothea Viehmann. There is ample evidence that they had become very close to her before the publication of their description of her in 1815; and their very introduction to her had been by way of the pastor of the French-speaking community in Cassel, which means that they had to have known that she was French-speaking and of French ancestry.[21] And that leaves only one conclusion: they deliberately published a deceptive description of her as part of their attempt to create a completely false impression of the status of their collection. Weber-Kellermann's determination not to face the most awkward questions raised by the true facts of Dorothea Viehmann's life and (even after realizing that this information was completely inconsistent with the prevailing view of the *KHM*) to close the argument with admiration for the Grimms inevitably limited the impact of her contribution to the field. For once more, when Rölleke mentioned this information too in his 1975 edition of the earliest versions of the *KHM*, the result was consternation.

Again, Rölleke was credited with the discovery, probably because no one could believe that a piece of information which was so devastating to the still prevailing attitudes toward the tales' authenticity could have been in print and known about for twenty years, without those attitudes having been abandoned years before. To name just three responses on these lines, Linda Dégh (1979), James McGlathery (1977), and Thomas Schumann (1977) credit Rölleke with having, as Schumann puts it, "finally destroyed" this stubbornly widespread legend about the *KHM*.[22] Once again, Schumann carefully makes this seem a legend with a life of its own, avoiding the question of who started it off, and how; and McGlathery and Dégh also just as carefully skirt the issue of the Grimms' clearly deceptive statements, and what kind of light such blatant misleading of the reading public might in itself throw on the authenticity of the tales and the reliability of *any* statement the Grimms might have made about them.

Before drawing any general conclusions about the Grimms' sources, we must first acknowledge that our evidence is not complete; we know much about the sources in many cases, but not in all. And that might seem to allow the possibility that the sources which are not identifiable may have been more authentic than those which are. But this theoretical possibility can be discarded with confidence. The Grimms used Dorothea Viehmann as their star informant—their best case. If there had been any significant sources with more impressive credentials as transmitters of a German folk oral tradition, we can be sure that the Grimms would have used them instead.

The conclusions to be drawn from this discussion are clear. First, the sources of the material the Grimms used were not older, untainted, and untutored German peasant transmitters of an indigenous oral tradition but, instead, literate, middle-class, and predominantly young people, probably influenced more by books than by oral tradition—and including a very significant presence of people who were either of French origin or actually French-speaking. Second, knowledge of the sources shows that they were largely limited to the brothers' family, friends, and acquaintances in their home area, which indicates both a very narrow base for the collection and that the brothers devoted very little energy and interest to collecting. Third, the Grimms deliberately deceived their public by concealing or actually misstating the facts, in order to give an impression of ancient German folk origin for their material which they knew was utterly false. Fourth, the essential facts which show all of these first three conclusions to be true have long been available. And fifth, scholars have shown considerable reluctance to admit that the evidence leads to the first and second conclusions, and complete and universal reluctance to admit that it must lead to the third.

4

The Grimms' Treatment of Their Sources in the Preparation of the First Edition

T he preceding chapter considered one of the two important issues involved in a judgment of the status of the
KHM—the authenticity of the sources of the tales. We
must now turn to the other, the Grimms' use of those sources
in preparing the printed text of the *KHM*. Here, too, the facts
are troublesome; they are consistent neither with the popular
view of the tales, nor with the various attempts by scholars familiar with all or part of the evidence to retain a modified version
of that view, nor even with the Grimms' account in the second
edition preface, that account having already retreated significantly from the popular view.

The first thing that must be said is that the Grimms destroyed
all of the manuscripts that they had used in preparing the first
publication of the *KHM*—surely an action which must seem
strange, given the reverence they professed for the material that
they had received from their informants. To be sure, the papers
left after the deaths of the brothers contain much manuscript
material, in various stages of completeness; but all of this material
dates from *after* the 1812 and 1815 volumes of the first edition
KHM, and appears to have been kept so that a possible third
volume (never actually issued) could be published. None of these
manuscripts can be compared with the printed texts of the first
edition of the *KHM*[1] in order to draw conclusions about
the Grimms' treatment of their sources because none were the

manuscripts from which the brothers produced the 1812 and 1815 *KHM* volumes.

The destruction by the brothers of the manuscript material which was the basis of the *KHM* could well have prevented any judgment as to whether they had accurately described their treatment of the original sources. In the absence of any other information, the solemn assurances of the prefaces that the brothers were scrupulously faithful to their sources might have had to stand. Wilhelm's compulsive rewriting of the text of the subsequent editions ought in any case to have aroused skepticism about the "purity" of the first edition too—though it did not; but any conclusion on this point could only have been speculative. Since they had, in destroying all the relevant manuscripts, effectively suppressed all the direct evidence as to what they really did with their source material in preparing the printed text of the first edition *KHM,* no one could know for sure what happened—or so it would seem. But an unforeseen circumstance thwarted the intent of the brothers. Clemens Brentano knew that the Grimms were collecting fairy tales and wrote asking for copies, intending to use them to provide ideas for the fairy tales he himself was writing—tales which did not pretend to be authentic folktales but instead his own imaginative compositions. The brothers made a set of copies and sent what they had by then collected on October 25, 1810; this material remained among Brentano's papers, and was eventually rediscovered many years after his death. An irony is that it was the consciously unscientific Brentano who preserved this original material, not the more scholarly Grimms; and only Brentano's material can provide the basis for a judgment as to how the Grimms reworked their sources.[2]

Even here we cannot be sure that we have material that is direct from the informants, without any change by the brothers. Only an informant's handwriting could guarantee that the 1810 material had not already been altered by them, but this material is largely already in the Grimms' hands.[3] Nevertheless, the differences between the manuscripts and the printed texts are sufficient to make this further caveat a relatively insignificant one, for the extent of the differences is sufficient to give a clear idea of the nature of the changes made by the brothers, regardless of any they may have made before passing on the manuscripts to Brentano. What the manuscripts in fact showed was an *enor-*

mous discrepancy between the source material and the first edition texts, one far greater than that between the first and seventh editions.

Before considering and interpreting the changes, however, let us look once again at what is by far the most puzzling feature of this situation. The manuscripts from the Brentano *Nachlaß* became available publicly over half a century ago, and there have been no fewer than four editions of the manuscripts published in that time—the first, in 1924, by Schulz; the second, in 1927, by Lefftz; the third, in 1964, by Lemmer; the fourth, in 1975, by Rölleke.[4] And yet these editions seem hardly to have made any impact on the popular view of the status of the *KHM*, nor to have changed the basic structure of the view taken by scholars. Once more, the critical response to the last of these four editions tells the story: Rölleke's edition proved startling to many, and yet there was absolutely no reason why it should. But when material presented three times before has not had its effect, it is not unnatural that the fourth occasion will seem like the first. Schumann, for example, welcomed Rölleke's edition as a work which now made it possible to compare the Grimms' sources with their reworked printed texts.[5] Now ever since 1924 it had been possible to pick up a copy of Schulz's edition in one hand and the *KHM* first edition in the other, and to compare these two; but it must have seemed to Schumann that, given the present state of attitudes to the authenticity of the *KHM*, no one could ever have done it. Yet in point of fact it *had* been done, as we shall see. How, then, was it possible for attitudes to remain virtually unchanged by the earlier editions of the 1810 material?

To be sure, Rölleke's edition is technically superior to that of his three predecessors; that is, exact spelling is retained in all cases, crossings out and additions are noted, and so on. But *all* editions presented the 1810 texts clearly enough that the huge discrepancy between them and the 1812 *KHM* printed texts was immediately obvious. And, if all of this was taken together with the *Notes*, as expanded by Bolte and Polívka, judgments about sources and treatment of them would not differ from those that could be made today. Differences between the editions, therefore, should not have been a factor. On the other hand, the fact that Schulz's edition has remained virtually unused may not be surprising; it can probably be explained by the obscure manner of its publication, taken together with the rapidly following edition of Lefftz. But why did Lefftz not cause more change in attitudes? Only the entire context of the *KHM,* and of the Grimms in German literary history, adequately explains a climate of opinion so inhibited that judgments about both could not go beyond very narrow limits.

It is possible to diagnose two major mechanisms through which these inhibitions expressed themselves. Lefftz himself provides an example of one of these mechanisms. When Lefftz published the 1810 manuscripts, he faced a decision about the tone of his presentation of the material. There was a great discrepancy between this material and what would have been expected, given the brothers' claims and prevailing attitudes to the *KHM.* How was Lefftz to handle this discrepancy? His answer was not to do anything with it: astonishingly enough, he made no mention of these problems whatsoever. Instead, he made his preface a hymn of praise to the brothers and to their respect for their source material:

> The noblest purpose of this book shall be to erect a new monument to the never-to-be-forgotten brothers Grimm and their friendship with Clemens Brentano. What the two young scholars took up at that time from the soil of the nation, they have unfolded before us so faithfully and respectfully, with the clearest feeling for what is genuine and natural, and so pure and untouched, that we today, in editing the early form of their fairy tales, handed down in manuscript form, must especially strive, like the brothers Grimm and above all in relation to them, to be faithful in our deeds and truthful in our work.[6]

Nothing captures the spirit of unreality in the scholarship on the *KHM* so well as this strange passage; for here we have a spirited tribute to the Grimms' passion for truth and authenticity on the part of the very man who is offering the public all the evidence it needs to reach the opposite conclusion!

This pattern recurs frequently in the history of the *KHM;* when Manfred Lemmer reissued the 1810 manuscripts in 1964, he too mentioned none of the problems which they involved, but instead offered them to the public simply as "charming" *(reizvoll)* material.[7] And, as we have seen, the alarming facts about the life of Dorothea Viehmann emerged from an anniversary celebration of her, and were first critically discussed fifteen years later in an essay which ended not in criticism but in another hymn of praise to the brothers. The rule appears to be: the more the facts throw a bad light on the brothers, the more the brothers must be praised in order to compensate.

The second mechanism through which inhibition of adverse judgments operated was a resort to the notion of "style": however big the discrepancies between one edition and another, or between manuscript sources and the Grimms' reworked printed texts, they could always be minimized by attributing them to stylistic differences or the process of stylization. Before the 1810 manuscript material became available, no comparison between the Grimms' sources and their printed texts was possible, but scholars could still be troubled by the considerable differences (which I shall examine below) between the seven editions. In 1912, Ernest Tonnelat undertook a detailed study of the changes which had occurred during the course of the editions, and his general conclusion was a pleasant, reassuring one: "The content of the tales remained the same from the first to the last edition. Not a single new trait was invented . . . Meanwhile, the style became more colorful, more alert, more alive."[8] Three years later, Johannes Bolte welcomed Tonnelat's study and its results, summarizing those results in a shorthand phrase which was to be repeated over and over again in the subsequent studies: "this process of gradual stylizing" ("dieser Prozess allmählicher Stilisierung").[9] After this, virtually any subsequent problems that surfaced would be attributed to "stylizing" and, as a result, not taken seriously. When, therefore, the 1810 manuscripts were discovered, a tool was readily available with which to blunt their impact; and yet the discrepancy between the manuscripts and the first edition *KHM* was huge even in comparison with those between first and seventh editions, and it required a completely different level of euphemistic disregard of the facts. The publication of the 1810 material provoked three major studies which looked at and evaluated the new material: by Elisabeth Freitag in 1929,[10] by Wilhelm Schoof in 1930, and by Kurt Schmidt in 1931. Yet, because of this willing reliance on the concept which they inherited from Ernest Tonnelat by way of Johannes Bolte, the almost incredible outcome of these new studies of the *KHM* in light of this startling new material was conclusions virtually identical to those of Tonnelat, who had had no knowledge of it. Freitag's words even echoed those of Tonnelat; while Tonnelat found that the *KHM* became stylistically more colorful and lively as they progressed from the first to the seventh edition, Freitag found that the 1810 material was made much clearer, more distinct, more expressive, more concrete in its more "stylized" version of the 1812 first edition.[11] Schmidt too, found the language of 1812 more "colorful" stylistically than that of 1810, and talked of the "concretizing" style; these are again Tonnelat's ideas.[12] Schoof in his 1930 study was mainly concerned with the informants and the origins of each manuscript, but soon joined in the prevalent habit of using the word "stylization" to cover any possible problem; but perhaps he may have found some difficulty in using the notion to cover the transition from 1810 to 1812, for he produced an amazing piece of convoluted thinking in order to turn attention away from that discrepancy and toward the more familiar traditional issue of the discrepancies between the seven editions—another example of the unreal quality of much writing on the Grimms:

> The original form of these not yet stylized folk fairy tales is very different from that of the last edition from Wilhelm's hand of 1857. While the printed fairy tales of the first volume of 1812 were still closest to the manuscript records of 1810, the later printed editions had to undergo stylistic changes that became more and more extensive. In contrast to Jacob, who was in favor of the most literal possible rendering of the traditional material, but who left the further editing after the year 1812 to his brother, Wilhelm gave the tales the artistic form which he himself created.[13]

Instead of focusing on the real problem—the huge discrepancy between the 1810 manuscripts and the 1812 printed texts—Schoof begins by mentioning the discrepancy between the manuscripts and the 1857 texts. Having begun thus, he can make several true statements: that the 1810 material is very different from that of 1857, that the closest to the 1810 material is the 1812 material (but how could it be otherwise than that stage 2 in a sequence of eight stages is closest to stage 1?), and that the later material moves further and further away from the 1810 material. Having positioned himself in this way, Schoof can blame Wilhelm for the whole problem, and can manage not to mention, and not to face, the fact that by far the biggest discrepancy between any two successive versions of the *KHM* is between the 1810 and the 1812 texts. Even the many biographies of the year 1970–71 did not allow the 1810 material seriously to influence their thinking. Michaelis-Jena, for example, says only that they provide "useful information on the early stages of the fairy-tale collections,"[14] and then goes back to making the conventional judgments on the status of the *KHM*. And while Peppard says that the manuscripts allow us "now to see their process of selection and editing," he avoids the real issues which they raise by saying that "as early as the Oelenberg manuscript, Jacob combined various sources as he saw fit . . . he sternly enjoined collaborators to transmit exactly without changes of any kind, yet he would combine and adjust himself."[15] But one did not need the 1810 material to conclude that the brothers "combined and adjusted"—they said as much themselves in the preface of 1819. What the 1810 material showed was far, far more than this. Small wonder that Rölleke's publication in 1975 of the 1810 material was a surprising event to many; there has still never been a serious attempt to assimilate its import.

Before we can compare any of the 1810 manuscripts with the 1812 first editon printed *KHM* texts, it is necessary to spell out some factors which place limits on the comparability of the two sets of texts. The point of the comparison is to make judgments about the modus operandi of the brothers through looking at characteristic differences between the two; but in order to do this we must first be sure when dealing with any particular story that the 1810 text is the material exclusively used and reworked by the brothers in the preparation of the 1812 text. The major difficulty here is that collecting went on after October 1810, when all the surviving manuscripts were sent to Brentano. The first volume of the *KHM* contained eighty-six tales, the complete collection twice that number, but the 1810 material probably comprised originally fifty-three texts.[16] Many *KHM* tales are therefore not represented among the 1810 texts, and in fact some 1810 manuscript tales were not included in the *KHM*. Moreover, the 1810 manuscripts are in some cases not the only versions of a given tale used by the brothers in preparing the first *KHM* edition. For some tales they had by 1812 two or three different manuscripts, sometimes basing themselves on one and ignoring the others, and in other cases drawing on all the sources for a single composite text. Care is therefore necessary to make sure that the 1810 and 1812 texts are directly comparable if we are to make valid inferences about the Grimms' procedure from the differences between them; we must be sure that those differences derive from the Grimms' editorial treatment rather than from a now lost alternative manuscript source.[17]

In order to make sure that a judgment of the Grimms' procedure is not contaminated by this kind of error, it is essential first of all to make an analysis of the status of the fifty-three manuscript tales. Three can immediately be discarded, because the brothers made no use of them whatsoever in the printed *KHM*. These are:

23 *Mährchen v. Fanfreuluschens Haupte (Story of Fanfreuluschen's Head)*
31 *Die alte Hexe (The Old Witch)*
(Unnumbered) *Vom König von England (The King of England)*

(The Grimms numbered the manuscripts consecutively from one to fifty-one, leaving two unnumbered, and these are the numbers I have used here.) In addition, eight more manuscripts cannot help us in judging the Grimms' editorial procedure because they have not survived; for one reason or another, they are now missing from the Brentano collection. In the following list of these eight I have also given after each title the corresponding number of the tale in the *KHM* first edition; and the title is also that given the tale in the *KHM:*

1 *Von einem tapfern Schneider (KHM 20) (The Valiant Little Tailor)*
24 *Von den Fischer un süne Fru (KHM 19) (The Fisherman and his Wife)*
28 *Der Sperling und seine vier Kinder (KHM 35, later 157) (The Sparrow and his Four Children)*
30 *Von dem gestohlenen Heller (KHM 7, later 154) (The Stolen Farthing)*
33 *Von dem Mäuschen, Vögelchen und der Bratwurst (KHM 23) (The Mouse, the Bird, and the Sausage)*
38 *Von der Nachtigall und der Blindschleiche (KHM 6, later dropped) (The Nightingale and the Slowworm)*
50 *Aschenputtel (KHM 21) (Cinderella)*
51 *Vom goldnen Vogel (KHM 57) (The Golden Bird)*

The fifty-three are already reduced to forty-two which both survive and have some relevance to the *KHM*. But this number must be reduced still further. Some were obviously not used as the basis of the 1812 texts, being in fact discarded in favor of other manuscript versions of a given tale, which the brothers must have considered superior ones. In these cases the brothers briefly summarized the 1810 manuscript in the notes to the *KHM*, presenting it only as an alternative version of the tale they printed; generally, there are significant variations in the plot which allow the 1810 manuscript clearly to be identified as this alternative version. In this category are the following, with titles once more those of the *KHM* printed tale rather than in the wording of the manuscript:

7   *Allerlei-rauh (KHM* 65) *(Allerleirauh)*
13 *Von dem Dummling, III, Die drei Federn (KHM* 64/III) *(The Three Feathers)*
15 *Vom dem Dummling, III, Die drei Federn (KHM* 64/III) *(The Three Feathers*—both this and the preceding are unused variants to the same *KHM* story)
42 *Rumpelstilzchen (KHM* 55) *(Rumpelstiltskin)*

Still others were only summarized in the notes to different stories in the *KHM,* because the Grimms considered them to be variants on the same basic theme expressed in the *KHM* story. For example, they considered a manuscript *Däumling* story to be thematically only a *Hansel and Gretel* variant. The list of those manuscripts only summarized in *KHM* notes to other tales is as follows (*KHM* titles here are in square brackets):

12 *Däumling [Hänsel und Gretel, KHM* 15] *(Thumbling)*
20 *Der Drache [Vom dem Sommer- und Wintergarten, KHM* 68] *(The Dragon)*
22 *Die goldne Ente [Die weiße und schwarze Braut, KHM* II/49] *(The Golden Duck)*
29 *Herr Hände [Von dem Schneider der bald reich wurde, KHM* 61] *(Mr. Hands)*
32 *Goldner Hirsch [Brüderchen und Schwesterchen, KHM* 11] *(The Golden Deer)*
36 *Der Mond und seine Mutter [Die drei Raben, KHM* 25] *(The Moon and his Mother)*
37 *Murmelthier [Frau Holle, KHM* 24] *(The Marmot)*
46 *Das stumme Mädchen [Marienkind, KHM* 3] *(The Dumb Girl)*

The number of manuscripts usable for our purposes has now shrunk to thirty. But still, that number must be reduced again.

Three more manuscripts were only partial sources for the 1812 texts, which in these cases combined a number of versions; again, titles are those given in the *KHM:*

10   *Die zwölf Brüder* (*KHM* 9) (*The Twelve Brothers*)
21   *König Droßelbart* (*KHM* 52) (*King Thrushbeard*)
43   *Sneewittchen* (*KHM* 53) (*Snow-White*)

Four more were fragments or a summary sketch, in which cases it could easily be argued that the brothers had of necessity to fill out and elaborate their source somewhat; that being so, no conclusions about the Grimms' general editorial practice could be drawn:

8   *Das arme Mädchen* (*KHM* 83, later 153) (*The Poor Girl*)
39   *Das gute Pflaster* (*KHM* 85d, later dropped) (*The Good Plaster*)
44   *Das Goldei* (*KHM* 60) (*The Golden Egg*)
45   *Prinz Schwan* (*KHM* 59) (*Prince Swan*)

Three more are very brief manuscripts of less than two hundred words, and for similar reasons general conclusions from these cases could be suspect:

5   *Strohhalm, Kohle und Bohne auf der Reise* (*KHM* 18) (*The Straw, the Coal, and the Bean*)
9   *Die wunderliche Gasterei* (*KHM* 43) (*The Strange Feast*)
47   *Die Wassernix* (*KHM* 79) (*The Water-Nixie*)

The remaining twenty, however, are all fairly full manuscript versions of the tales corresponding to the *KHM* texts, and used by the brothers in preparing those texts. But there is one further caveat. A number of these twenty were dropped in later editions of the *KHM*. There are only twelve of these twenty manuscripts which were the basis of the *KHM* first edition texts and continued to be so used throughout all of the editions:

2   *Vom Kätzchen und Mäuschen* (*KHM* 2) (*Cat and Mouse*)
3   *Läuschen und Flöhchen* (*KHM* 30) (*The Louse and the Flea*)
6   *Der Wolf und die sieben jungen Geislein* (*KHM* 5) (*The Wolf and the Seven Little Kids*)
11   *Hänsel und Gretel* (*KHM* 15) (*Hansel and Gretel*)

14 *Des Schneiders Daumerling Wanderschaft* (*KHM* 45) (*Thumbling's Travels*)
18 *Vom dem Dummling: Die Bienenkönigin* (*KHM* 64/II) (*The Queen Bee*)
19 *Dornröschen* (*KHM* 50) (*Sleeping Beauty*)
25 *Der Froschkönig oder der eiserne Heinrich* (*KHM* 1) (*The Frog-King, or Iron Henry*)
26 *Vom Fundevogel* (*KHM* 51) (*Fundevogel*)
27 *Von dem Dummling: Die goldene Gans* (*KHM* 64/IV) (*The Golden Goose*)
34 *Marienkind* (*KHM* 3) (*Our Lady's Child*)
(Unnumbered) *Herr Korbes* (*KHM* 41) (*Mr. Korbes*)

Two of the *KHM* first edition tales for which the 1810 manuscripts served as the basis were subsequently completely omitted from the *KHM* late editions:

35 *Prinzessin Mäusehaut* (*KHM* 7) (*Princess Mice-Skin*)
49 *Vom Schreiner und Drechsler* (*KHM* 77) (*The Joiner and the Turner*)

(In addition, the fragmentary 35, *Das gute Pflaster,* already listed above, was also later abandoned.) Three more 1810 manuscripts which were used as the basis of the 1812 texts were not so used in subsequent editions; later *KHM* editions had their texts of these stories based on a different, now lost manuscript:

4 *Vom treuen Gevatter Sperling* (*KHM* 58) (*The Dog and the Sparrow*)
17 *Von dem Dummling: Die drei Federn* (*KHM* 64/III) (*The Three Feathers*)
41 *Der Räuberbräutigam* (*KHM* 40) (*The Robber Bridegroom*)

(In addition, the fragmentary 44, *Das Goldei,* and the very brief 9, *Die wunderliche Gasterei,* already listed above, were also abandoned in favor of other manuscript versions of the same tale.) Another tale which had been based on its one surviving manuscript in the 1812 *KHM* was rewritten in later editions as a version combined from that manuscript and another, now lost:

40 *Die drei Raben* (*KHM* 25) (*The Three Ravens*)

Finally, two more 1812 tales which had been based on surviving 1810 manuscripts were in subsequent editions omitted from the

collection and instead mentioned only in notes to different stories as variants on the same kind of theme:

16   *Von dem Dummling: Die weiße Taube* (*KHM* 64/I) (*The White
     Dove*)
48   *Von Johannes-Wassersprung und Caspar-Wassersprung* (*KHM*
     74) (*Johann-Waterspring and Casper-Waterspring*)

(The same fate befell the fragmentary 45, *Prinz Schwan*, already
listed above.)

To sum up: there are twenty tales where the differences between the 1810 and 1812 texts reflect the modus operandi of
the brothers without the intervention of any other factors, but
if we wish to trace the brothers' treatment of a particular text
throughout the seven editions of the *KHM*, this number shrinks
to twelve. While this is no more than one-tenth of the full *KHM*,
it is still enough to allow some firm conclusions to be drawn,
conclusions which, moreover, are fully supported by a comparison of the *general* character of all the 1810 manuscripts with
that of the entirety of the 1812 texts.

A major source of the information necessary to clarify the
manuscript situation in this way is the brothers' notes to the tales;
the notes allow us to interpret the relation of a particular manuscript to a printed text and to avoid, for example, the danger of
comparing a particular manuscript to a first edition text when
in fact that text was based wholly or partly on a variant manuscript which the Grimms had received *after* they had sent this
material to Brentano in October 1810. Generally, when they had
only one manuscript version of a tale, they would simply note
its place of origin. Where, on the other hand, they composed
the printed text by combining different manuscript versions,
they noted that the printed version is "nach verschiedenen Erzählungen" or "nach vielfachen Erzählungen" ("after various
stories"). Or when there were divergent manuscript versions of
a particular tale of which they followed one and *not* the others,
they would summarize the distinctive plot features of those others, usually beginning, "es wird auch erzählt . . ." (the story is
also told, of . . .").[18]

Through use of this information it is often possible to say with
near certainty that a particular manuscript was or was not the
exclusive basis of an 1812 *KHM* tale. To take one example: *Rumpelstilzchen* in the 1812 *KHM* begins with a girl in distress because

she must spin gold out of flax; the 1810 manuscript begins the other way around, the girl being given the task of spinning flax and being unable to spin anything but gold. The plot understandably develops differently in the two cases. In their notes,[19] the Grimms tell us that "the story is also often begun differently, as follows . . ." and they then summarize a plot which is clearly that of the 1810 manuscript. Here, evidently, one can conclude nothing about their editorial procedure by comparing manuscript and first edition, for that edition was based on a different manuscript entirely.

The same is true of *Sneewittchen (Snow-white):* here the notes say that "another story varies only in the fact that the Queen goes into the wood with Snow-White, and asks her to pick a bunch of the pretty roses that are there; while she picks them the Queen goes off and leaves her alone." This variant substitutes for the part of the *KHM* version in which the Queen orders the hunter to take Snow-White into the forest and kill her. The 1810 manuscript is clearly the variant version in question; its relevant part reads:

> Wie nun der Herr König einmal in den Krieg verreist war, so ließ sie ihren Wagen anspannen u. befahl in einen weiten dunkeln Wald zu fahren, u. nahm das Schneeweißchen mit. In dem selben Wald aber standen viel gar schöne rothe Rosen. Als sie nun mit ihrem Töchterlein daselbst angekommen war, so sprach sie zu ihm: ach Schneeweißchen steig doch aus u. brich mir von den schönen Rosen ab! Und sobald es diesem Befehl zu gehorchen aus dem Wagen gegangen war, fuhren die Räder in größter Schnelligkeit fort, aber die Frau Königin hatte alles so befohlen, weil sie hoffte, daß es die wilden Thiere bald verzehren sollten.[20]

> (When the King had gone off to the war, she had her carriage made ready and commanded to be taken with Snow-white to a large, dark forest. But in this same wood there were many very pretty red roses. When she arrived there with her little daughter, she said to her: oh, Snow-white, get out and pick some of the pretty roses for me! And as soon as Snow-white had got out of the carriage to do as she said, the wheels went off at great speed, but the Queen had commanded it all to happen, because she hoped that the wild animals soon would eat the child.)

Again, no simple inference can be made from the comparison of the manuscript to the first edition,[21] since here a different manuscript, not preserved, would be the only real basis for that comparison.

König Droßelbart (King Thrushbeard) is an example of a different problem; information contained in the marginalia to the Grimms' copy of the 1812 *KHM* and in the notes of 1822 (second edition) indicate that the 1812 text combines the 1810 manuscript with another which has not survived. Again, the texts of 1810 and 1812 are not directly comparable. But where the notes do not mention a second or more versions, or where variant versions are mentioned and then described as having features not found in the 1810 manuscript, we may be fairly sure that a direct comparison between the 1810 and 1812 versions will indicate how the Grimms reworked the former to produce the latter, and the results are so consistent from one story to another that any error of inference in a specific case will not alter the resulting picture substantially.

To be sure, information provided by the Grimms themselves can never be free of suspicion when it is already clear that they intended to deceive their public about the status of the *KHM;* but there are good reasons to regard their *Notes* as reliable sources of information. For the manuscripts which appeared in the Brentano *Nachlaß* showed that whenever the Grimms referred in their notes to the 1810 materials, they did so quite truthfully and even scrupulously, and yet they had no reason to suppose that their readers would ever see this material. The point is that the brothers had no reason to lie about which particular manuscripts were the basis of their printed texts—what they wanted to conceal was what they had routinely done to *any* manuscript, and the question of precisely which manuscripts they had treated in their characteristic way was immaterial once they had destroyed them all. This, surely, is the reason why the results obtained from comparing the texts are, as I have said, so consistent from one text to another. Moreover, one very important conclusion about the general relation between the 1810 and 1812 texts can be determined quite easily, almost regardless of the question of whether particular texts in either group are directly comparable: the latter are generally very much longer than the former. In fact, the 1812 text is commonly twice as long as its 1810 counterpart,[22] and sometimes two and a half times as long. There is nothing like a comparable increase in the progress of the *KHM* from the first to the seventh editions. There are, to be sure, odd cases in which a noticeable increase in the length of a text can be seen in the seventh edition. *Die sieben Raben (The Seven Ravens)* is an example. However, this case represents not the elaboration and lengthening of the same text that existed in the first edition, but rather the introduction of much new material from a different manuscript and in many ways a different story. The title shows as much, for in the first edition the title was *Die drei Raben (The Three Ravens);* and the motivation for the brothers being changed into ravens is both altogether different and a much longer part of the tale in the seventh edition. Even so, the story is only lengthened by a half, not doubled, as is often the case in the transition from the manuscripts to the first edition.

Apart from the odd case of this kind, the lengthening involved in the progress from the 1810 manuscripts to the 1812 printed texts is far greater than any subsequent edition's elaboration of its predecessor; evidently the Grimms rewrote and elaborated their manuscript material very freely indeed, and in a way that cannot be made consistent with any of their programmatic statements in the first and second edition prefaces. To double the length of a text obviously makes nonsense of the claim in the first preface that nothing has been improved or altered. And even though the terms of the statement in the second preface would allow editorial changes, it is difficult to reconcile the kind and extent of change that really took place with the rationale for editorial changes set out in that preface. For here, still, it was insisted that only the expression had been changed, that nothing had been *added* or improved, and that the point of all this was in any case to search for what would be simpler, and purer *(das Einfachere, Reinere)*. But on the contrary the Grimms moved precisely in the opposite direction: they gave the texts not a simpler but a much more elaborate verbal structure; their original form had been far more simple and bare. The result was not refining of material (which might suggest a *decrease* in wording, cutting and perhaps making the text more pointed) but instead expansion and elaboration. So great an increase in sheer wordage of the texts created an altogether different sense of fullness and explicitness, and a totally different aura. But in any case, once we recall the circumstances of the second edition preface, it will become obvious that it is pointless to try to reconcile the considerable rewriting and expansion of the manuscripts for the first edition with the programmatic statement of the second edition. For that programmatic statement, it will be remembered, is introduced only because of the problem created by the changes between the first and second editions; the Grimms would scarcely have used it to defend the far greater changes that they had already made before the first edition—changes which they thought their public would never know about, and which they knew could only be defended by concealing them completely and suppressing their manuscripts.

It is important to recall again just why the voice of the actual storyteller is important, and why so many scholars have insisted that the Grimms' respect for that voice is a central feature of their work: versions of the same tale occur in many countries, and the *only* ethnographical importance of the Grimms' *KHM* lies precisely in its being evidence of the specific character of German storytelling. A freely retold version of the Grimms' sources may result in a better story, a smoother story or a more attractive story—and the history of the *KHM* proves that these were indeed the results. But it certainly did not make the kind of story which those printed in the *KHM* are claimed to be in the Grimms' prefaces, and which, on the basis of those prefaces, were then hailed by scholars as important testimony of storytelling by the German *Volk;* for the degree of the Grimms' recasting and rewriting, even if judged only in terms of the sheer extent of new material added, was sufficient to swamp the voice of the informant storytellers, and to obliterate their characteristic tone or style.

Once more, scholars have struggled hard to find ways of avoiding this knowledge. Max Lüthi, for example, sets out parallel passages from the 1810 and 1812 texts which show changes of very great extent, and can only bring himself to say, with evident reluctance: "It is clear: the Grimm brothers did not tell the fairy tales exactly in the same way that they heard them."[23] But to say that they did not tell them *exactly* as they heard them is an understatement so great as to amount to a complete misdescription of what Lüthi has just set out; it suggests a minor change here and there, not a complete recasting and doubling or tripling of the extent of the text. And what is truly remarkable here is that Lüthi speaks as if he had only just discovered that the Grimms were not *completely* faithful to the expression of their sources, whereas in 1819 the brothers had already confessed that the expression of the tales was *largely* their own! But Lüthi is an instructive and typical example of the way in which so many have been so attracted to the popular view of the *KHM* based on the first edition prefaces that they refused even to accept the admission the Grimms made in 1819—though that admission, too, considerably understated the seriousness of the problem.

Schoof tried another way of explaining away the very large gap between the manuscripts and the first edition. He argued that the Grimms were simply seeking a *unified* style for their collection *(eine Stileinheit)*.[24] But this too is just as obviously inconsistent with the facts of the various texts as it is with the brothers' claims in both prefaces. What the Grimms were doing was not leveling the style of the stories, or standardizing it so that all should be in the same style, but instead creating a degree of fullness and explicitness entirely different to that present in *any* of their oral sources.

To sum up so far: even if we consider the extent of the Grimms' reworking of their source material only from a stylistic point of view, it is still wholly inconsistent with their own claims, or with those of their apologists, or with the possibility that their printed texts retain the voice or style of the German folktale teller, and hence have any significance for Germanic folklore. But in addition, given so great a degree of expansion of the texts, it was impossible not also to introduce new elements of substance into the tales: new aspects of events, characters, motivation, and theme. The Grimms simply could not avoid changing the substance of the stories as well as their verbal fabric in tampering with them to so great an extent.

The tale of the Daumerling (or Däumerling) provides a good example of the sheer weight of the new material added by the Grimms' elaboration and its impact on the content of the story. Information in the notes to the *KHM* allows a firm conclusion that *Des Schneiders Daumerling Wanderschaft (Thumbling's Travels)* in the first edition derives from the 1810 manuscript *Vom Schneiderlein Däumerling*. Daumerling's first experience after setting out on his travels is, in the manuscript, as follows:

> Zuerst kommt er zu einem Meister in Arbeit, da ist ihm das Eßen nicht gut genug, u. wie er nicht eßen will, wird die Meisterfrau bös u. will ihn schlagen, er kriecht aber behend

untern Fingerhut u. macht allerlei Streiche u. verbirgt sich unter den Lappen, Tischritzen u.s.w. sobald man an ihn will, endlich wird er fortgejagt.

(At first he goes to work with a Master, but the food there is not good enough, and when he won't eat, the Master's wife becomes angry and wants to beat him, but he nimbly crawls under a thimble and pulls all sorts of tricks and hides under the cloth, in crevices in the table, and so on, every time she wants to get at him. Finally he is chased out.)

But here is the corresponding passage in the first edition of 1812:

Das Schneiderlein zog aus in die Welt und kam zuerst bei einem Meister in die Arbeit, da war ihm aber das Essen nicht gut genug. "Frau Meisterin, wenn sie uns kein besser Essen giebt, sagte der Daumerling, schreib ich morgenfrüh mit Kreide an ihre Hausthüre: 'Kartoffel zu viel, Fleisch zu wenig, Adies, Herr Kartoffelkönig!' und gehe fort."—"Was willst du wohl, du Hüperferling" sagte die Meisterin, ward bös, ergriff einen Lappen und wollte ihn schlagen, mein Schneiderlein kroch behend unter den Fingerhut, guckte unten hervor und streckte der Frau Meisterin die Zunge heraus. Sie hob den Fingerhut auf, aber der Daumerling hüpfte in die Lappen und wie die Meisterin die Lappen auseinander warf und ihn suchte, machte er sich in den Tischritz: "he! he! Frau Meisterin," rief er und steckte den Kopf in die Höhe, und wenn sie zuschlagen wollte, sprang er immer in die Schublade hinunter. Endlich aber erwischte sie ihn doch, und jagte ihn zum Haus hinaus.

(The little tailor set off into the world, and first went to work with a Master, but there the food was not good enough for him. "Mistress, if you don't give us better food, said Thumbling, I'll write tomorrow morning on your door with chalk: 'too much potatoes, too little meat, farewell Mr. Potato-king' and I'll leave." "What are you about, you grasshopper," said the Mistress, became angry, seized a cloth, and wanted to hit him, but my little tailor crawled nimbly under a thimble, looked out from under it, and put his tongue out at the Mistress. She picked up the thimble, but the Thumbling hopped into the cloth, and when the Mistress shook the cloth out to look for him, he got into the crevice in the table: "Ho! Ho! Mistress," he cried out and raised his head, and when she wanted to strike, he always jumped down into the drawer. But at last she caught him, and drove him out of the house.)

The number of words here is two and a half times that of the original, and because of the volume of the new material, there can be no question of the style and tone of the finished product being close to that of the original; the new material dominates, and sets the tone. Even if the original *had* been of genuine folk origin, and evidence of the tone and voice of German folk story telling (which it was not, in any case), that crucial characteristic would have been quite lost. But the new detail has an obvious impact on the substance of the story. In the 1812 version, we see the Thumbling sticking his tongue out at the Mistress and speaking to her in a decidedly rude way, and it is this misbehavior that causes his departure; but in the 1810 version the emphasis is on her behavior, nor his, leading to that departure. It is her exaggerated anger over his failure to eat a poor meal, not his rudeness, that causes the trouble. And so we have a rather different Thumbling, and thus a different story, in the Grimms' rewriting. To say that the Grimms have not told the story in the same *manner* as the original does not do the situation justice; for this is in one important respect no longer the same story.

This was not the only case in which the Grimms, possibly without meaning to do so, changed part of the essential character of the figure of the Thumbling. (The name is variously given in different manuscripts as Daumerling, Däumerling, Däumling, Dummling or Dümmling.) The 1810 manuscript *Die drei Königssöhne (The Three King's Sons)* is a Thumbling story in which the youngest son outwits his two older brothers by performing a number of tasks set for the three by their father, the king, while his brothers could not do so. The third of these tasks is to find the most beautiful woman possible, the winner being promised the kingdom as a reward. As in his previous tasks, the smallest son (here "Däumling") gets help from a maiden who lives in an underground cave:

> Wie Däumling hinunter kommt, sagt ihm das Mädchen, er solle nur weiter in das Gewölbe gehn in das goldne Gemach, da werde er die schönste Dame findet [sic]. Er eilt hin, und öffnet ein Gemach das von Gold und Edelsteinen blitzt, aber drinnen sitzt keine Dame sondern eine [sic] entsetzlich häßlicher Frosch. Doch faßt er Muth, und trägt ihn herauf zu einem nahen Teich, wo er ihn hinabwirft, kaum aber berührt der Frosch das Waßer, so verwandelt er sich in die schönste Dame, die je gelebt hat.

(As Thumbling descends, the girl says to him, he must go further into the vault, into the golden room, where he will find the most beautiful lady. He hurries there, opens a room that sparkles with gold and precious stones, but in it is not a lady but a horribly ugly frog. But he takes courage, and carries him up to a nearby pond, where he throws him in, but no sooner does the frog touch the water than he changes into the most beautiful lady who ever lived.)

Of course, the frog turns into the required beautiful woman, and Däumling wins the contest. This tale was included in the *KHM* first edition as *Von dem Dummling: III. Die drei Federn (The Three Feathers)*, and the manuscript was subjected to the Grimms' usual elaboration. The passage cited above was doubled in length, to become the following:

Da ging er hinunter und klagte dem Mädchen, was sein Vater wieder für ihn so schweres aufgelegt habe, das Mädchen aber sagte, es wolle ihm schon helfen, er solle nur weiter in dem Gewölbe gehen, da werde er die schönste auf der Welt finden. Der Dummling ging hin und kam an ein Gemach, worin alles von Gold und Edelsteinen schimmerte und flimmerte, aber statt einer schönen Frau, saß ein garstiger Frosch mitten darin. Der Frosch rief ihm zu: "umschling mich und versenk dich!" Er wollte aber nicht, da rief der Frosch zum zweiten und drittenmal: "umschling mich und versenk dich!" De faßte der Dummling den Frosch, und trug ihn herauf zu einem Teich, und sprang mit ihm hinein, kaum aber hatte das Wasser sie berührt, so hielt er die allerschönste Jungfrau in seinen Armen.

(Then he descended and complained to the girl, what a difficult task his father had imposed upon him again, but the girl said that she would help him, he had only to go further into the vault, where he would find the most beautiful woman in the world. Thumbling went and came to a room, where everything sparkled and shimmered of gold and precious stones, but instead of a beautiful woman a horrible frog sat there. The frog called to him: "Embrace me and immerse yourself!" He did not want to do it, and the frog called out a second and third time: "Embrace me and immerse yourself!" Then Thumbling grasped the frog, and carried him up to a pond, and jumped in with him, but hardly had they touched the water when he held the most beautiful maiden in his arms.)

It is possible to regard some of this elaboration as lengthening for its own sake, according to recognizable formulas; for example, the frog has to ask three times before the Dummling will do as he asks, and this threefold repetition is found many times in the *KHM*. But here it is completely out of place: a stock lengthening formula has changed the character of what is happening. Essential to the traditional character of the Thumbling are two related characteristics. First, he usually grasps the right thing to do immediately and instinctively, and does it without any hesitation or thought. And second, he is absolutely undaunted by anything: he acts easily and confidently, rarely betraying any anxiety. Now the Grimms' lengthening formulas may have a generalized quaint fairy-tale effect, but they are in this case antithetical to the character of the Thumbling. They make the Thumbling hesitate out of fear of the frog's ugliness, thus removing the essential self-confidence of this figure. The original text had him showing the courage we expect of him, and in the face of a much uglier frog than that of the rewritten first edition text.

The little boy's hesitation in the first edition text is uncharacteristic whatever the reason. But the elaboration makes another important change in Thumbling's character. In the original, he does not even need telling what to do: the little boy knows instinctively. Simply in having the frog explain what he must do, the Grimms have changed the Thumbling in a critical way; they have removed his easy, assured grasp of what is necessary in any situation. In changing the form of the expression here, the Grimms have cut into an essential part of the substance of the Thumbling.

Dornröschen (Sleeping Beauty) presents another good example of the effects of the Grimms' elaborations. Again, the evidence suggests that the 1810 text was the exclusive basis of that of 1812. The 1810 version reads:

> Nach langer langer Zeit kam ein Königssohn in das Land, dem erzählte ein alter Mann die Geschichte, die er sich erinnerte von seinem Großvater gehört zu haben, u. daß schon viele versucht hätten durch die Dornen zu gehen, aber alle hängen gelieben wären. Als sich aber dieser Prinz der Dornhecke näherte, so thaten sich alle Dornen vor ihm auf u. vor ihm schienen sie Blumen zu seyn, u. hinter ihm wurden sie wieder zu Dörnern.

(After a long, long time a king's son came into the land, he
was told the story by an old man who remembered hearing
it from his grandfather and that already many had tried to
get through the thorns, but had all remained hanging in them.
But when this prince went up to the thorn hedge, all the
thorns parted in front of him and seemed to be flowers, and
behind him they turned into thorns again.)

But in the *KHM* printed text this passage has been reworked to
become the following:

Prinzen, die von dem schönen Dornröschen gehört hatten,
kamen und wollten es befreien, aber sie konnten durch die
Hecke nicht hindurch dringen, es war als hielten sich die
Dornen fest wie an Händen zusammen, und sie blieben darin
hängen und kamen jämmerlich um. So währte das lange,
lange Jahre: da zog einmal ein Königssohn durch das Land,
dem erzählte ein alter Mann davon, man glaube, daß hinter
der Dornhecke ein Schloß stehe, und eine wunderschöne
Prinzessin schlafe darin mit ihrem ganzen Hofstaat; sein
Großvater habe ihm gesagt, daß sonst viele Prinzen gekommen wären und hätten hindurchdringen wollen, sie wären
aber in den Dornen hängen geblieben und todtgestochen worden. "Das soll mich nicht schrecken, sagte der Königssohn,
ich will durch die Hecke dringen und das schöne Dornröschen
befreien"; da ging er fort, und wie er zu der Dornhecke kam,
waren es lauter Blumen, die thaten sich von einander, und er
ging hindurch, und hinter ihm wurden es wieder Dornen.

(Princes, who had heard of the beautiful Thorn-rose, came
and wanted to free her, but they could not penetrate through
the hedge, it was as if the thorns held fast together like clasped
hands, and they remained hanging in them and died pitifully.
That went on for many long years: then once a king's son
traveled through the land, an old man told him of the fact
that people believed that behind the thorn-hedge stood a castle, and a wondrously beautiful princess was sleeping in it with
her whole court; his grandfather had told him that many other
Princes had come and wanted to penetrate, but had remained
hanging in the thorns and had been pierced to death. "That
shall not frighten me, said the king's son, I will penetrate
through the hedge and free the beautiful Thorn-rose"; then
he went off, and as he came to the thorn hedge, there was
nothing but flowers which moved apart, and he went through,
and behind him they became thorns again.)

Of course, this much elaborated passage has destroyed any characteristic "voice" or style of the original; but it has also added motivational factors to the story which change its characters and indeed its logic in important respects. An obvious addition, for example, is emphasis on the bravery of the prince; but an important change in the story's very logic lies in the added information that all of the would-be rescuers had been princes. In the original version, there had been many *(schon viele)* who had failed in their attempts to rescue Dornröschen, until one unique individual succeeded, and he was a prince. The implication is that only a prince was adequate for the task, and a fit match for Dornröschen. But in the Grimms' rewritten version, one prince succeeds where *other princes* have failed; and so, his success is not a matter of his being a prince. Why, then, does this one succeed where others have failed? To this, there is no answer; a gap has opened up in the logic of the story's plot which was not there in the original.

My point here is not that the Grimms wanted to impose a different conception on the plot of the original version; I very much doubt that the effects of these particular changes are the result of a clear intent on their part to change the story, its plot, or its characters. But the story is certainly changed, and some such changes of substance are inevitable, given the extent of the Grimms' elaboration of their sources. So much new material necessarily has an impact on the motivation of the story. Still, the *kind* of change is significant: while the Grimms' intent may well have been to fill out the story, the result is an inherently less well-motivated plot, and a correspondingly greater reliance on fairy tale clichés which substitute on occasion for the original motivation.

A recurrent pattern in the Grimms' elaborations is the addition of language intended to clarify motivation, and to explain the events more thoroughly. We have already seen this tendency clashing with an essential part of a particular story, that is, the Daumerling's being able to seize the right path swiftly and surely without any explanation being offered him. But there are many other cases in which the Grimms' attempts to make the motivation of the tales clearer simply results in their narrowing down the possible range of explanations or motives, on occasion excluding those that seem the most interesting through the addition of explicit explanatory material which restricts motivation to a single possibility.

An interesting case in point is the beginning of *Von Johannes-Wassersprung und Caspar-Wassersprung*. Here is the opening of the 1810 manuscript:

> Ein König hatte eine Prinzeßin, welche nicht heirathen sollte; er ließ ihr daher ein Haus im Walde bauen. Nicht weit davon wahr [sic] eine wohlthätige Quelle; sie ließ sich hiervon reichen und trank es; und die Folge davon war daß sie 2 Prinzen gebahr. Sie zieht sie groß und der König, welchem es lange nachher gemeldet wurde, läßt sie die Jägerei lernen.

> (A King had a princess, who was not to marry. Because of this he had a house built for her in the forest. Not far from it was a beneficial spring; she had water fetched from it and drank it; the result of this was that she bore 2 princes. She raises them and the king, to whom this was told long after, has them taught hunting.)

Once more, there is much elaboration of this in the first edition's text:

> Ein König bestand darauf, seine Tochter sollte nicht heirathen, und ließ ihr in einem Wald in der größten Einsamkeit ein Haus bauen, darin mußte sie mit ihren Jungfrauen wohnen, und bekam gar keinen andern Menschen zu sehen. Nah an dem Waldhaus aber war eine Quelle mit wunderbaren Eigenschaften, davon trank die Prinzessin, und die Folge war, daß sie zwei Prinzen gebar, die darnach Johannes-Wassersprung und Caspar-Wassersprung genannt wurden, und wovon einer dem andern vollkommen ähnlich war. Ihr Großvater, der alte König, ließ sie die Jägerei lernen, und sie wuchsen heran, wurden groß und schön.

> (A king insisted upon the fact that his daughter should not marry, and had a house built for her in the forest in the greatest solitude, in which she had to live with her maidens, and never saw any other person. Nearby the house in the forest, however, was a spring with supernatural properties, from which the princess drank, and the consequence was, that she bore two princes, who accordingly were named Johannes-Waterspring and Casper-Waterspring and one was exactly like the other. Their grandfather, the old king, had them taught hunting, and they grew tall and handsome.)

At first sight, the Grimms' explanatory additions may seem no more than legitimate extensions of the original; but a closer look shows that they have excluded very important possibilities in the situation. In the original the situation is described very sketchily, but in a way typical of fairy tales: many connecting links are missing, and the point here is that the vagueness and mystery is an essential part of the original. We get some outlines of the situation, but not enough. A daughter is not to marry. Why? We are not told. Whose is this decision? We do not know. Her father builds for her a secluded house. Why? Probably something to do with the first two questions. She bears two children in mystifying fashion, keeping it from her father. When he finds out, he helps to raise them just as if they were his own. What does he think of her behavior? Is he angry? Is he curious as to who the father is? We are not told.

If we think about all of this, and especially of the gaps in what seems a pointedly incomplete text, we surely must entertain one obvious possibility: incest. That would explain a great deal of what happens, and fill in some of those odd gaps of motivation. The answer to the puzzle of why the daughter is not to marry would lie in her incestuous relationship with her father; the reason for his building a secluded house for her is to hide this shocking secret from the world; the answer to the mysterious birth of the two sons without any visible father would lie in her own father's role; the answer to his accepting them and raising them is the fact that they are his own; and the reason for his lack of anger about her possible misconduct is his knowing very well that this is not the case.

My point is not that this is the correct interpretation, but that it is a strong possibility that the odd gaps, taken together, at least suggest. And now it will be clearer how the Grimms have done violence to the original text in rewriting, elaborating, and clarifying it. In the reworked 1812 text, many details introduced by the Grimms lead us well away from the possibility of incest. For example, the princess lives with her women in the 1812 version, and sees no other person—which excludes her father, too. In 1812, he is explicitly the grandfather of the children, and the *old* king while the original leaves his relationship with the children open, as well as his age, and thus his vigor. The reason for the daughter's not marrying lies now in her father's explicit command—thus excluding the possibility of its being the result of their mutual understanding based on their relationship. In addition, the Grimms try to make the story of the childrens' birth seem more plausible, and thus shift it further away from possible natural causes, by giving the spring supernatural properties. In the original it had only been a beneficial spring. In all of these details, the Grimms' filling in the gaps and making motivation more explicit committed the story to a particular kind of explanation and excluded another; but what was excluded was precisely the kind of explanation that characteristically lurks in those murky gaps in fairy tales, and should be allowed to remain there. The story is damaged if it is removed. But perhaps the Grimms were conscious here of what they were doing. For their revision of the tale for the 1812 text still did not satisfy them; after the first edition, they threw this story out of the *KHM* altogether. It is altogether possible that they thought the suggestion of incest and illegitimate birth was too strong even after their attempts to remove it. To this matter I shall return in the following chapter when looking at the common characteristics of all of the tales that were gradually removed from the *KHM*.

A different kind of damage occurs through clarification of motivation in the story of the golden goose, one of the *Dummling* tales in the 1812 *KHM*. (Dummling/Simpleton is a variant of the Däumling/Thumbling.) In this story the Dummling and his brothers are all in turn asked by a little gray man in the forest to share their food with him, and all but the Dummling refuse. The consequence is that the two older children suffer injuries while working in the forest, while Dummling finds a golden goose, and eventually marries a princess. In the 1810 version the gray man is a shadowy figure, and we do not experience any description of him or any speech from him. When the little boy meets him in the forest, this is what happens: "Nun geht der dritte in Wald u. gibt dem Männchen seinen Kuchen. Darauf haut er den Baum ab u. findet unter dem Baum eine goldene Gans" ("Now the third child goes into the forest and gives the little man his cake. Then he chops down the tree and finds under it a golden goose"). For the 1812 first edition, the brothers rewrote this as follows:

> Endlich ging der Dummling hinaus, das Männchen sprach ihn, wie die andern, um ein Stück Kuchen an. "Da hast du

ihn ganz," sagte der Dummling, und gab ihn hin. Da sagte
das Männchen: "hau diesen Baum ab, so wirst du etwas finden." Der Dummling hieb da zu, und als der Baum umfiel,
saß eine goldene Gans darunter.

(Finally the Simpleton went out, and the little man asked him,
as he had asked the others, for a piece of cake. "Have it all,"
said the Simpleton and gave it to him. Then the little man
said; "Chop down this tree and you will find something." The
Simpleton began chopping, and when the tree fell, a golden
goose was sitting under it.)

Again, the elaboration looks plausible enough; but more has
changed than is apparent at first glance. One point here will
already be clear from the discussion above of another story of
the Daumerling/Dummling group; in 1810, the Dummling knows
instinctively exactly what to do, while in 1812 he has to be told.
But there is also a change in the figure of the little gray man.
In the original he is a mysterious figure, and the link between
the Dummling's good fortune and the gray man is not entirely
clear. Perhaps the gray man himself is rewarding the Dummling
for his kindness; or perhaps the world is rewarding the Dummling for his kind acts towards the gray man. In the 1812 text,
the former is explicit; in the process of this clarification, the
world of the story has become a more rational, practical place,
instead of the slightly more mysterious and supernatural one of
the original. And the ending of the reworked text makes motivation more explicit still:

Der Dummling ging noch einmal in den Wald, da saß das alte
graue Männchen, dem er seinen Kuchen gegeben, und sagte:
"ich hab für dich getrunken und gegessen, ich will dir auch
das Schiff geben, das alles thu' ich, weil du barmherzig gegen
mich gewesen bist." Da gab er ihm das Schiff, das zu Land
und zu Wasser fuhr, und als der König das sah, mußte er ihm
seine Tochter geben.

(The Simpleton went into the forest again, there sat the old
gray little man, to whom he had given his cake, and said:
"Because of you I have eaten and drunk, and will likewise
give you the ship, because you were good to me." Then he
gave him the ship, which could go on land and water, and
when the king saw this, he had to give him his daughter.)

Here there is quite simple moralizing, and a world with a clear rational structure; the supernatural has been tamed and deprived of some of its dangers and unpredictability. And indeed, the most general effect of the Grimms' clarifying and elaborating of motivation in the tales is just that; even where motivation is not altered, distorted, or simplified, the character of the world of these tales has been changed. It has lost a great deal of its mystery.

In the cases I have discussed so far, new material appears to have been introduced largely as a result of an intent to fill out the text and to elaborate for the sake of elaboration; the disturbance to the meaning of the original is somewhat random, though predictably leading in the direction of greater reliance on fairy tale clichés and to that extent less on the rationale of the original tale. But it is also possible to see patterns in the Grimms' elaborations which represent typical alterations of the thematic structure of the texts and alter the content of the tales in more fundamental and almost certainly more deliberate ways.

There are, for example, typical ways in which the elaboration results in major changes in the relationships among members of a family; and since family relationships are a large part of the content of the tales, the brothers were in this respect interfering in an important way with the basic material available to them.

A good example is *Hänsel und Gretel (Hansel and Gretel)*. The manuscript entitled *Das Brüderchen und das Schwesterchen (Little Brother and Little Sister)* is by the usual indications clearly the basis for the *KHM* first edition *Hansel und Gretel*,[25] and the latter is twice as long as the former, the usual relationship in the proportions of the two groups of texts. But a significant feature of the large amount of material added to the 1810 text by the Grimms' elaborations is the difference of emphasis given to the role of the children's father. In the 1810 text, both father and mother wake up the children on the morning of the first attempt to abandon them, but in the *KHM* first edition the mother is the prime mover: "Morgens früh, ehe die Sonne noch aufgegangen war, kam die Mutter und weckte sie alle beide: steht auf, ihr Kinder, wir wollen in den Wald gehen" ("Early next morning, still before the sun had risen, the mother came, and woke them both: 'get up, you children, we will go into the forest' "). Similarly, the second attempt to abandon the children is rewritten so as to exonerate the father and place all the blame on the mother; for in the 1810 version the two parents had cooperated: "Als sie mitten in den großen Wald gekommen, machte der Vater wieder ein großes Feuer an, die Mutter sprach wieder dieselbigen Worte, und beide gingen fort" ("When they had come to the middle of the great forest, the father again made a great fire, the mother again said the same words, and both went away"). But in 1812 it is the mother who does the deed: "Die Mutter aber führte sie noch tiefer in den Wald hinein, wo sie ihr Lebtag nicht gewesen waren, da sollten sie wieder einschlafen bei einem großen Feuer, und Abends wollten die Eltern kommen und sie abholen" ("But the mother took them even deeper into the forest, where they had not been in all their days, there they were to go to sleep again by a great fire, and in the evening the parents would come and fetch them"). Of course, the father acquiesces in the plot against the children even in the printed text, but the Grimms attempted to ease that problem too. For example, the manuscript of 1810 quickly passes over the decision by the parents to make a second attempt to abandon the children: "das Brüderchen hörte wieder Abends im Bett, wie die Mutter zu dem Vater sagte, er solle die Kinder hinaus in den großen Wald bringen" ("the little brother heard again in the evening in bed, how the mother said to the father, he should take the children out into the great forest again"). But the *KHM* first edition follows with an elaborate account of the father's reluctance to treat his children so: "Dem Mann fiels schwer aufs Herz, und er gedachte, es wäre doch besser, wen du den letzten Bissen mit deinen Kindern theiltest, weil er es aber einmal gethan hatte, so durfte er nicht nein sagen" ("The husband felt sad about it and he thought, yet it would be better if you shared your last bite with your children, but because he had done it once, he could not say no").

In the 1810 text the children return to their father and bring him jewels which make him rich; but the Grimms must have been offended by this undeserved fortune on his part after his behavior toward the children, and so they make a point of talking of his regret at what he has done: "Der Vater freute sich als er sie wieder sah, er hatte keinen vergnügten Tag gehabt, seit seine Kinder fort waren, und ward nun ein reicher Mann. Die Mutter aber war gestorben" ("The father was joyful to see them again, he had had not one happy day since his children had gone, and now became a rich man. But the mother was dead"). Clearly, the results of all these individual changes add up to an attempt by the Grimms to present the father as a basically good man who loves his children and whose only fault is that he is weak enough to be pushed into wrongdoing by an evil wife, and in this way they motivate his becoming rich and living happily every after with the children without his seeming unworthy of this. This change also has the effect of reducing emphasis on the conflict between parents and children—a persistent tendency of the Grimms, to which I shall return.

The rather fragmentary story *Vom Schreiner und Drechsler (The Joiner and the Turner)* presents an especially intriguing example of series of changes in the manuscript which when taken individually seem too small to matter but when taken together can be seen to have changed the world and the ethos of the story considerably. Once more, the 1812 text is a lengthened and elaborated version of the 1810 manuscript, and subtle changes in the plot outline are made continually during the rewriting. In the original, the prince's motivation for flying in at the window of the beautiful princess is that he is "neugierig, sie su sehen" ("curious to see her"). The rewritten version changes this slightly, so that on hearing of the princess, the prince simply becomes curious: "Nun wurde er höchst neugierig" ("Now he became very curious"). The change is slight, shifting emphasis toward a general curiosity, rather than a specific curiosity to experience the sight of this great beauty—but still merely a small change of emphasis if this passage is only taken by itself. Another such small change is the elaboration of the manuscript's terse statement that he is discovered ("wird entdeckt") to "wie sie aber nicht lange Zeit beisammen, wurde die Sache verrathen" ("but when they had not been together for very long, the thing was betrayed"). Note here that the Grimms' 1812 version introduces the notion that the two had not been together long, which is absent in the original; this appears to be meaningless unless intended to convey the idea that they had not been together long enough for anything improper to develop. And the change from "discovered" to "betrayed" also seems to bear on the question of the innocence of the encounter. To be *entdeckt* somewhat suggests being caught out doing something one should not be doing, but to be betrayed suggests instead that guilt is located in the person doing the betraying, while those who are betrayed are wronged, and innocent. Still, all of these changes give only very subtle suggestions, nowhere near the level of explicit statement; their significance could be open to doubt.

It is when we reach the end of the story that we really see the point of the rewriting. After the prince escapes with the princess, the king offers a bargain, with the following result in the 1810 manuscript: "Nach einiger Zeit erfährt er daß der Vater der Prinzeßin, das halbe Konigreich demjenigen geben wolle, dem ihm s. Tochter wiederbringe. Er reist mit einem Heere und d. Prinzeßin zu ihrem Vater und zwingt ihn, sein gegebenes Versprechen zu leisten, nachdem er ihm seine Tochter wieder geschenckt hat" ("After some time he learns that the father of the princess will give a half of his kingdom to whoever will bring him back his daughter. He travels with an army and with the princess to her father, and compels him to fulfill his promise, after he has given him his daughter back again"). But in the Grimms' *KHM* first edition this is changed to the following: "Nach einiger Zeit aber ließ der Vater der entführten Prinzessin bekannt machen, daß derjenige das halbe Königreich bekommen sollte, der ihm seine Tochter wiederbringe. Dies erfährt der Prinz, rüstet ein Heer aus und bringt die Prinzessin selbst ihrem Vater zu, den er zwingt, ihm sein Versprechen zu erfüllen" ("After some time the father of the kidnaped princess let it be known, that whoever should bring back his daughter would get one half of his kingdom. The prince learns this, equips an army, and takes the princess to her father, whom he compels to fulfill his promise").

Now, at last, we can see where the Grimms' rewriting was headed. In the original there is no ambiguity: the prince *exchanges* the beautiful princess for half the king's kingdom. He gives her up, and gets something in return; she is treated as a commodity to barter. But this is missing from the Grimms' rewritten version. There the prince receives half the kingdom simply for taking her to her father. We are not told what happens next to their relationship, but the 1812 text does not exclude the possibility that the two may stay together and live happily ever after as a married couple, for the prince is not said to give the princess back to her father, but only to bring her to see him. The 1810 text, on the other hand, certainly did not allow that possibility. With the small, subtle changes which they introduced into the 1812 text, the Grimms actually did something very far-reaching: they have changed the entire world of the story from an Arabian Nights world of sexual opportunism and adventure, in which beautiful women are prizes to win by daring, but also to exploit and to barter, to the world they developed in their *KHM*, a world in which princes and princesses fall in love and live happily ever after, outwitting the older generation and obtaining riches and a kingdom to secure their happiness. And it is this very fundamental change in the story that those two apparently small changes in its middle section were moving toward.[26]

Both in *Hänsel und Gretel* and in *Vom Schreiner und Drechsler,* the Grimms' rewriting moved the texts visibly in the direction of what was by their standards an emotionally and ethically more congenial world; but in so doing they removed highly characteristic features of their sources. Some negative evidence for the proposition that their rewriting had in large part this ethical goal can be seen in the few stories they left relatively intact, for these were stories about animals, rather than people. *Läuschen und Flöhchen,* for example, is a rare case of a tale changed almost not at all from the 1810 manuscipt all the way through to the final edition of 1857; the manuscript is reproduced almost verbatim in the printed versions.[27] The story is a simple one of two small creatures, posing no ethical problems—and it was probably for this reason that the Grimms showed no interest in rewriting it. In this case it is intriguing to note, however, that the manuscript derives from Dorothea Catharina Wild—the mother of Wilhelm's wife Henriette Dorothea Wild ("Dortchen"); could it be that the Grimms' unwillingness to tamper with this text reflected also their awareness that this one really *was* from an older woman?

One of the manuscripts—that which was the basis for the first edition text *Vom Fundevogel (Fundevogel)*—has an unusual character which throws more light on what the Grimms were trying to do when they reworked the manuscripts in preparation for the printed text of the *KHM*. Alone among the manuscripts, it really does look like a genuine example of oral transmission by an unschooled storyteller, as the following passage shows:

> Den Morgen früh geht der Forster um zwey Uhr auf die Jagd, wie er weg ist so spricht das Lehnchen zum Karl verläßest du mich nicht so verlaß ich dich auch nicht, so spricht der Karl nimmermehr, da spricht das Lehnchen ich will dir es nur sagen die Köchin hat gestern so viel Waßer ins Haus getragen

so fragte ich sie warum sie so viel Waßer ins Haus trug so sagte sie wann ich es vor keinen Menschen sagen wollte, dann wollte sie mir es sagen so sagte ich ich wolte es vor keinen Menschen sagen, so sagte sie sie wolte morgen früh wann mein Vater auf die Jagd wäre dann wollte sie einen Keßel voll Waßer kochen und dich hinein werfen und kochen.

(Early next day the forester goes hunting at two o'clock, when he is gone Lehnchen says to Karl if you don't leave me I won't leave you either, then Karl says never, then Lehnchen says I just want to tell you the cook carried so much water into the house yesterday so I asked her why she carried so much water into the house so she said if I would tell no one she would tell me so I said I'd tell no one, so she said she wanted tomorrow morning when my father had gone hunting she wanted to boil a cauldron of water and throw you into it and boil you.)

The succession of phrases such as "so she said" and "so I said" could well be characteristic of oral peasant storytelling. The manuscript is in a hand that is not identifiable, while the others are largely in the hands of the two brothers. And it is unusual in yet another way: it does not stem from the family or friends of the two brothers, but instead (according to Wilhelm Grimm's handwritten note) from one Friederike Mannel of Allendorf—to be sure still in Hessen. To judge from her language, she really sounds like a popular voice—not like the literate Wilds and Hassenpflugs. What, then, did the Grimms do when faced with this real example of the natural speech of the people? Alas, they did not melt in admiration, and praise its simplicity and natural eloquence. Instead, they quickly tidied it up and recast it in that form which they professed to despise—a literary language *(Schriftsprache)* that no peasant would ever have uttered:

Und des andern Morgens in aller Frühe stieg der Forster auf und ging auf die Jagd, und als er weg war, lagen die Kinder noch im Bett, da sprach Lehnchen zum Fundevogel: verläßt du mich nicht, so verlaß ich dich auch nicht!" so sprach der Fundevogel: nun und nimmermehr. Da sprach Lehnchen: "ich will es dir nur sagen, die Sanne schleppte gestern Abends so viel Eimer Wasser ins Haus, so fragte ich sie, warum sie das thäte, so sagte sie: wenn ichs keinem Menschen sagen wollte, so wollte sie es mir wohl sagen; so sprach ich: ich wollte es gewiß keinem Menschen sagen, da sagte sie, morgen früh, wenn der Vater auf die Jagd wäre, wollte sie den Kessel voll Wasser sieden, und dich hineinwerfen und kochen.

(And early the next morning the forester got up and went hunting, and when he was gone, the children still lay in bed, then Lehnchen spoke to Fundevogel: if you don't leave me, I won't leave you either! and so Fundevogel said: now and never. Then Lehnchen said: "I will tell you now, Sanna carried so many buckets of water into the house yesterday, so I asked her why she did it, so she said: if I would tell no one she would tell me; so I said: I would certainly not tell anyone, then she said, tomorrow morning, when my father had gone hunting, she would boil the cauldron full of water and throw you into it and cook you.)

What is happening here is all too familiar in human affairs; there is all the difference in the world between an intellectual's romantic protestations of love of the simple life and the common folk, on the one hand, and his ability to live with its actual conditions, on the other.

We can sum up the typical relationship between the Grimms' source material and the texts which they printed as follows. First, the source material is completely recast and rewritten, and heavily elaborated, the result commonly being a doubling in length. Second, this process has totally destroyed the style and flavor of the original, the resulting tone being the creation of the brothers themselves. Third, any sense of the "voice" of the original storytellers is completely obliterated in this process. Fourth, the added material adds many new elements of substance to the tales, which commonly result in important changes in plot, theme, character and motivation of the tales. Fifth, there are characteristic patterns in the brothers' changes in the content of the tales, for example the removal or softening of such disturbing elements as violent conflict between parents and children, incest, and sexuality, all of which tend to be replaced by harmless fairy-tale clichés of princes and princesses, and living happily ever after. Sixth, traditional characters and situations are altered in ways that are fairly significant. And last, the mysterious, magical and often threatening world of these tales is tamed and made more rational, predictable, and benevolent.

Now let us compare these summary statements of what the Grimms really did to their source material with what they claimed to be doing in their various prefaces. Some conclusions are unavoidable. First, the discrepancy between the claims of the two first edition prefaces, on the one hand, and the Grimms' part in the production of the first edition text, on the other, is so great that the brothers cannot possibly have been unaware of it; in other words, they were clearly and consciously lying when they claimed there not to have changed or improved anything, or to have added anything of their own. And as for their claim to have reproduced exactly the common speech of the people and the voice of the untutored popular storyteller without tidying it up or allowing a compromise with a *Schriftsprache*—that too can only have been conscious deception on their part. Second, the modified version of the first edition's claims which has become the general view of scholarship—that those claims were more or less true, though the brothers had to use editorial discretion in combining different versions, restoring corrupt passages, making style consistent, etc.—this, too, is completely untenable; the brothers created a fullness and a style absent in any of their sources or partial sources. Third, even the much milder claim of the second edition preface, which admitted that the expression of the tales was largely due to the brothers but still insisted that they had added otherwise nothing of their own and had not attempted to improve the stories, was still very far from the truth; and the continued insistence in that preface on the inferiority of "eine geläuterte Schriftsprache" ("a purified literary language") and on the beauty of the speech of the common folk shows that the brothers were still intent on the same deception as previously, except that the discrepancy between their first and second printed editions had compelled them to modify their previous statement. And, it must be remembered, all of this would nullify and render fraudulent the Grimms' claims *even if* the 1810 material genuinely derived from folk traditions of the German-speaking area; but this judgment of those claims can be even clearer in view of the fact that this, too, is false, and that middle-class literate people, heavily contaminated by French culture in particular and by books in general, were the actual sources.[28] No wonder the Grimms' treatment of their sources showed no real respect for the characteristic qualities of those sources; from a folklore point of view, they in fact possessed none whatsoever. What was there for the brothers to respect?

5

The Further Development of the Text of the Tales

Once the character of the differences between the 1810 manuscripts and the first edition has been assessed, it is not difficult to see that the further changes introduced between the first and seventh editions, though smaller in scale, have that same character; the gradual reworking of the succeeding editions is thus very much a part of what the Grimms did from the beginning. That there is a correlation between the brothers' initial deviation from the manuscripts of 1810 and their subsequent tinkering is shown in an interesting, odd case: *Läuschen and Flöhchen* is atypical of the stories in being hardly changed throughout all of the seven printed editions—but then it was just as atypical in the first editon of 1812, being a virtually intact reproduction of the 1810 manuscript. The more typical cases, which had been substantially changed by 1812, show most clearly the continuity between the Grimms' further reworking and what they had already done in the first edition.

Hänsel und Gretel is a good example. As we have seen, when the brothers rewrote and elaborated the manuscript which was its basis, they softened the father's role, so that his involvement in and guilt over the mistreatment of the children is much reduced.[1] The effect of this is to change in a more general way the relations between parents and children in the story; instead of the horrendous situation of both parents deciding to abandon their children, we have the much less disturbing situation of only one parent wanting to do so, with the other resisting and giving in only through weakness. One evil parent can be regarded as aberrant and atypical; for both to be so malevolent is an altogether different and more frightening matter. Now the subsequent editions carry this process of removing the dangerous idea of the threatening parents even further. The first edition cut the number of malevolent parents from two to one; by the final edition the number is reduced to zero. The wicked mother has become a wicked stepmother; now *neither* parent plots malevolently against the children.

This change is introduced relatively casually; in the fourth edition a sentence is simply amended to read "Die zwei Kinder hatten vor Hunger auch nicht einschlafen können und hatten gehört, was die Stiefmutter zum Vater gesagt hatte." ("The two children had also not been able to go to sleep because they were hungry, and had heard what the stepmother had said to the father.") But even after this change, the Grimms were evidently still not satisfied that the point was clear enough. The story was rewritten once more for the fifth edition, and a stepmother's wickedness as the sole source of the children's problems was emphasized by a number of further changes. For example, her command to the children in the early editions: "steht auf, ihr Kinder" ("get up, you children") becomes "steht auf, ihr Faullenzer" ("get up, you lazybones!"), emphasizing her malevolent disposition.

But the brothers were also still worried by the father's acquiescence, and so the fifth edition introduces more material designed to exonerate him. First, his wife's pressuring him to agree to her plan to abandon the children is made more severe. In the early editions, she tells him "Wenn du das nicht thust . . . so müssen wir alle miteinander Hungers sterben" ("if you don't do it . . . we shall all have to die of hunger together"), but in the fifth edition this becomes the more brutal "Oh du Narr . . . dann müssen wir alle viere Hungers sterben, du kannst nur die Bretter für die Särge hobelen" ("Oh you fool . . . then we shall all four have to die of hunger, you can just smooth the boards for the coffins"). And after the father gives in to her, the Grimms, still trying to further lighten his burden of guilt, could not resist inserting a sentence which is in fact weak and foolish in its effect: " 'Aber die armen Kinder dauern mich doch,' sagte der Mann" (" 'But I still feel sorry for the poor children,' said the husband"). What the Grimms wanted to achieve is clear enough; they were not comfortable with the idea of parents abusing their children, and slowly removed that notion from the story. But this presents a very serious problem: the tales in the collection are frequently much concerned with intrafamily strife—with the tensions between siblings, or between children and parents as the children grow up; what the Grimms were actually trying to do was to remove a central and essential feature of their material, part of what might make the material important, as if it were merely an unnecessarily offensive excrescence.

The fate of *Sneewittchen (Snow-white)* as it progressed through the seven editions provides an especially striking example of how the Grimms practically destroyed the whole point of a story in their zeal to render it less offensive to sensibilities which expected the *KHM* to be above all charming, and never threatening. The manuscript tale—its basic elements still largely preserved in the first edition, though disturbed as early as the second edition—is the story of ambivalence in a relationship between mother and daughter. A woman wishes for a daughter of great beauty—a narcissistic wish on the part of a woman herself celebrated for her beauty. But when she gets her wish the mother realizes too late that this is not simply the further extension of her own beauty which her narcissistic wish had contemplated, but instead a separate person whose beauty rivals and eventually outdoes her own. Seeing what a dangerous threat she has invoked, mother tries to destroy the daughter and, when she fails, is eventually destroyed by her. Now here is a dramatic version of mother-daughter rivalry and sexual jealousy, in which the older woman, at first identifying with the flesh of her flesh, later sees herself eclipsed by a younger woman who really is a separate person and thus a rival. The daughter's active participation in the rivalry is more than hinted at; for it is at her wedding—the celebration of her own beauty and sexuality—that her mother is put to death in grisly fashion, being forced to dance in red-hot shoes until she drops dead. Thus, she is destroyed at the very celebration of her daughter's sexual power.

This is certainly a provocative story—a fascinating study of the way in which a child begins its life as a narcissistic extension of its parent, and in growing up becomes a separate human being with all the problems that that entails. But in the second edition of this tale the Grimms introduced a key sentence which destroyed its meaning. After the sentence announcing the birth of the child the queen had wished for—as beautiful as she had wished—the text now adds: "Und wie das Kind geboren war, starb die Königin. Über ein Jahr nahm sich der König eine andere Gemahlin, sie war eine schöne Frau, aber stolz auf ihre Schönheit, und konnte nicht leiden, daß sie von jemand darin sollte übertroffen werden" ("When the child was born, the queen died. A year later, the king took another wife, but she was a beautiful woman, but proud of her beauty, and could not bear the fact that anyone might surpass her in that").

In this version the woman who wishes for a beautiful daughter and gets her is *not* the same woman who envies her beauty or who is destroyed at her wedding; gone is the *ambivalence* of the battle of the generations, and the crucial link between the mother's narcissistic wish and its later results. The Grimms again shrank from the real conflict between parents and children which derives from the children's growing up and becoming separate people. In the stage of conflict they substituted a stranger for the parent, and this softening of the impact of the tale removes its real interest.[2] Now the tale has become one about the vanity of a specific person—it is not any longer a symbolic fantasy on the nature of a wish for a child and the danger of the fulfillment of that wish.

There is already in *Sneewittchen*'s first printed text a discrepancy between the manuscript and the first edition which seems not unrelated to the discrepancy between the first two editions I have just discussed, though its significance is somewhat harder to judge. As I have noted above, the *Notes* indicate that the manuscript of *Sneewittchen* was not the basis of the first edition, since a feature of the manuscript not present in the 1812 text is described there as being part of a different version of the story. Thus, the 1810 manuscript must be that other version, while the manuscript that was the basis of *Sneewittchen* must have been destroyed. Yet the 1812 text deviated from the extant manuscript in a far more important way, and, strangely, *this was not mentioned in the notes at all:* whereas in the 1812 version a prince rescues Snow-white, in the 1810 manuscript it is Snow-white's *father* who rescues her.

This is a most interesting feature of the manuscript, and one that would obviously add more depth to the meaning of the first edition's text than it would to that of the second edition. Like the first edition's use of the real mother (rather than the step-mother) as the wicked queen, the manuscript's use of the father as rescuer concentrates the action into Snow-white's immediate family circle, and provides an added dimension to the rivalry between mother and daughter. The general competition be-tween mother and daughter for preeminence in physical beauty then has a specific context of competition for the affection of the father/husband. And rescue by her father represents victory for Snow-white in the second sphere, just as the mirror tells us she won in the first. The substitution of a prince for the father is very much the same kind of move, therefore, as the substi-tution of a stepmother for a real mother.

Curiously, the notes—usually informative as to the salient out-lines of versions other than those used—make no mention of this particular variant motif. More than this, the notes actually stress that the *only* variant in the 1810 manuscript concerns the intended means of killing Snow-white; here Snow-white is aban-doned in the woods by the queen, while in the first edition the queen orders a hunter to kill Snow-white in the woods. And yet the different identity of the rescuer is surely a more striking variant than the relatively minor matter of a different way of murdering Snow-white. Why, then, did the Grimms not mention it? I suspect that the 1810 manuscript did *not* in fact deviate from the manuscript used as the basis of the first edition in this critical respect, but that instead the two manuscripts agreed with each other here while the Grimms' 1812 printed text deviated from *both* manuscripts. This supposition would at least explain why the Grimms did not note that the 1810 manuscript was aberrant in having Snow-white's father as her rescuer, since it would not then be aberrant.

If the Grimms did make this unannounced change of a feature present in both manuscripts, it would have been the kind of change that was entirely characteristic of them. As usual, they would have moved the text away from stark intrafamilial violence and substituted a harmless fairy-tale cliché, here the rescuing prince. Though this conclusion is speculative, there can be no doubt that we can only choose between two possibilities: either the Grimms misstated the extent of the difference between the two manuscripts, or they changed an ending common to both manuscripts in a way which is frequently visible in their reworking of the *KHM* for publication. Of the two possibilities, the second is certainly the more likely.[3]

Many other changes in the *KHM* which took place after the first edition are certainly consistent with this interpretation. In general, the Grimms continued to make the tales more and more acceptable from a moral standpoint.[4] For example, in *Der Hund und der Sperling (The Dog and the Sparrow)*, the bird's persecution of the man who runs over his friend the dog may seem excessively bitter and somewhat disproportionate to the man's crime in the early versions, for there the dog is run over by the man's cart because he is lying dead drunk in the road, and so his death is partly his own fault. But though the dog's drunkenness survived into the first edition, by the seventh it had vanished, and there instead the dog merely lies down to sleep because he is tired. And while the dog becomes more blameless, in the later editions the man becomes more bad-tempered and ill-intentioned than formerly, and he provokes the bird by challenging it to do him harm after killing the dog: "was könntest du mir schaden!" ("What harm can you do me"). Meanwhile the bird's personality is softened, so that his bloodthirsty challenge of the first version (both the manuscript and 1812 *KHM*)—"Fuhrmann thus nicht, rief der Sperling, es kostet dein Leben" ("Waggoner, don't do it, cried the sparrow, it will cost you your life")—is weakened to the seventh edition's "Fuhrmann, tus nicht, oder ich mache dich arm" ('Waggoner, don't do it, or I will make you poor"). The sum total of all this is that to make the rather cruel revenge of the bird for his friend's death more palatable, the Grimms first make the dog more lovable, then make the man, not the bird, the irascible and provocative character of the tale, and finally make the bird simply reactive and far less obviously ready for a bloody fight. As a result, what seemed a needlessly cruel punishment on the bird's part becomes a more justifiable one.

The progress of a story like *Das Mädchen ohne Hände (The Girl with No Hands)* through the various editions shows again the character of the Grimms' moral concerns, and in particular their anxiety to soften depictions of serious intrafamily violence, a concern somewhat similar to that which emerges from their reworking of *Sneewittchen*. Here, however, it is suggestions of incest which they suppress. In the first edition, the daughter loses her hands as the result of a series of events initiated by her father's making a bargain with the devil. He promises to give the devil whatever is at that moment behind his mill in exchange for a fortune, without knowing that at that very moment his daughter is standing there. The daughter's mutilation occurs as a consequence of attempts to extricate her from this pact—successful attempts, since she escapes the devil's clutches. This beginning of the tale remains into the seventh edition, and yet there are good reasons why it should not. For in the final edition of their notes, the Grimms tell of two versions of the tale, one of the two obviously having turned up *after* the 1812 *KHM* was printed, and they say quite unreservedly that the second version "übertrifft die andere an innerer Vollständigkeit" ("surpasses the other in inner completeness"). For this stated reason they prefer the second manuscript, following it in the later editions in preference to that which they had followed in the first edition— except that they keep the *beginning* of the first manuscript. But why would they not have preferred to use the *whole* of the second version, instead of inconsistently retaining part of an admittedly inferior version of the tale?

The reason becomes immediately obvious when we read the very brief summary which the brothers include in their notes. There, we are told, it was not the devil who set in motion the train of events leading to the girl's mutilation and subsequent helpless wandering about the world; instead: ". . . ein Vater habe seine eigene Tochter zur Frau begehrt, und als diese sich geweigert, ihre Hände (und Brüste) abschneiden und ein weißes Hemd anthun lassen, darauf sie in die Welt fort gejagt" (". . . a father had wanted to take his own daughter as his wife, and when she had refused, had cut off her hands (and breasts) and made her put on a white shirt, and then driven her out into the world"). Once more, the Grimms wanted nothing to do with incest and intrafamily violence; again, they removed this highly problematic material and filled up the gap in the motivation of the tale with a fairy-tale cliché—the devil. But as a result the motivation works far less well. For example, in the final version it is not at all clear in the printed text why the girl has to leave home after her mutilation; and one would have felt that, in that state, she would need and have to rely on her family instead of wandering abroad. The girl simply announces: "hier kann ich nicht bleiben" ("I cannot stay here"), but it is not clear why not; nor does the rest of the tale shed any light on the question.

It would be a mistake, however, to think of the Grimms' reworking of the tales as invariably producing a softening and blunting of everything that was violent or shocking in them.[5] To be sure, they softened whatever was shocking to their own moral outlook, and reduced the level of violence where it ran counter to that outlook; but they retained and even *increased* the level of violence and brutality when, for example, those in the tales who suffered it deserved it according to their moral outlook. To put the matter more succinctly: the innocent are treated more gently, but the evil or guilty are punished even more brutally. And, once again, this tendency is maintained throughout the progress of the *KHM* from the 1810 manuscript to the later editions.

Take, for example, the final exit of the thwarted and cheated Rumpelstiltskin. In the 1810 manuscript he simply leaves: "Wie das Männchen das hört erschrickt es und spricht: das muß dir der Teufel gesagt haben, und fliegt auf dem Kochlöffel zum Fenster hinaus" ("When the little man hears this he starts, and says: the devil must have told you that, and flies out of the window on a spoon"). But in the first edition he becomes more angry: "Das hat dir der Teufel gasagt! schrie das Männchen, lief zornig fort und kam nimmermehr wieder" ("The Devil told you that! cried the little man, ran off angrily, and never came back"). And finally, by the second edition he has become so violent that he tears himself apart: "Das hat dir der Teufel gesagt! das hat dir der Teufel gesagt! schrie das Männlein und stieß mit dem rechten Fuß vor Zorn so tief in die Erde, daß es bis an den Leib hineinfuhr, dann packte es in einer Wuth den linken Fuß mit beiden Händen und riß sich mitten entzwei" ("The Devil told you that! The Devil told you that! cried the little man, and stamped his right foot in rage so far into the earth, that it went in up to his body. Then in a fury he grasped his left foot with both hands and tore himself in half").

This is not an isolated example, for much the same kind of increase in the level of violence and bloodiness occurs also in *Aschenputtel*. At the end of the tale in the first edition, Cinderella gets her prince, and no harm comes to anyone; the villains are shaken, but that is all: "Die Stiefmutter und die zwei stolzen Schwestern erschracken und wurden bleich, aber der Prinz führte Aschenputtel fort" ("The stepmother and the two proud sisters were startled and turned pale, but the prince led Cinderella away"). But already in the second edition there is a brutal and bloody punishment for the sisters:

> Als die Hochzeit mit dem Königssohn sollte gehalten werden, kamen die falschen Schwestern, wollten sich einschmeicheln und Theil an seinem Glück nehmen. Als es nun zur Kirche ging, war die älteste zur rechten, die jüngste zur linken Seite, da pickten die Tauben einer jeden das eine Aug aus, hernach als sie heraus ging war die älteste zur linken und die jüngste zur rechten, da pickten die Tauben einer jeden das andere Auge aus und waren sie also für ihre Bosheit und Falschheit mit Blindheit auf ihr Lebtag gestraft.

> (When the wedding with the Prince was to be held, the false sisters came and wanted to ingratiate themselves, and take part in her good fortune. When they were going to the church, with the oldest on her right and the youngest on her left, doves pecked out one eye of each of them, and after that as they were coming out, with the oldest at the left and the youngest to the right, the doves pecked out the other eye of each of them, and so they were punished for their wickedness and dishonesty with blindness for all of their days.)

Similarly, when the ugly sisters are trying to fit their oversized feet into the tiny slipper, the first edition has one sister cut off part of her toes ("so schneide lieber vorne an den Zehen ab"—"then cut something off your toes," advises her mother) but the second and subsequent editions have the toes taken clear off ("hau die Zehe ab"—"cut off your toes" says her mother, and, indeed, "Das Mädchen hieb die Zehe ab"—"the girl cut off her toes"). When the deceit is discovered, "Der Prinz sah nieder, da waren die weißen Strümpfe der Braut roth gefärbt und das Blut war hoch herauf gedrungen" ("The prince looked down, the bride's white stockings were stained red, and the blood had penetrated up through them"). But in the second and later editions, "da blickte er auf ihren Fuß und sah wie das Blut herausquoll" ("then he looked at her foot and saw the blood gush out").

Whenever the Grimms make changes in the later editions of the *KHM,* it is always necessary to consider the possibility that these may originate in new manuscript versions of the story concerned which became available only after the printing of the first edition. In a few cases it can be shown that this is indeed what happened. The new and more violent ending of *Rumpel-*

stilzchen, for example, is foreshadowed in marginalia to Wilhelm's copy of the 1812 *KHM,* where it is attributed to "Lisette," i.e., Lisette Wild, Dortchen's sister. Whether this is also true of *Aschenputtel* is uncertain; already in the first set of notes published in a separate volume (in 1822) the printed text is said to be "nach drei Erzählungen aus Hessen" ("after three tales from Hessen"), and it is conceivable that others arose later. But in this case it is surely not likely, for the archetype of most of these versions of *Cinderella* must have been Perrault's *Cendrillon,* especially in view of the very frequent contamination of the Grimms' material by educated French sources; and Perrault's text is free of the bloody cruelty of the later editions of the *KHM.* Compare, for example, the fate of the ugly sisters in the final edition of the *KHM* to what happens in Perrault; in Perrault's story, the sisters throw themselves at Cendrillon's feet and beg her forgiveness, after which "Cendrillon les relève, et leur dit en les embrassant qu'elle leur pardonnait de bon coeur et qu'elle les priait de l'aimer bien toujours" ("Cinderella raises them up, embraces them, and tells them that she forgives them completely, and that she wants them to love her always"). In Perrault there is forgiveness and goodwill; in the *KHM* there is a cruel vengeance.[6]

But a judgment of the Grimms' introducing more blood and violence does not in any case depend on what was available in their sources. Even if they never introduced such details simply through their own invention (which I do not believe), the fact remains that on many occasions, when a choice was available between alternative texts differing in their degrees of bloodiness and cruelty, the Grimms frequently—as in *Aschenputtel* and *Rumpelstilzchen*—chose the most extreme versions.

One more general point can be made about the progress of the *KHM* through the seven editions. The Grimms were surely aware of the very disparate nature of the material they started with, and of the fact that their programmatic statements required a more homogenous collection. If indeed there was an indigenous Germanic tradition of storytelling, its products should have a characteristic stamp—the stamp of that tradition. But the manuscripts were far too discrepant to display such a stamp; and even the first edition *KHM* was by no means uniform in tone and style. As the editions progressed, editorial changes were introduced which were evidently in part designed to knit the collection more firmly together. With each new edition, not only did language and style become more uniform, but motifs and typical developments in a given situation were imported from one story into another. In this way, a predominant "voice" of the stories was cultivated, and stock figures, situations, and motifs progressively emerge. Yet this voice is *not* the voice of the Germanic tradition, but, instead, one supplied by the Grimms.

To the extent that one (but only one) of the things the Grimms did to pull their collection together was to create a more unified style, Schoof was partly justified in saying that the changes made by the Grimms involved a search for a stylistic unity. But it is important also to see that even in making this partly justified assertion, Schoof still misconceived the situation in important ways. To begin with, he thought of it simply as a process of making a predominant voice uniformly audible in all of the tales; in other words, he saw the Grimms making more audible a voice which was found in the tales already, and so enhancing the folk quality and origin of the collection. Nothing could be further from the truth. For as Panzer pointed out in the introduction to his reprint of the first edition *KHM*, the changes move the texts away from popular, oral narration and in the direction of a "für diese Literatur kaum erwünschte Annäherung an die Schriftsprache"[7] ("an approximation to a literary language which is scarcely desirable for this kind of literature"). The polished, still simple, but in some ways quaint tone which the Grimms imposed was one of their own creation, and it was indeed a kind of literary language, in spite of their earlier protestations that they wanted the natural speech of the people—at all costs to avoid a *Schriftsprache*.

But Schoof's concept was insufficient in yet another respect: for the knitting together of the collection involved far more than stylistic changes. Situations, characters, and motifs all tended to be changed to create uniformity. Take, for example, the case of *Dornröschen*. Both in the 1810 manuscript and in the early editions, the animal which crawls out of the water to prophesy the girl's birth is a crab; but by the third edition it has become a frog. In their notes, the brothers are strangely silent regarding this change—even in the final, much elaborated notes of 1856; and yet this is the kind of change of motif which they usually dealt with in those notes. The answer to this puzzle is not hard to find. The notes do not mention the changes from crab to frog because it almost certainly does not originate in a new manuscript at all—it surely originates in an analogy introduced by the brothers with the story which opens the *KHM*, *Der Froschkönig oder der eiserne Heinrich*. What emerges, then, is a kind of stock figure of the frog who crawls out of the water to precipitate a crisis in a young girl's life. But here we find another example of that almost willful scholarly blindness which so regularly afflicts the scholarship on the *KHM;* for Bolte and Polivka, in their extensive notes to the tales, discuss the frog's prophecy as one of the four basic motifs of the tale without ever mentioning the fact that it did not exist until introduced late in the history of the *KHM* in order to create a connection to another tale.

Something similar was surely at work in the elaboration introduced into late editions of that part of the *KHM* tale *Brüderchen und Schwesterchen (Little Brother and Little Sister*—not to be confused with the 1810 manuscript of the same name, which became the *Hänsel und Gretel* of the *KHM)* which describes the life of the two children in the forest. The first edition of the story is much shorter than the second and subsequent editions. One significant aspect of the lengthening involves the difference between the children's simply living in the woods in the first edition, and their finding *ein kleines Haus* ("a little house") in the second. The analogy with *Hänsel und Gretel* is obvious; and so this story, too, is in effect decorated with another of the stock fairy-tale motifs of the collection. And, once more, the Grimms' notes are silent on this new episode; they had evidently decided, here too, to introduce it for their own purposes, which were to spread a net of common motifs over the collection.

As I have already observed, one of the Grimms' concerns was to narrow the differences of style among the stories. But a special case of stylistic change is the effect which they gradually introduced of symmetrical or nearly symmetrical repetition, for this kind of repetitive pattern has become accepted as a distinctive characteristic of the collection. In *Aschenputtel (Cinderella)*, for example, the two ugly sisters try on the slipper one after the other, so that there are two events to be described. In the first edition, the two are related in very different language, and they are of different length; the first is the longer, the second much abbreviated. The first sister cuts off part of her foot to get it into the slipper, and goes to her prince in the following language:

> Da ging die älteste in ihre Kammer und probirte den Pantoffel an, die Fußspitze kam hinein, aber die Ferse war zu groß, da nahm sie das Messer und schnitt sich ein Stück von der Ferse,

bis sie den Fuß in den Pantoffel hineinzwängte. So ging sie heraus zu dem Prinzen, und wie der sah, daß sie den Pantoffel anhatte, sagte er, das sey die Braut, führte sie zum Wagen and wollte mit ihr fortfahren.

(Then the oldest went to her chamber, and tried the slipper on, the front part of her foot went in, but the heel was too big, then she took a knife and cut a part of the heel off, until she forced her foot into the slipper. Then she went out to the Prince, and when he saw that she had the slipper on, he said, this is the bride, led her to the carriage, and wanted to drive her away.)

In the case of the second sister, the language changes considerably:

Da nahm sie den Pantoffel in ihre Kammer, und als der Fuß zu groß war, da biß sie die Zähne zusammen und schnitt ein groß Stück von den Zehen ab, und drückte den Pantoffel geschwind an. Wie sie damit hervortrat, meinte er, das wäre die rechte und wollte mit ihr fortfahren.

(Then she took the slipper into her chamber, and when she saw that her foot was too big, she clenched her teeth, and cut off a large part of her toes, and quickly pushed the slipper onto her foot. As she came forward, he thought, this is the right one, and wanted to go off with her.)

But by the seventh edition the variety of language of those episodes has given way to a cultivated symmetry; the first reads:

Das Mädchen hieb die Zehe ab, zwängte den Fuß in den Schuh, verbiß den Schmerz und ging heraus zum Königssohn. Da nahm er sie als seine Braut aufs Pferd und ritt mit ihr fort.

(The girl cut off her toes, forced her foot into the shoe, suppressed the pain, and went out to the prince. Then he took her on his horse as his bride, and rode off with her.)

But the second is almost the same:

Das Mädchen hieb ein Stück von der Ferse ab, zwängte den Fuß in den Schuh, verbiß den Schmerz und ging heraus zum Königssohn. Da nahm er sie als seine Braut aufs Pferd und ritt mit ihr fort.

(The girl cut off part of her heel, forced her foot into the shoe, suppressed the pain, and went out to the prince. Then he took her on his horse as his bride, and rode off with her.)

What variety there is between the two separate events is now a small variation exploiting the otherwise symmetrical framework, and this effect has become part of the atmosphere of the *KHM* in its final edition.

So far, I have dealt with certain patterns which can be discerned in the extensive changes which the Grimms made both in the material which they had received, and also in their own printed versions in the later editions. But these still do not give any real impression of the scope of the brothers' rewriting both of their sources and of their own texts. To anyone who has studied the manuscripts and the various editions, what is most striking is not finally the changes that appear to be purposive and motivated by attempts to achieve certain goals—whatever they may have been—but, on the contrary, the constant changing of the verbal fabric of the tales from one edition to another in what most of the time can only seem a random and arbitrary way. The Grimms appear to have been guilty of a pervasive habit of tinkering idly and uninhibitedly with the language of the texts; and this ever-present activity leaves a strong impression about their real, as opposed to their expressed, attitude to their material: it shows that they had in fact very little respect for the original quality of their material, and that they were only concerned to make as much of it as they could. This ceaseless rephrasing can only mean that their aim was to produce a text that was maximally pleasing to them—not one that had any fidelity to a tradition.

This impression will become clear if I juxtapose four different versions of certain passages from the *KHM*. Take, for example, the passage in which the princess in the *Froschkönig* loses her golden ball in the well. Here are four versions of that passage:

1. *Manuscript version*
Sie sah wie sie in die Tiefe fiel und stand an dem Brunnen und war sehr traurig.

(She saw how it fell into the depth and stood by the well and was very sad.)

2. *First edition*

Die Königstochter blickte ihr erschrocken nach, der Brunnen war aber so tief, daß kein Grund zu sehen war. Da fing sie an jämmerlich zu weinen und zu klagen: "ach! wenn ich meine Kugel wieder hätte, da wollt' ich alles darum geben, meine Kleider, meine Edelgesteine, meine Perlen und was es auf der Welt nur wär'."

(The king's daughter looked after it and was alarmed, but the well was so deep that she could not see the bottom. Then she began to weep and lament pitifully: "Oh! if I had my ball again, I would give everything for it, my clothes, my jewels, my pearls, and anything in the world.")

3. *Second edition*

Erschrocken sah ihr die Königstochter nach; aber die Kugel sank hinab und der Brunnen war so tief, daß kein Grund zu erkennen war. Als sie nun ganz verschwand, da fing das Mädchen gar jämmerlich an zu weinen und rief: "ach! meine goldene Kugel! hätte ich sie wieder, ich wollte alles darum hingeben: meine Kleider, meine Edelsteine, meine Perlen, ja meine goldene Krone noch dazu."

(Alarmed, the king's daughter looked after it, but the ball sank down and the well was so deep that no bottom could be seen. As it now completely disappeared the girl began to weep most pitifully, and cried: "Oh! my golden ball! if I had it again, I would give everything for it: my clothes, my jewels, my pearls, even my golden crown as well.")

4. *Seventh edition*

Die Königstochter folgte ihr mit den Augen nach, aber die Kugel verschwand, und der Brunnen war tief, so tief, daß man keinen Grund sah. Da fing sie au zu weinen und weinte immer lauter und konnte sich gar nicht trösten.

(The king's daughter followed it with her eyes, but the ball disappeared, and the well was deep, so deep, that no bottom was visible. Then she began to weep, and wept louder and louder, and was inconsolable.)

In this passage, we see a constant substitution of words and phrases for others, even where no changes of substance are made. Here is another example, from the same tale. The frog obtains the agreement of the princess to his conditions for retrieving the ball, and dives into the water:

1. *Manuscript version*

Und als sie es versprochen, tauchte er unter und kam bald die Kugel im Maul wieder in die Höhe, und warf sie ans Land.

(And when she had promised it, he plunged down and soon came back up to the surface with the ball in his mouth, and threw it onto land.)

2. *First edition*

Der Frosch steckte seinen Kopf unter das Wasser und tauchte hinab, es dauerte auch nicht lange, so kam er wieder in die Höhe, hatte die Kugel im Maul und warf sie ans Land.

(The frog stuck his head under the water and plunged down, and it was not long before he came back up again to the surface, had the ball in his mouth and threw it onto land.)

3. *Second edition*

Als sie das gesagt hatte, tauchte der Frosch seinen Kopf wieder unter das Wasser, sank hinab und über ein Weilchen kam er wieder in die Höhe gerudert, hatte die Kugel im Maul und warf sie heraus ins Gras.

(When she had said that the frog plunged his head under the water again, sank down, and a little while later came swimming up to the surface again, had the ball in his mouth and threw it out into the grass.)

4. *Seventh edition*

Der Frosch, als er die Zusage erhalten hatte, tauchte seinen Kopf unter, sank hinab, und über ein Weilchen kam er wieder heraufgerudert; hatte die Kugel im Maul und warf sie ins Gras.

(When the frog had received her agreement, he plunged his head under, sank down, and a little while later came swimming back up; had the ball in his mouth, and threw it into the grass.)

One last example: in *Daumerlings Wanderschaft, (Thumbling's Travels)* when the Daumerling meets the robbers in the wood, they suggest that his size would make it easy for him to help them to steal:

1. *Manuscript version*

. . . die tragen ihm auf, er soll sich in die Schatzkammer schleichen u. ihnen das Geld zum Fenster hinaus werfen.

(They give him the task of slipping into the treasury and throwing the money out of the window to them.)

2. *First edition*
Und als sie das Schneiderlein sehen, denken sie, der kann uns viel nützen, reden es an, sagen, es sey ein tüchtiger Kerl, es solle mit zur Schatzkammer gehen, sich hineinschleichen und ihnen das Geld herauswerfen.

(And when they see the little tailor, they think, he can be very useful to us, talk to him, tell him he is a good fellow, he must go with them to the treasury, slip into it, and throw the money out to them.)

3. *Second Edition*
Als sie das Schneiderlein sahen, dachten sie, so ein Instrument kann uns viel nützen. "Heda, rief einer, du gewaltiger Kerl, willst du mit zur Schatzkammer gehen, du kannst dich hineinschleichen und das Geld herauswerfen."

(When they saw the little tailor, they thought, a tool like that can be very useful to us. "Ho there, cried one, you tough fellow, do you want to go to the treasury with us, you can slip yourself in and throw the money out.")

4. *Seventh edition*
Als sie das Schneiderlein sahen, dachten sie "so ein kleiner Kerl kann durch ein Schlüsselloch kriechen und uns als Dietrich dienen." "heda," rief einer, "du Riese Goliath, willst du mit zur Schatzkammer gehen? du kannst dich hineinschleichen und das Geld herauswerfen."

(When they saw the little tailor, they thought, "a little fellow like that can crawl through the key-hole and serve as a picklock for us." "Ho there," cried one, "you giant Goliath, do you want to go with us to the treasury? You can slip yourself in and throw out the money.")

All of these examples show the same thing: a continual readiness to change any and every word in a text, and then to change the already changed version in the next edition once more—and then again in the next printing; and so on. What will strike any unprejudiced observer is the Grimms' willingness to devote considerable energy to this continual search for a better effect—but most decidedly not their devotion to the preservation of the qualities of what they started with.

There is, in fact, substantial rewriting in every edition except the final one; the seventh is close to a reprint of the sixth. In 1819, 1837, 1840, 1843, and 1850, therefore, there was major rewriting of the *KHM*—an extraordinary fact in itself. This does not mean that all of the tales were treated in the same way; but a typical pattern emerges from a comparison of the different editions, and it holds for most of the tales. Typically, a tale was rewritten to a major extent twice after the first edition; in addition, there would be varying degrees of minor rephrasing in the rest of the editions—sometimes only here and there, in other cases in every other line; and, occasionally, one edition would largely reprint the text of its predecessor in a given tale. This means that any particular edition may contain a major rewriting of some tales, much rephrasing of others, a little rephrasing of still others, and in some cases no changes at all. The fifth edition, for example, virtually reprints the fourth's version of *Der Frosch-könig oder der eiserne Heinrich* but, on the other hand, contains important changes in *Hänsel und Gretel* and minor changes in *Daumerlings Wanderschaft*. The second commonly contains major rewriting, for example in the cases of *Daumerlings Wanderschaft*, *Dornröschen* and *Der Froschkönig*. While the fourth edition text is critical for the development of *Hänsel und Gretel,* however, it is of no importance for *Daumerlings Wanderschaft*, but has some rephrasings for *Der Froschkönig* and *Dornröschen*. In most cases, then, there are four critical texts: the manuscripts, the first edition, and two subsequent major rewritings; and this is why I gave four versions in the examples given above. But to give my reader a clearer view of the Grimms' activity in their constant tinkering with the *KHM* text, I have given, in an appendix, the four critical texts of three different tales: *Der Froschkönig, Dornröschen,* and *Hänsel und Gretel.* In addition to those complete texts, the many variant rephrasings of the editions not given in their entirety are also given in a set of notes to these basic four texts for each tale, so that a full view of the changing shape of each text throughout the seven editions is possible.

It is not only the Grimms' continued rewriting of their material that we need to take into account in order to judge how they gradually changed the character of their collection; its character also changed through another means. Throughout the editions, the Grimms dropped some stories and added others, and the sum of these changes is a definite shift of direction for the *KHM*.

As we have seen, the brothers omitted three of the surviving manuscript stories from the first edition, but in these cases their reasons were in fact reasonably close to their stated rationale for the collection; all three had been very close to printed sources. But the pattern of their later changes suggested very different motives, and it had a very different effect: the exclusion of themes and subject matter uncongenial to the brothers.

Some care is needed in drawing up a list of tales included in the first edition and subsequently omitted from the collection. Number 7 of the 1812 *KHM* first volume, for example, is *Von dem gestohlenen Heller (About the Lost Farthing)*, but this tale is replaced already in the first volume of the second edition by the new story *Der gute Handel (The Good Bargain)*. But this does not mean that the tale is no longer part of the *KHM;* it has simply been relegated to number 154 of the second volume, and is now entitled *Der gestohlene Heller (The Lost Farthing)*. Other stories were replaced by other versions of the same tales with different titles; for example, number 14, *Von dem bösen Flachsspinnen (About the Evil Flax Spinning)* becomes *Die drei Spinnerinnen (The Three Spinsters)*. And others were relegated to the notes of related tales and summarized there.

Several, however, are dropped in the later editions, and no trace of them remains, either in the text or the notes. A look at them is very instructive. Take, for example, the following 1812 *KHM* tales:

6   *Von der Nachtigall und der Blindschleiche (The Nightingale and the Slow-worm)*
8   *Die Hand mit dem Messer (The Hand with the Knife)*
22 *Wie Kinder Schlachtens mit einander gespielt haben (How Children Played Butcher with Each Other)*
27 *Der Tod und der Gänsehirt (Death and the Gooseherd)*
33 *Der gestiefelte Kater (Puss-in-Boots)*
54 *Hans Dumm (Silly Hans)*
62 *Blaubart (Bluebeard)*
77 *Vom Schreiner und Drechsler (The Joiner and the Turner)*

All of these were abandoned in later editions. Reasons have been suggested in individual cases for the Grimms' action in dropping a given story; but before considering those reasons, let us survey the content of this group. In number 6, a nightingale cheats a slow-worm, who as a result remains blind, and the nightingale enjoys the results of his cheating without punishment or misfortune. In number 8, brothers cheat their sister and again go unpunished, in fact thriving after their misdeed. In number 22, children literally butcher each other. In number 27 the central figure commits suicide. In number 33, the trickster Puss-in-Boots deceives a king into believing that his pauper master is a rich count in order to secure a favorable marriage for him. Number 54 opens with the birth to a princess of an illegitimate child, the identity of the father being unknown. Number 62 is the story of Bluebeard, who marries and butchers one woman after another. Number 77 is the story I have discussed above in which a prince is excited by the stories of a beautiful princess and manages secretly to gain access to her room, for which she and he are condemned to death.

It is not difficult to conclude here that the Grimms, in dropping these stories, were purging the *KHM* of content they found objectionable: successful crime, sex, suicide, illegitimate birth, wanton violence by children and family members. In the final collection, this kind of content is minimized; crime is punished; only the good prosper; relations between the sexes are reduced to clichés which do not allow sexual promiscuity, immorality, or incest to come into view; only sorcerers and witches usually mistreat other people;[8] violence is generally reserved for those who deserve it; and life is too rational and just to allow suicides.

Even the stories which were relegated to the notes, but not abandoned altogether, show something of this tendency. In the preceding chapter, for example, I showed how the brothers rewrote the manuscript story which became the *KHM Von Johannes-Wassersprung und Caspar-Wassersprung* to try to remove its strong suggestions of incest and illegitimate birth. But they were evidently not satisfied that their work had been able to completely hide these suggestions, for they dropped it as early as the second edition, replacing it by *Der Fuchs und die Frau Gevatterin (The Fox and the Gossip)* and summarizing it in the notes to number 60, *Die zwei Brüder (The Two Brothers)*.

To be sure, one reason for some of these omissions seems plausible enough: several of them are of foreign origin, and the Grimms' second edition preface had announced: "Es ist noch einmal geprüft, was verdächtig schien, d.h. was etwa hätte fremden Ursprungs . . . seyn können" ("We have once more examined whatever might look suspect, i.e., what might be of foreign origin"). An intention to purify the collection of tales of foreign origin would seem to be an inherently reasonable one, though it could not account for more than about half of the cases involved, such as numbers 6, 8, 33 and 62. But this explanation is bound to raise some questions. If a rejection of foreign source material was the reason for these changes, why did the Grimms not also remove tales like *Aschenputtel,* which obviously derived from Perrault's *Cendrillon,* or *Dornröschen,* deriving from *La Belle au bois dormant?* The brothers explicitly rejected *Blaubart* because of its dependence on Perrault, according to their notes, and they certainly could claim the same in the case of *Der Gestiefelte Kater,* also omitted after the first edition. But they acted this way only in some cases, and not in others.

The second problem raised by this explanation is that of the Grimms' willing reliance on sources heavily contaminated by French speakers; they accepted material from Dorothea Viehmann, and from the Hassenpflug family, without seemingly being concerned in principle with this contamination—though they tried to conceal it, showing that they were indeed concerned about its being known publicly. Indeed, the first edition's *Blaubart* and *Der gestiefelte Kater* had both derived from the Hassenpflug family. The impression remains, therefore, that their omissions were due to a wish to avoid certain kinds of subject matter, and that their explanation of some of those omissions was a justification after the fact for what they wanted to do for a different reason.[9]

It is very important to understand how the Grimms restricted the content of the *KHM,* because they have in so doing helped significantly to give the word "fairy tale" its unambiguously positive meaning—for example, a "fairy-tale marriage" is one of unproblematic happiness. The world of the *KHM* sources was by no means so consistently benevolent and sunny.

A close look at the changes in the *KHM* as it progressed from the first to the seventh edition leads, therefore, to the following conclusions. First, throughout the first six editions the brothers never stopped recasting, rewriting, and rephrasing the tales over and over again; and this ever-present readiness on their part to tinker with the language of the tales is impossible to square with their professed reverence for the authentic folk quality of their material since it is obviously motivated by a desire to maximize the literary effect and impact of the *KHM.* Second, they continued to make changes of substance in the texts, which had the effect of slowly changing the world of the *KHM*, making it a more rational and less mysterious or dangerous one, particularly with regard to violence and sexuality. And, third, changes in the composition of the *KHM* achieved by dropping some tales and substituting new ones also contributed in a major way to the same process of changing the world of the collection. Once more, it is very hard to imagine that they could have been unaware of the discrepancy between their insistance on authenticity, on the one hand, and their disregard for it in these actions, on the other.

6

The Status of
the Tales and Their
Historical Context

It has often been said, and reasonably enough, that any final judgment on the *Kinder- und Hausmärchen* and on the brothers' work on the collection can only be made in the context of the ethnographic standards of their own time. But it is far too easily assumed that those standards would be completely undemanding ones. That assumption arises typically because figures like Musäus are invoked in order to set the Grimms in historical perspective. Here, for example, is Michaelis-Jena's way of doing so: "The Weimar schoolmaster [Musäus] could not refrain from manipulating the language, and giving it a stiltedness alien to genuine tradition. . . . The Grimms' approach was different."[1]

Hermann Hettner puts the matter in a more pointed way: "Musäus entered the scene with his 'Fairy Tales of the Germans,' 1782–86. . . . We now know that Musäus had not yet found the genuine fairy tale style."[2] By contrast, it would seem the Grimms *did* find that genuine fairy tale style.

But the comparison with Musäus is not and never has been one which could yield the perspective of contemporary ethnographic standards as a framework within which to judge the Grimms. For Musäus did not embody those standards, and had no interest in them; like Perrault before him, and Brentano after him, Musäus was interested in using the folkloric material as an artist, to create an independent work of art. The Grimms offered

94

the *KHM* as folkloric material in original form, with professed reverence for that original form; Musäus by contrast expressed contempt for the original form of his material.

To gain a historical perspective on the brothers we must look to those who *did* have or profess an interest in folkloric material for its own sake, not to those who had none; in practice the comparison with Musäus has only functioned to provide an excuse for the Grimms' transgressions, not to illuminate the key issues of what they did and why.

As it happens, there is a celebrated eighteenth-century controversy which was both extensive enough to provide us with plenty of evidence on contemporary attitudes and sufficiently similar in its issues to the case of the *KHM* to allow us to see fairly clearly just what contemporary judgments might have been of the Grimms' procedure, had the truth been known. This is the controversy over Macpherson's *Ossian.*

Around the beginning of the eighteenth century, interest in the systematic study of the language and literature of ancient cultures was beginning to spread; and one of the factors involved in this serious philological study was a new interest in writers like Homer. Influenced by this climate, the Scot James Macpherson (1736–96) studied ancient Celtic poetry. In 1760 he published his *Fragments of Ancient Poetry,* which he announced as translations of original Gaelic ballads, following this with two similar publications in 1762 and 1763, the first of these being the epic *Fingal.* The impact of these publications on the European scene was tremendous. In Germany, admiration for what seemed to be the natural expression of these "Ossianic" poems (named after the third-century Gaelic poet Ossian or Oisín) became a major part of the literary program of the Sturm und Drang movement, and Herder's essay on Ossian was the occasion for praise of the natural expression of primitive folk poetry which helped to set the stage for the Grimms and their *KHM.* But immediately there was skepticism as to the authenticity of Macpherson's material, and the skeptics were prominent and influential, including no less a figure than Dr. Samuel Johnson. The skeptics charged that those "translations" were largely Macpherson's own inventions, and that they had only the loosest relationship with ancient legends. Macpherson was challenged to produce the originals which he had translated. When he did not do so, public opinion soon concluded that his published texts were "fakes" and his claims for them fraudulent.

It is worthwhile to compare this case to that of the Grimms, for the issues it raised had become well known throughout Europe before they began to collect and publish their tales, though the whole incident was still very recent.

Apparently like the Grimms, Macpherson published his collection as an attempt to preserve and disseminate material from an oral folk tradition; and in both cases serious questions were eventually raised about the authenticity of what was published. But there the similarity ends; for in his own time, Macpherson was branded a fraud and a forger, while the Grimms have been celebrated in their lifetime and ever since as devoted scholars of an indigenous folk culture. Yet from Macpherson's case we can get a good idea of what was counted as fraud and forgery in ethnographic matters in the eighteenth century.

Let us look first at the facts of the two cases. In the case of the Grimms we can sum up the situation as follows. The brothers claimed to collect from indigenous folk sources in order to record and preserve a folk tradition of storytelling, but in fact they collected almost exclusively from their own middle-class, literate family and friends, who were contaminated both by knowledge of books, including foreign books, and by French family origin. To disguise this, the Grimms concealed the identity of their sources, referring vaguely to regions of origin to give an impression that the folk of that region was the source, and then deceptively described as their archetypal source an old German peasant woman who was actually middle-class, literate, and of French origin. Having thus claimed fraudulently that they had much genuine folk material, they at first claimed to have published it intact, without alteration or improvement, destroying their manuscripts to make sure that no one would know that they had in fact extensively elaborated and rewritten all their source material, changing form and content at will, and doubling and sometimes tripling the length of a text. Later, however, when their having tampered freely with the second edition text made it necessary to abandon the claim of intactness, they admitted to changing expression, but not content. This was still a lie, for the resulting collection bore absolutely no relation to an indigenous storytelling tradition in its expression and also very little in its content.

Now, let us compare this record with what is known of Macpherson's Ossianic material. While Ossian generated much heated debate, the main facts of the situation are now fairly clear; but before setting them out we should recall what happened to Macpherson: he was fairly quickly branded as a forger, and in spite of later qualifications attached to this view, the popular sense has remained that *Ossian* is to a large extent a "fake."

Here are the facts which are now agreed upon, and which were indeed very soon largely clear at the time. Diligently and energetically, Macpherson collected authentic manuscripts of the Gaelic ballads which are the basis (in a sense to be set out in a moment) of his printed texts. Derick Thomson, in his very thorough study *The Gaelic Sources of Macpherson's Ossian*, concludes:

> The evidence shows that Macpherson cast his net wide, and collected a large amount of Ossianic materials. The picture emerges of an eager investigator, travelling through Invernesshire, Perthshire, Argyll, and the Inner and Outer Hebrides. He employed scribes to record oral traditions . . . he wheedled MSS. from their owners, sometimes by personal interview, sometimes by letter.[3]

No greater contrast with the Grimms could be imagined. Macpherson collected energetically from many areas; they from one. He traveled widely to find his material; they stayed at home. He sought out reliable sources carefully; they collected from their friends and family. He made sure his informants were really part of the Gaelic folk tradition he was trying to document; they allowed serious contamination from foreign sources and from literate people whose sources might be simply books. They had as a consequence nothing like the same quantity and quality of genuine traditional material available to them, but instead only material which, judged by Macpherson's standards, was of very poor quality indeed. They lied and dissembled to conceal from their public the nature of their sources, which Macpherson most assuredly did not: his sources were what he claimed they were— real folk sources, real transmitters of genuine oral tradition material. Macpherson had no reason to conceal the nature of his sources or to invent a fictitious tale teller.

So much for the quality of Macpherson's original material and his sources. Now what of his treatment of that material? Only on this point is Macpherson more like the Grimms, though here he still stands somewhat better. Like the Grimms, Macpherson first claimed that his published texts were faithful transcripts (in his case, translations from the Gaelic) of authentic folk material; and like them, he later had to retreat from that absolute claim. In fact, Macpherson paraphrased, elaborated, refined and combined elements of different stories[4]—all processes we have observed in the Grimms' case. The result was, as Thomson remarks, that "Macpherson's refining and bowdlerising pen has often changed the atmostphere of the ballads almost beyond recognition."[5] This may sound like the kind of judgment I have made on the Grimms' treatment of their material; yet we should note that Thomson refers to the *atmosphere* of the stories, not to their events and episodes. The Grimms, on the other hand, changed those in important ways too. Furthermore, the 1805 *Report of the Highland Society of Scotland,* the conclusions of which have held up well over the years since its publication, cites a number of witnesses who mention passages in Macpherson's text which they found similar to those which they had independently heard recited orally.[6] Thomson's own comparison of extant authentic manuscripts with the Macpherson text supports this judgment. The Grimms, on the other hand, rewrote and elaborated their manuscripts to such a degree, and their manuscripts themselves were so far inferior to Macpherson's in their remoteness from authentic folk sources, that it is probably doubtful whether the details of any passages in the *KHM* would be recognized by those familiar with folk sources—where such existed, and whatever they might have been.

To sum up: Macpherson worked hard to collect much genuine material, but misled his public to a substantial degree about his own role in editing and recasting it; the Grimms never bothered to collect material of real quality, lied to their public about its nature and their sources, destroyed their basic material, and again lied about the extent of their own role in creating the text which they published, that role being rather more active than Macpherson's had been. Yet Macpherson generally counts as the faker and forger, not the Grimms. The facts, if viewed dispassionately, should have made the Grimms subject to far more severe criticism than Macpherson; yet Macpherson's image as a forger has softened only a little with the passage of time, while even today, long after all of the essential facts became available, the Grimms are still excused, and are never judged by the standard used in Macpherson's case.

There are many ironies in this situation. The controversy over *Ossian* was famous by the time the *KHM* appeared, and it has remained so. What emerged from that controversy was a historical fact that should have been impossible to ignore, then or since: that Macpherson claimed a very strict standard of ethnographic recording, and that everyone who criticized him accepted that standard as an appropriate one to use in judging him. And this makes nonsense of one of the standard defenses of the Grimms' reworking of their material; for if standards of faithfulness in ethnographic recording were so much weaker in the Grimms' time, as is often alleged, it would be very strange indeed that Macpherson was so heavily censured for transgressions that were noticeably less than those of the Grimms half a century before their *KHM* was published. Moreover, the terms of the *Ossian* controversy also make nonsense of the sentimental claim that the Grimms were pioneers in the methodology of folklore, and they would do so even if the Grimms had been doing what they claimed to be doing. But perhaps the most eloquent evidence as to contemporary standards is provided by the Grimms themselves; their efforts to conceal the true nature of their procedure betray a clear awareness on their part that, by the early nineteenth century, much more was required of folklorists than they had done or were prepared to do.

But what are we to make of this difference of reception— maximally hostile and disbelieving in the case of *Ossian,* and exactly the opposite in the case of the *KHM?* One important difference may well lie in the length of time which elapsed before the appearance of evidence which allowed an informed and accurate assessment. Experience shows that once misconceptions are really firmly entrenched in a body of scholarship, they develop a life of their own and are not easily eradicable; like a giant oil tanker, they have enormous directional momentum and take a very long time to turn around. In the Grimms' case, the misconceptions had a chance to take firm root and to go unchallenged for a very long period of time; the situation was very different for Macpherson.

Knowledgeable collectors in the Celtic area existed already in Macpherson's time, while they seem to have been largely absent where fairy tales were concerned in the German-speaking area.

Thus the necessary evidence was soon available in Macpherson's case, and he was quickly challenged; but the crucial evidence as to the real status of the *KHM* became available mostly in the second and third decades of this century, by which time the *KHM* had become an indispensable classic, a status which made for very considerable emotional resistance to the kind of language (e.g., "fraud") with which Macpherson was assailed. To be sure, the actions of the principals also played a role in creating this difference of conditions, and again the Grimms must be contrasted unfavorably with Macpherson. For they destroyed the primary evidence, while he preserved the manuscripts from which he worked.[7]

A second factor undoubtedly lies in the much broader and more innocuous popular appeal of the *KHM*. But it is impossible not to discern a third factor which operated strongly, though differently, in the two situations: nationalism. Just how important such a factor can be in situations involving controversies over the authenticity of folklore material can be seen from the simple fact that Macpherson's *Ossian* was immediately attacked by Anglo-Saxon scholars, and defended by Scottish ones.[8] By contrast the Grimms' immediate audience was that of their own nation, not an ethnically distinct group predisposed to a skeptical attitude toward their culture. But more than this, the Grimms appealed strongly to German nationalism because their *own* motives were nationalistic; and so this factor is dominant both in the brothers' fabrications and deceit, and in the strong reluctance of later scholars to acknowledge what they had done when the evidence emerged. The Grimms wanted to create a German national monument while pretending that they had merely discovered it; and later on, no one wanted to seem to tear it down.

I described above the way in which the literary scene in Germany became consciously nationalistic with the appearance of the romantic movement, but the historical circumstances of Germany in 1812 also make the Grimms' patriotic motives easier to understand. The military successes of Frederick the Great had produced an atmosphere of confidence that Prussia could stand up to Napoleon, but the resulting battles of 1806 were military disasters, and devastating blows to a German pride that had only recently been raised. The entire German territory was for the moment effectively dominated by France. That the Grimms' motives were in large part patriotic has been generally recognized, but there has been less awareness of how those motives helped to distort the truth about the *KHM*. Murray Peppard, for example, in the following passage, recognized the Grimms' patriotic motives, without questioning the integrity of the results of activities that had been so motivated:

> It is ironic that this gift to the world had its origins in the Grimms' patriotic fever. What was originally a collection of tales from Hesse, with a few from Westphalia, became an enduring part of international cultural heritage. The brothers presented the book to their nation as an encouraging reminder of its spiritual history at a time when Germany was about to rise with renewed courage from its days of defeat and despair; in fact, so much of what they wrote is suffused with this love of their country and its culture.[9]

Louis Snyder goes even further in arguing that the tales "were designed originally to stimulate German national sentiment";[10] but, though it may be going too far to attribute to the Grimms so exclusive a conception of the purpose of their *KHM* collection, it remains true that they did create a German national monument. Whatever its origin, the *KHM* quickly achieved and has maintained that status, a fact which goes a long way toward explaining the reluctance of scholars and lay readers alike to subject the myth of their provenance to the scrutiny which the emerging evidence so clearly demanded.

Any situation in which a popular misconception is in effect protected for patriotic reasons is a potentially dangerous one; and Snyder's study illustrates this in an interesting way. For Snyder, like Peppard, saw only the Grimms' patriotic motives, but not how those motives had led them to misrepresent what they had done; and he thus believed what the Grimms meant him to believe, i.e., that their collecting had been "laborious," that they "took down the tales with almost fanatical accuracy," and that they "obtained their folk-tales from the lips of peasant women, shepherds, waggoners, vagrants, old grannies, and children."[11] From this, Snyder deduced that an analysis of the content of the tales would yield "important elements of the German national character."[12] And his conclusion, after that analysis, is as follows:

> An analysis of the Märchen gives ample evidence to show an emphasis upon such social characteristics as respect for order, belief in the desirability of obedience, subservience to authority,

respect for the leader and the hero, veneration of courage and the military spirit, acceptance without protest of cruelty, violence, and atrocity, fear of and hatred for the outsider, and virulent anti-Semitism.[13]

These conclusions would be all very well if the *KHM* were really the product of the German *Volk;* but since they are not, Snyder's analysis tells us more about the attitudes of the Grimms than of the German people. To be sure, Snyder sometimes cites evidence from the later *KHM* tales which have no counterparts in the 1810 manuscripts, and in these cases the character of the Grimms' sources and of their treatment of them cannot be known. But when he does cite a tale for which the existence of an 1810 manuscript does allow such knowledge, it is often apparent that Snyder's quarrel is with the Grimms' contribution, not with that of their sources.

A case in point is his discussion of *Aschenputtel.* To demonstrate his contention that the tales are full of cruelty and violence, Snyder points to the fate of Cinderella's sisters;[14] but this is a feature added by the brothers. And to show that "the concept of obedience is emphasized again and again," he refers to the daughter's willingness to allow her father to cut off her hands in order to placate the Devil in *Das Mädchen ohne Hände;*[15] but this is part of the awkward and unconvincing alteration of the more plausible beginning of the tale, omitted by the Grimms, in which the father mutilates his daughter in anger because of her refusal to become his wife. To show the "fear of and hatred for the outsider, characteristic of primitive tribalism and modern nationalism," Snyder points to the unsympathetic portrayal of and brutal treatment of stepmothers, e.g., in *Hänsel und Gretel;*[16] but here and elsewhere, the Grimms introduced that figure themselves in order to soften the much more direct and frightening intrafamily strife of the original. In all of these cases, then, the object of Snyder's analysis is really the brothers themselves, not the German people.

Nationalism is often a dubious force, and it has worked in many different ways in the history of the *KHM;* first to promote its acceptance, then to obscure its real status, and finally to call it into question. But fortunately, there is no longer any reason to treat the *KHM* as having been authored by a nation. And if we ignore national boundaries and judge Macpherson and the

Grimms by the same international standard, the inevitable conclusion must be that the charge of fraud and forgery is not entirely fair to Macpherson but is far more appropriate to two men who have been treated more kindly by history—the brothers Grimm.

7

Conclusion

There is a strange paradox in the history of the Grimms'
KHM; though seemingly nothing more than delicate fantasy, the tales have proved to be far more durable than
could possibly have been imagined. And the same is true of the
brothers' fantasy tale about the nature and origin of their collection. Only a few years ago, Alfred Riemen cast it into *KHM*
style: "There were once two brothers who loved nothing as much
as listening to stories which old women and young girls told
them . . . and because friends encouraged them, they went deeper
and deeper into the fairy-tale forest, and collected all the pretty
leaves that they found, and took them home, and preserved them
as a precious treasure."[1] Now the context of the passage shows
just how sturdy and durable this fantasy is: it is actually the
beginning of a review of Rölleke's edition of the 1810 manuscript
material. Even when faced with a body of evidence which should
make nonsense of this story, the writer sets it out in almost ritual
fashion. This is essentially what has happened ever since the appearance of the *KHM,* and it shows no real signs of abating.
Consider the historical sequence of events relating to the *KHM.*

During the Grimms' lifetimes (Wilhelm died in 1859, Jacob in
1863) the only available evidence was the seven editions and
their prefaces. On the basis of that evidence, one could have
been concerned about the rewriting of the editions and the ir-
reconcilable differences between the various prefaces, but could

have believed that the two major statements were the work of Jacob on the one hand, Wilhelm on the other. In 1881–87, Wilhelm's collected shorter papers were published, and they included the preface for the first edition; that should have made it impossible to continue believing that different brothers wrote the two prefaces. But this information had no effect whatsoever. In 1899, Johannes Bolte received the brothers' own copies of the *KHM*, including marginalia indicating sources for the stories and Wilhelm's having written most of them. That should have destroyed the notion that the first edition was free of Wilhelm's rewriting, and should have shown that the brothers lied about the nature of their sources. But Bolte only published the information, without comment, in 1912, and in the absence of his drawing attention to its crucial importance, no one saw any importance in it. As a result, major studies such as those of Tonnelat (1912) and Panzer (1913a, 1913b), of the differences between the seven editions, lacking this information, both took positions which perpetuated past attitudes and strengthened the perseverance of those attitudes into the future. In 1924, the 1810 manuscript material was published by Schulz; no one paid any attention, though now the extent of the deception of the 1812 preface was completely clear, and any last vestige of a belief in the first edition's being unspoiled by Wilhelm's reworking was now impossible. Lefftz republished the same material three years later, and, though this provoked a small flurry of activity in studies by Freitag (1929), Schoof (1930) and Schmidt (1931)— all examining the new material and its significance—every one of them in effect retained the preexisting conceptual framework of *KHM* scholarship. Instead of seeing how the new evidence made the old ideas obsolete, Freitag, Schoof, and Schmidt simply forced that evidence to fit into the framework of the old ideas as best they could. Since those who were most knowledgeable did all they could to minimize the impact of the discoveries, the old view of the *KHM* survived virtually intact. Less knowledgeable readers must of course have found it reassuring that, for example, Lefftz sounded not the least bit alarmed. All was silent for another quarter of a century.

In 1955 the devastating revelation about Dorothea Viehmann still caused no alarm; though it is mentioned on occasion in studies appearing sporadically over the next fifteen years, no one commented on its significance. During that time, attitudes continued as before, for example, in studies by Schoof (1959), Winter (1962), Lüthi (1962), Woeller (1965), and the four full-length biographies of 1970–71 by Denecke, Michaelis-Jena, Peppard, and Gerstner. The 1810 material is even published once more (in 1964, by Lemmer) without being noticed at all.

By the beginning of the 1970s, *KHM* studies were in a truly strange condition. The field had retained all of its old attitudes while having managed for many decades to assimilate large amounts of material which should be lethal to those attitudes. The odd result is that when during the 1970s this material was published again (in 1970, by Weber-Kellermann, on Dorothea Viehmann; in 1975, the 1810 manuscript material and the Grimms' handwritten notes on this information, by Rölleke), only writers who obviously knew little about Grimm scholarship (e.g., Schumann) welcomed it (correctly) as startling material which clashed with previous attitudes to the *KHM*, while more knowledgeable scholars did not. Not unnaturally, such people could not believe that this material was ever published before (how could it have been, since it would have to have caused a great commotion, surely?) and attribute the new discoveries to scholars (e.g., Rölleke) who are merely reissuing long-since printed material.

What can we expect to happen next? There are signs that the disturbing information is slowly, after so many years, becoming better known. On the other hand, this knowledge seems only to be producing a new crop of excuses and attempts to explain the facts away. We have already seen some of them above: some scholars have tried to treat the new information merely as a corrective to common misconceptions, as if the Grimms had nothing to do with those misconceptions; others have argued that the Grimms' failure to give sufficient information about their methods allowed misconceptions to arise, ignoring the fact that the Grimms' silences concerned matters where their explicit statements would have been exposed as lies had they not remained silent.

Two other major new excuses have been set forward recently, one concerning the problem of the specifically German quality of the collection, the other concerning the standing and literacy of the informants.

The first tries to understate the issue of national origin of the *KHM*, and its exponents are Schumann and Rölleke. Schumann tells us that the Grimms never intended their fairy tales to be viewed as a *German* collection because they did not use the word "German" in the title of the collection, in contrast to their *Deutsche Sagen (German Legends).*[2] If the titles of these collections were the only available evidence of the Grimms' intentions, Schumann might have a point; but unfortunately, the Grimms said many things in many contexts which create an overwhelming case for the opposite conclusion. In the preface of 1815, they said that their collection contained "pure ancient Germanic myth" *(ur-deutscher Mythus);* in the preface of 1812, they said that theirs was the first collection of its kind in Germany, and that with a few exceptions, everything had been collected in Hessen and Hanau from oral tradition; in the 1819 preface, they said that they had reexamined "anything that might be suspect, that is, of foreign origin;" and so on. Over and over again, they insisted that the collection was the product of an indigenous folk tradition, i.e., a German one.

Rölleke's contribution to this argument is a logical sleight-of-hand which can only succeed if it confuses the reader and makes him lose sight of the issue he is dealing with. He sets out some of the facts about the informants, and then remarks: "One must nevertheless warn against conclusions that are too extreme. One cannot, just from the fact that some of the main contributors were of Huguenot origin, simply conclude that the Grimms' Fairy Tales originate in France."[3] Rölleke is trying to shift our attention to an irrelevance; if we let ourselves be persuaded that the real issue here is whether the tales are all French in origin, we can certainly say that that is not so and, having dealt easily with that issue, stop worrying about the whole question of foreign elements in the collection. But this trick of argument will not really solve the problem so simply; the question is not whether the tales are essentially all French but whether they are essentially all German. If we keep our eyes on the real issue, rather than the red herring which substitutes for it here, we shall still have to go on being disturbed by the fact that there is very considerable French presence and influence in a collection which the Grimms tried to pass off as German through and through, knowing that not to be the case.

The second of these new excuses tries to persuade us not to worry too much about the fact that the Grimms' informants were middle-class and literate; its exponents are Rölleke and Dégh.

Rölleke argues that the middle-class story repertoire of the early nineteenth century in any case goes back to generations of workers and peasants;[4] Dégh extends this idea when she redefines the status of the Grimms' informants—they are, apparently, not informants at all but a "small collecting team."[5] And so, the Grimms collected material from the middle class, which had collected it in turn from the peasants. Oddly enough, Rölleke, having exposed the myth of "old Marie," now creates a hypothetical whole series of "old Maries"—all unfortunately, unnamed, invisible, and conjectural, but the advantage of their being so is that, unlike the specific "old Marie," they cannot be exposed. Still, this argument suffers from many fatal flaws. Its major problem, once more, lies in the Grimms' false statements. If there is indeed a reasonable explanation for what the Grimms did, one which preserves the rationale for their collection, why did they themselves not state it? Why did they need to mislead their public? For Dorothea Viehmann, we must remember, is described by the brothers not as a member of the collecting team but as the archetypal folk narrator. And what, on this explanation, can we make of their insistence on the very words of the folk narrator, if they never found one, and largely created the fabric of the tales themselves? At best, these middle-class "collectors" collected some scraps of plot material for the finished product, but they did not collect the substance and style of folk narration; and given the widespread distribution of their tales throughout Europe and beyond, nothing else really mattered anyway. Rölleke's conjecture is, therefore, irrelevant. Even if it were true, it would not help in any way to preserve the Grimms' rationale for their collection, or to prevent the kinds of judgments I have made in the course of this study. And, in fact, this conjecture appears to me only to represent an attempt on Rölleke's part to cling to one of those myths about the "common folk" which the Romantic movement in general and the Grimms in particular had cherished; there is no evidence for it.

The Grimms, it will be remembered, were part of a cultural context which rejected the artificial, stilted quality of neoclassicism and was drawn to the poetry of earlier cultures, which it regarded as closer to nature and a more simple, primal way of life. Homer and Ossian were considered representative of such poetry. The brothers, like Herder before them, thought of the simpler folk of their time as having this same natural expression because of their simpler way of life. But there is a large gap in the logic of this train of thought; the "primitive" way of life of earlier cultures cannot be equated with the way of life of the lower classes of a stratified modern society, and certainly Homer and Ossian—who most surely would have been among the most outstandingly literate members of those societies—cannot be juxtaposed to the illiterate members of a literate nineteenth-century European nation. When the Grimms *did* find illiterate tale-tellers,[6] they responded to the results as one would expect—they found them illiterate, and had to impose on this material the particular literate, even literary, style which they created in order to give the *illusion* of a simple, unsophisticated folktale teller. The nearest equivalent of the Homers and the Ossians in nineteenth-century Germany were gifted storytellers like Wilhelm Grimm, not the romanticized peasants that they and even some of their critics imagined.[7]

The events of the 1970s seem in many ways to have been a repetition of those of 1912–24: once again, all of the evidence was published which shows plainly enough the fraudulence of the Grimms' claims for their collection, but, as before, the scholars who published it accompanied that publication with a commentary so full of excuses for the Grimms that its impact was blunted. This pattern causes considerable confusion: onlookers see what seems to be highly damaging evidence offered to them by more knowledgeable scholars who seem not to worry about it to anything like the degree that they would expect. Dégh reflects this confusion when she asks: are the tales "prototypes of genuine oral narratives?" and answers herself: "This is not quite so, or perhaps it is."[8] And this confusion allows everyone to go on as before; the same judgments will be made about the Grimms as pioneers in folklore, and Alfred Riemen's charming fairy tale will continue essentially unchanged. Even analysis of the contents of the *KHM* is allowed to go on much as before by the confusion that publications such as Rölleke's leave behind. Faivre, for example, published in 1978 a study of the mythological content of the *KHM,* a study which depends on the assumption that the tales are what they were announced to be— genuine folktales. Yet in his introduction Faivre had referred to and summarized some (though not enough) of the recent publications of contrary evidence. Dégh, too, was mainly interested in pursuing a sociological analysis of the content of the *KHM.*

Both these scholars move on from an inconclusive presentation of some of the troubling material to the kind of analysis they are really interested in, but in so doing they are building on sand; they could scarcely have done so if the situation they found in recent publications had not been so confusing. And this is the result of a great irony in the history of the *KHM:* no child has ever been so charmed and beguiled by one of the Grimms' tales as the most knowledgeable Grimm specialists seem to have been by the brothers' fairy tale about the origin of their collection.

Yet one example from the year 1906 shows that it was not so very hard to see through at least some of what the Grimms had done, even before the publication of any of the major discoveries. Hermann Hamann looked at a number of the first edition *KHM* tales which seemed related to prior printed sources. He noticed that the relationship between the printed source and the *KHM* story was the *same* in all cases: it was as if the Grimms had taken each printed source, one by one, and subjected it to the same treatment to convert it to a *KHM* tale. From this he generalized: "To be sure, the material is not exhausted, because in my treatment the fairy tales from oral tradition are not included, but from an examination of a fairly small part of the collection one can draw conclusions about the stylizing of the whole."[9] Years later, it would turn out that Hamann had in fact guessed correctly: what he observed in these few cases is what the Grimms typically did to all of their sources. It is interesting to see how much one scholar was able to see with so little evidence to work with, by contrast with which more recent scholars have been determined to see as little as possible in far stronger and more extensive evidence.

The *KHM* collection presents two hundred tales that are both charming and full of interest; surely, by now, we should dispense with that added fairy tale with which they launched the collection—it is altogether one too many.

Texts of Three
of the Tales, from the
Manuscripts to the
Seventh Edition

Reproduced below are the texts of *Der Froschkönig oder der eiserne Heinrich; Dornröschen;* and *Hänsel und Gretel.* There three are among the small group of twelve for which there are eight fully comparable surviving versions—the 1810 manuscript and the texts of all seven editions in each case. Only in these twelve cases was the 1810 manuscript the basis of the 1812 edition and all later editions; no other manuscript was substituted at a later stage, either wholly or partly, and none of the tales was dropped to make way for other tales in late editions. It is unnecessary, however, to give all eight versions of each tale. The last edition is little more than a reprint of the sixth, which means that we can restrict our attention largely to the first seven texts. In all other editions (one through six) some major rewriting or recasting is present, but not uniformly in the case of each tale. In any one tale, for example, there may be great changes in one edition followed by none in its successor; or a little reworking in one edition, followed by rather more in another; or major reworking in three consecutive editions, followed by relatively much less in any of the subsequent editions; or any combination of these developments. The three tales I have chosen are fairly representative of the different kinds of development in the texts during the course of the seven editions. All show complete rewriting of the 1810 manuscript for the 1812 first edition. Thereafter, in one case the next two editions are considerably rewritten once more, while two of the subsequent four editions show re-writing of a lesser extent; in another the second and sixth editions are the texts showing much change, with less in the third and fourth only; and in the last case the second and fifth editions are the most important subsequent texts, with the third and fourth both showing a good deal of piecemeal rewriting and, in the fourth only, one very important change in a major character. In each of these cases it has been possible to give a complete account of the history of a tale by reproducing four critical texts, and giving variations from the versions not printed in their entirety as footnotes to those which are; the differences between the versions which are printed complete were far too great to be dealt with in this way. I have not indicated all variants in the notes, however: it would have made an unnecessarily cluttered and confusing presentation of this material to include changes of punctuation and spelling as well as minor grammatical changes (e.g. *lud* for *ladete*), and for these reasons I have restricted the footnote changes to actual changes of wording. The extent of the Grimms' continual rewriting of the texts will in this way come more sharply into focus. Readers who wish to work with exact copies of the texts not reproduced whole here are referred to the extant copies of the relevant edition in university and other libraries. The four texts of each tale which are reproduced here, however, are given exactly in their original spelling and punctuation; even inconsistencies of spelling have been retained. The translations given in each case are my own; for a note on their character, see the Preface.

1. Der Froschkönig oder der Eiserne Heinrich (The Frog-King, or Iron Henry)

The four basic texts of *Der Froschkönig* are the first four of the sequence of eight: the manuscript of 1810, and the first three editions of 1812, 1819, and 1837. These four differ substantially; there was considerable recasting for each edition. The text of the third edition remains in general the basis of the further editions, but there was a good deal of rephrasing in the sixth edition, and some in the fourth. The fifth edition is virtually a reprint of the fourth, as the seventh is of the sixth. I give below the full texts of the manuscript and the first three editions, with variants introduced into the fourth and sixth editions as footnotes to the text of the third.

MANUSCRIPT: *die Königstochter*
                und der verzauberte Prinz.
                Froschkönig

Die jüngste Tochter des Königs ging hinaus in den Wald, und setzte sich an einen kühlen Brunnen. Darauf nahm sie eine goldene Kugel und spielte damit, als diese plötzlich in den Brunnen hinabrollte. Sie sah wie sie in die Tiefe fiel und stand an dem Brunnen und war sehr traurig. Auf einmal streckte ein Frosch seinen Kopf aus dem Waßer und sprach: warum klagst du so sehr. Ach! du garstiger Frosch antwortete sie, du kannst mir

doch nicht helfen, meine goldene Kugel ist mir in den Brunnen
gefallen. Da sagte der Frosch, wenn du mich mit nach Haus
nehmen willst, so will ich dir deine goldene Kugel wieder holen.
Und als sie es versprochen, tauchte er unter und kam bald die
Kugel im Maul wieder in die Höhe, und warf sie ans Land. Da
nahm die Königstöchter eilig ihre Kugel wieder und lief eilig
fort, und hörte nicht auf den Frosch der ihr nachrief sie solle
ihn mitnehmen, wie sie ihm versprochen. Und als sie nach Haus
kam, setzte sie sich an die Tafel zu ihrem Vater, und wie sie eben
eßen wollte, klopfte es an die Thüre und rief: Königstochter
jüngste mach mir auf! Und sie eilte hin und sah wer es war, da
war es der häßliche Frosch und sie warf eilig die Thüre wieder
zu. Ihr Vater aber fragte, wer da sey und sie erzählte ihm alles.
Da rief es wieder

> Königstochter jüngste
> mach mir auf
> weißt du nicht was gestern
> du zu mir gesagt,
> bei dem kühlen Brunnenwaßer
> Königstochter jüngste
> mach mir auf.

Und der König befahl ihr dem Frosch aufzumachen, und er
hüpfte herein. Dann sprach ihr: setz mich zu dir an den Tisch,
ich will mit dir eßen. Sie wollte es aber nicht thun, bis daß es
der König auch befahl. Und der Frosch saß an der Seite der
Königstochter und aß mit. Und als er satt war, sprach er zu ihr:
bring mich in dein Bettlein ich will bei dir schlafen. Das wollte
sie aber durchaus nicht, denn sie fürchtete sich sehr vor dem
kalten Frosch. Aber der König befahl es wiederum, da nahm sie
den Frosch und trug ihn in ihre Kammer und voll Zorn faßt sie
ihn und warf ihn mit aller Gewalt, wieder die Wand in ihrem
Bett. Wie er aber an die Wand kam, so fiel er herunter in das
Bett und lag darin als ein junger schöner Prinz, da legte sich die
Königstochter zu ihm.

Und am Morgen kam ein schöner Wagen mit dem treuen
Diener des Prinzen, der hatte ein solch großes Leid über die
Verwandelung deßelben gehabt, daß er drei eiserne Bande um
sein Herz legen mußte. Und der Prinz und die Königstochter
setzten sich in den Wagen, und der treue Diener stellte sich
hinten auf, und sie wollten in sein Reich fahren. Und wie sie

ein Stück Wegs gefahren sind, hört der Prinz hinter sich ein lautes Krachen. Da ruft er

> Heinerich der Wagen bricht!
> Nein Herr der Wagen nicht,
> Es ist ein Band von meinem Herzen,
> das da lag in großen Schmerzen
> als ihr an dem Brunnen saßt
> als ihr eine Fretsche wart.   Frosch

FIRST EDITION

Es was einmal eine Königstochter, die ging hinaus in den Wald und setzte sich an einen kühlen Brunnen. Sie hatte eine goldene Kugel, die war ihr liebstes Spielwerk, die warf sie in die Höhe und fing sie wieder in der Luft und hatte ihre Lust daran. Einmal war die Kugel gar hoch geflogen, sie hatte die Hand schon ausgestreckt und die Finger gekrümmt, um sie wieder zufangen, da schlug sie neben vorbei auf die Erde, rollte und rollte und geradezu in das Wasser hinein.

Die Königstochter blickte ihr erschrocken nach, der Brunnen war aber so tief, daß kein Grund zu sehen war. Da fing sie an jämmerlich zu weinen und zu klagen: "ach! wenn ich meine Kugel wieder hätte, da wollt' ich alles darum geben, meine Kleider, meine Edelgesteine, meine Perlen und was es auf der Welt nur wär'." Wie sie so klagte, steckte ein Frosch seinen Kopf aus dem Wasser und sprach: "Königstochter, was jammerst du so erbärmlich?"—"Ach, sagte sie, du garstiger Frosch, was kannst du mir helfen! meine goldne Kugel ist mir in den Brunnen gefallen."—Der Frosch sprach: "deine Perlen, deine Edelgesteine und deine Kleider, die verlang ich nicht, aber wenn du mich zum Gesellen annehmen willst, und ich soll neben dir sitzen und von deinem goldnen Tellerlein essen und in deinem Bettlein schlafen und du willst mich werth und lieb haben, so will ich dir deine Kugel wiederbringen." Die Königstochter dachte, was schwätzt der einfältige Frosch wohl, der muß doch in seinem Wasser bleiben, vielleicht aber kann er mir meine Kugel holen, da will ich nur ja sagen; und sagte: "ja meinetwegen, schaff mir nur erst die goldne Kugel wieder, es soll dir alles versprochen seyn." Der Frosch steckte seinen Kopf unter das Wasser und tauchte hinab, es dauerte auch nicht lange, so kam er wieder in die Höhe, hatte die Kugel im Maul und warf sie ans Land. Wie die Königstochter ihre Kugel wieder erblickte, lief sie geschwind darauf zu, hob sie auf und war so froh, sie wieder in ihrer Hand zu halten, daß sie an nichts weiter gedachte, sondern damit nach Hause eilte. Der Frosch rief ihr nach: "warte, Königstochter, und nimm mich mit, wie du versprochen hast;" aber sie hörte nicht darauf.

Am andern Tage saß die Königstochter an der Tafel, da hörte sie etwas die Marmortreppe heraufkommen, plitsch, platsch! plitsch, platsch! bald darauf klopfte es auch an der Thüre und rief: "Königstochter, jüngste, mach mir auf!" Sie lief hin und machte die Thüre auf, da war es der Frosch, an den sie nicht mehr gedacht hatte; ganz erschrocken warf sie die Thüre hastig zu und setzte sich wieder an die Tafel. Der König aber sah, daß ihr das Herz klopfte, und sagte: "warum fürchtest du dich?"— "Da draußen ist ein garstiger Frosch, sagte sie, der hat mir meine goldne Kugel aus dem Wasser geholt, ich versprach ihm dafür, er sollte mein Geselle werden, ich glaubte aber nimmermehr, daß er aus seinem Wasser heraus könnte, nun ist er draußen vor der Thür und will herein." Indem klopfte es zum zweitenmal und rief:

> "Königstochter, jüngste,
> mach mir auf,
> weiß du nicht was gestern
> du zu mir gesagt
> bei dem kühlen Brunnenwasser?
> Königstochter, jüngste,
> mach mir auf."

Der König sagte: "was du versprochen hast, mußt du halten, geh und mach dem Frosch die Thüre auf. Sie gehorchte und der Frosch hüpfte herein, und ihr auf dem Fuße immer nach, bis zu ihrem Stuhl, und als sie sich wieder gesetzt hatte, da rief er: "heb mich herauf auf einen Stuhl neben dich." Die Königstochter wollte nicht, aber der König befahl es ihr. Wie der Frosch oben war, sprach er: "nun schieb dein goldenes Tellerlein näher, ich will mit dir davon essen." Das mußte sie auch thun. Wie er sich satt gegessen hatte, sagte er: "nun bin ich müd' und will schlafen, bring mich hinauf in dein Kämmerlein, mach dein Bettlein zurecht, da wollen wir uns hineinlegen." Die Königstochter erschrak, wie sie das hörte, sie fürchtete sich vor dem kalten Frosch, sie getraute sich nicht ihn anzurühren und nun sollte er bei ihr in ihrem Bett liegen, sie fing an zu weinen und wollte durchaus nicht. Da ward der König zornig und befahl ihr bei seiner Ungnade, zu thun, was sie versprochen habe. Es half nichts, sie mußte thun, wie ihr Vater wollte, aber sie war bitterböse in ihrem Herzen. Sie packte den Frosch mit zwei Fingern und trug ihn hinauf in ihre Kammer, legte sich ins Bett und statt ihn neben sich zu legen,warf sie ihn bratsch! an die Wand; "da nun wirst du mich in Ruh lassen, du garstiger Frosch!"

Aber der Frosch fiel nicht todt herunter, sondern wie er herab auf das Bett kam, da wars ein schöner junger Prinz. Der war nun ihr lieber Geselle, und sie hielt ihn werth wie sie versprochen hatte, und sie schliefen vergnügt zusammen ein. Am Morgen aber kam ein prächtiger Wagen mit acht Pferden bespannt, mit Federn geputzt und goldschimmernd, dabei war der treue Heinrich des Prinzen, der hatte sich so betrübt über die Verwandlung desselben, daß er drei eiserne Bande um sein Herz legen mußte, damit es vor Traurigkeit nicht zerspringe. Der Prinz setzte sich mit der Königstochter in den Wagen, der treue Diener aber stand hinten auf, so wollten sie in sein Reich fahren. Und wie sie ein Stück Weges gefahren waren, hörte der Prinz hinter sich ein lautes Krachen, da drehte er sich um und rief:

> "Heinrich, der Wagen bricht!"—
> "Nein Herr, der Wagen nicht,
> es ist ein Band von meinem Herzen,
> das da lag in großen Schmerzen,
> als ihr in dem Brunnen saßt,
> als ihr eine Fretsche (Frosch) was't." (wart)

Noch einmal und noch einmal hörte es der Prinz krachen, und meinte: der Wagen bräche, aber es waren nur die Bande, die vom Herzen des treuen Heinrich absprangen, weil sein Herr erlöst und glücklich war.

SECOND EDITION

Es war einmal eine Königstochter, die wußte nicht was sie anfangen sollte vor langer Weile. Da nahm sie eine goldene Kugel, womit sie schon oft gespielt hatte und ging hinaus in den Wald.

Mitten in dem Wald aber war ein reiner, kühler Brunnen, dabei setzte sie sich nieder, warf die Kugel in die Höhe, fing sie wieder und das war ihr so ein Spielwerk. Es geschah aber, als die Kugel einmal recht hoch geflogen war und die Königstochter schon den Arm in die Höhe hielt und die Fingerchen streckte, um sie zu fangen, daß sie neben vorbei auf die Erde schlug und gerade zu ins Wasser hinein rollte.

Erschrocken sah ihr die Königstochter nach; aber die Kugel sank hinab und der Brunnen war so tief, daß kein Grund zu erkennen wär. Als sie nun ganz verschwand, da fing das Mädchen gar jämmerlich an zu weinen und rief: "ach! meine goldene Kugel! hätte ich sie wieder, ich wollte alles darum hingeben: meine Kleider, meine Edelsteine, meine Perlen, ja meine goldene Krone noch dazu." Wie es das gesagt hatte, tauchte ein Frosch mit seinem dicken Kopf aus dem Wasser heraus und sprach: "Königstochter, was jammerst du so erbärmlich?" "Ach, sagte sie, du garstiger Frosch, was kannst du mir helfen! meine goldene Kugel ist mir da in den Brunnen gefallen." Der Frosch sprach weiter: "deine Kleider, deine Edelsteine, deine Perlen ja deine goldene Krone, die mag ich nicht; aber wenn du mich willst zu deinem Freund und Gesellen annehmen, soll ich an deinem Tischlein sitzen zu deiner rechten Seite, von deinem goldenen Tellerlein mit dir essen, aus deinem Becherlein trinken und in deinem Bettlein schlafen, so will ich dir deine Kugel wieder herauf holen." Die Königstochter dachte in ihrem Herzen: was der einfältige Frosch wohl schwätzt! ein Frosch ist keines Menschen Gesell und muß im Wasser bei seines Gleichen bleiben, vielleicht aber kann er mir die Kugel herauf holen; und sprach zu ihm: "ja meinetwegen, schaff mir nur erst meine goldene Kugel, es soll dir alles versprochen seyn."

Als sie das gesagt hatte, tauchte der Frosch seinen Kopf wieder unter das Wasser, sank hinab und über ein Weilchen kam er wieder in die Höhe gerudert, hatte die Kugel im Maul und warf sie heraus ins Gras. Da freute sich das Königskind, wie es wieder sein Spielwerk in den Händen hielt. Der Frosch rief: "nun warte, Königstochter, und nimm mich mit," aber das war in den Wind gesprochen, sie hörte nicht darauf, lief mit ihrer Goldkugel nach Haus, und dachte gar nicht wieder an den Frosch.

Am andern Tag, als sie mit dem König und allen Hofleuten an der Tafel saß und von ihrem goldnen Tellerlein aß, kam, plitsch, platsch! plitsch, platsch! etwas die Marmor-Treppe herauf gekrochen und als es oben war, klopfte es an der Thür und rief: "Königstochter, jüngste, mach mir auf!" Sie lief und wollte sehen wer draußen wär, als sie aber die Thür aufmachte, so saß der Frosch davor. Da warf sie die Thüre hastig zu und setzte sich ganz erschrocken wieder an den Tisch. Der König sah, daß ihr das Herz gewaltig klopfte und sprach: "ei, was fürchtest du dich, steht etwa ein Riese vor der Thür und will dich holen!" "Ach nein, sprach das Kind, es ist kein Riese sondern ein garstiger Frosch, der hat mir gestern im Wald meine goldne Kugel aus dem Wasser geholt, dafür versprach ich ihm, er sollte mein Geselle werden, ich dachte aber nimmermehr, daß er aus seinem Wasser heraus könnte, nun ist er draußen und will zu mir herein." Indem klopfte es zum zweitenmal und rief draußen:

> "Königstochter, jüngste,
> mach mir auf!
> weißt du nicht, was gestern
> du zu mir gesagt
> bei dem kühlen Brunnen-Wasser?
> Königstochter, jüngste,
> mach mir auf!"

Da sagte der König: "hast du's versprochen, mußt du's auch halten, geh und mach ihm auf." Sie ging und öffnete die Thüre, da hüpfte der Frosch herein, ihr immer auf dem Fuße nach, bis zu ihrem Stuhl. Da saß er und rief: "heb mich herauf zu dir!" Sie wollte nicht, bis es der König befahl. Als der Frosch nun oben auf einem Stuhl neben ihr saß, sprach er: "nun schieb dein goldenes Tellerlein näher, damit wir zusammen essen. Voll Verdruß that sie auch das und der Frosch ließ sichs wohl schmecken, aber ihr blieb jedes Bißlein im Hals. Dann sprach er: "nun hab ich mich satt gegessen, und bin müd, trag mich hinauf in dein Kämmerlein, und mach dein seiden Bettlein zurecht, da wollen wir uns schlafen legen." Da fing die Königstochter an zu weinen, gar bitterlich, und fürchtete sich vor dem kalten Frosch, den getraute sie sich nicht anzurühren und der sollte nun in ihrem schönen, reinen Bettlein schlafen. Der König aber blickte sie zornig an und sprach: "was du versprochen hast, sollst du auch halten, und der Frosch ist dein Geselle." Da half nichts mehr, sie mogte wollen oder nicht, sie mußte den Frosch mitnehmen. Sie war aber in ihrem Herzen bitterböse, packte ihn mit zwei Fingern und trug ihn hinauf und als sie im Bett lag, statt ihn hinein zu heben, warf sie ihn aus allen Kräften an die Wand: "nun wirst du Ruhe haben, du garstiger Frosch!

Was aber herunter fiel, war nicht ein todter Frosch, sondern ein lebendiger, junger Königssohn mit schönen und freundlichen Augen. Der war nun von Recht und mit ihres Vaters Wille ihr lieber Geselle und Gemahl. Da schliefen sie nun vergnügt zusammen ein und am andern Morgen, als die Sonne sie aufweckte, kam ein Wagen herangefahren mit acht weißen Pferden bespannt, die waren mit Federn geschmückt und gingen in goldenen Ketten, und hinten stand der Diener des jungen Königs, das war der treue Heinrich. Der treue Heinrich hatte sich so betrübt, also sein Herr in einen Frosch verwandelt worden, daß er drei eiserne Bande hatte müssen um sein Herz legen lassen, damit es ihm nicht vor Weh und Traurigkeit zerspränge. Der Wagen sollte den jungen König in sein Reich abholen, der treue Heinrich hob beide hinein und stellte sich wieder hinten auf, voller Freude über die Erlösung. Und als sie ein Stück Wegs gefahren waren, hörte der Königssohn hinter sich, daß es krachte, als wär etwas zerbrochen. Da drehte er sich um und rief:

"Heinrich, der Wagen bricht!"—
"Nein, Herr, der Wagen nicht,
es ist ein Band von meinem Herzen,
das da lag in großen Schmerzen,
als ihr in dem Brunnen saßt,
als ihr eine Fretsche (Frosch) was't (wart)."

Noch einmal und noch einmal krachte es auf dem Weg, und der Königsohn meinte immer, der Wagen bräche und es waren doch nur die Bande, die vom Herzen des treuen Heinrich absprangen, weil sein Herr wieder erlöst und glücklich war.

THIRD EDITION

In den alten Zeiten, wo das Wünschen noch geholfen hat, lebte ein König, dessen Töchter waren alle schön, aber die jüngste war so schön, daß sich die Sonne selber, die doch[1] so vieles gesehen hat, darüber[2] verwunderte so oft sie ihr ins Gesicht schien.

1. iv: schon
2. iv and vi: sich

Nahe bei dem Schlosse des Königs lag ein großer dunkler Wald, und in dem Walde unter einer alten Linde war ein Brunnen: wenn nun der Tag recht heiß war, so gieng das Konigskind hinaus in den Wald, und setzte sich an den Rand des kühlen Brunnens, und wenn sie Langeweile hatte, so nahm sie eine goldene Kugel, warf sie in die Höhe und fieng sie wieder; und das war ihr liebstes Spielwerk.

Nun trug es sich einmal zu, daß die goldene Kugel der Königstochter nicht in das Händchen fiel, das sie ausgestreckt[3] hatte, sondern neben[4] vorbei auf die Erde schlug, und geradezu ins Wasser hinein rollte. Die Königstochter folgte ihr mit den Augen nach, aber die Kugel verschwand, und der Brunnen war tief, und gar kein Grund zu sehen.[5] Da fieng sie an zu weinen, und weinte immer lauter, und konnte sich gar nicht trösten. Und wie sie so klagte, rief ihr jemand zu "was hast du vor, Königstochter, du schreist ja, daß sich ein Stein erbarmen möchte." Sie sah sich um, woher die Stimme käme, da erblickte sie einen Frosch, der seinen dicken häßlichen Kopf aus dem Wasser streckte. "Ach, du bists, alter Wasserpatscher, sagte sie, ich weine über meine goldne Kugel, die[6] in den Brunnen hinab gefallen ist." "Gib dich zufrieden,"[7] antwortete der Frosch, "ich kann wohl Rath schaffen, aber was gibst du mir, wenn ich dein Spielwerk wieder heraufhole?" "Was du[8] willst, lieber Frosch," sagte sie, "meine Kleider, meine Perlen und Edelsteine, dazu[9] die goldne Krone, die ich trage." Der Frosch antwortete "deine Kleider, deine Perlen und Edelsteine, deine goldne Krone, die mag ich nicht: aber wenn du mich lieb haben willst, und ich soll dein Geselle und Spielkammerad seyn, an deinem Tischlein neben dir sitzen, von deinem goldnen Tellerlein essen, aus deinem Becherlein trinken, in deinem Bettlein schlafen: wenn du mir das versprecht, so will ich dir die goldne Kugel wieder aus dem Grunde hervor holen."[10] "Ach ja," sagte sie, "ich verspreche dir alles,[11] wenn du mir nur

3. iv and vi: in die Höhe gehalten
4. iv and vi: "neben" omitted
5. vi: war tief, so tief, daß man keinen Grund sah
6. iv and vi: "mir" inserted
7. iv: Laß dein Jammern; vi: Sei still und weine nicht
8. iv and vi: "haben" inserted
9. vi: auch noch
10. iv: "herauf" substituted for "hervor"; vi: "herauf" substituted and "aus dem Grunde" omitted
11. iv and vi: "was du willst" inserted

die Kugel wieder bringst." Sie dachte aber "was der einfältige Frosch schwätzt, der sitzt im Wasser bei seines Gleichen und quackt, und kann keines Menschen Geselle seyn."

Der Frosch, als er die Zusage erhalten hatte, tauchte seinen Kopf unter, sank hinab, und über ein Weilchen kam er wieder herauf gerudert, hatte die Kugel im Maul, und warf sie ins Gras. Die Königstochter war voll Freude, als sie ihr schönes Spielwerk wieder erblickte, hob es auf, und sprang damit fort. "Warte, warte," rief der Frosch, "nimm mich mit, ich kann nicht so laufen, wie du." Aber was half ihn daß er sein quack quack so laut nachschrie als er konnte! sie hörte nicht darauf, eilte nach Haus, und hatte bald den armen Frosch vergessen, der wieder in den tiefen Brunnen[12] hinab steigen mußte.

Am andern Tage, als sie mit dem König und allen Hofleuten an der Tafel saß,[13] und von ihrem goldnen Tellerlein aß, da kam, plitsch platsch, plitsch platsch, etwas die Marmortreppe herauf gekrochen, und als es oben angelangt war, klopfte es an der Thür und rief "Königstochter, jüngste, mach mir auf." Sie lief und wollte sehen wer draußen wäre, als sie aber aufmachte, so saß der Frosch davor. Da warf sie die Thür hastig zu, setzte sich wieder an den Tisch, und war ihr ganz angst. Der König sah[14] daß ihr das Herz gewaltig klopfte, und sprach "ei,[15] was fürchtest du dich, steht etwa ein Riese vor der Thür, und will dich holen?" "Ach nein," antwortete das Kind,[16] "es ist kein Riese, sondern ein garstiger Frosch,[17] der hat mir gestern im Wald meine goldene Kugel aus dem Wasser geholt, dafür versprach ich ihm, er sollte mein Geselle werden, ich dachte aber nimmermehr, daß er aus seinem Wasser heraus könnte: nun ist er draußen und will zu mir herein." Indem klopfte es zum zweitenmal und rief

"Königstochter, jüngste,
    mach mir auf,

12. iv and vi: "seinen" for "den teifen"
13. vi: sich zur Tafel gesetzt hatte
14. iv and vi: "wohl" inserted
15. iv and vi: "mein Kind" for "ei"
16. iv and vi: sie
17. vi: period after "Frosch," followed by elaboration: "Was will der Frosch von dir?" "Ach, lieber Vater, als ich gestern im Wald bei dem Brunnen saß und spielte, da fiel meine goldene Kugel ins Wasser. Und weil ich so weinte, hat sie der Frosch wieder herausgeholt, und weil er durchaus verlangte, so versprach ich ihm . . ."

weißt du nicht was gestern
du zu mir gesagt
bei dem kühlen Brunnenwasser?
Königstochter, jüngste,
mach mir auf"

Da sagte der König "hast du's versprochen,[18] mußt[19] du's auch halten; geh[20] und mach ihm auf." Sie gieng und öffnete die Thüre, da hüpfte der Frosch herein, ihr immer auf dem Fuße nach, bis zu ihrem Stuhl. Da saß er und rief "heb mich herauf zu dir." Sie wollte nicht bis es der König befahl.[21] Als der Frosch[22] auf den Stuhl gekommen[23] war, sprach er "nun schieb mir dein goldenes Tellerlein näher, damit wir zusammen essen." Das that sie auch,[24] aber man sah wohl daß sies nicht gerne that. Der Frosch ließ sichs gut schmecken, aber ihr blieb fast jedes Bißlein im Halse. Endlich sprach er "nun[25] hab ich mich satt gegessen, und bin müde, trag mich hinauf in dein Kämmerlein, und mach dein seiden Bettlein zurecht, da wollen wir uns schlafen legen." Da fieng die Königstochter[26] an zu weinen, und fürchtete sich vor dem kalten Frosch, den sie nicht anzurühren getraute, und der nun in ihrem schönen reinen Bettlein schlafen sollte. Der König aber blickte sie zornig an, und sprach "was du versprochen hast, sollst du auch halten, und der Frosch ist dein Geselle."[27] Es half nichts, sie mochte wollen oder nicht, sie mußte den Frosch mitnehmen.[28] Da packte sie ihn, ganz biterböse,[29] mit zwei Fingern, und trug ihn hinauf, und[30] als sie im Bett lag, statt ihn hinein zu heben,[31] warf sie ihn aus allen Kräften an die Wand,

18. vi: was du versprochen hast
19. iv: "so" inserted before "mußt"; vi: "das" inserted
20. iv and vi: "nur" inserted
21. iv: Sie that es nicht bis es der König befahl. vi: Sie zauderte bis es endlich der König befahl.
22. vi: "erst" inserted
23. vi: "gekommen" omitted
24. iv: nun; vi: zwar
25. vi:"nun" moved to before "trag mich"
26. vi: die Königstochter fieng an
27. iv and vi: "und der Frosch ist dein Geselle" omitted; iv: Der König aber ward zornig, und sprach "wer dir geholfen hat als du in der Noth warst, den mußt du dernach nicht verachten, und was du versprochen hast das mußt du auch halten"; vi: as in iv, omitting last ten words
28. iv and vi: sentence omitted
29. iv and vi: "ganz bitterböse" omitted
30. iv and vi: "und setzte ihn in eine Ecke" inserted
31. iv and vi: "statt ihn hinein zu heben" omitted; new sentence recast and

and sprach[32] "nun wirst du Ruhe haben, du garstiger Frosch." Was aber herunter fiel war nicht ein todter Frosch, sondern ein lebendiger junger Königssohn[33] mit schönen und freundlichen Augen. Der war nun von Recht[34] und mit[35] ihres Vaters Willen ihr lieber Geselle und Gemahl.[36] Da schliefen sie vergnügt zusammen ein,[37] und am andern Morgen, als die Sonne sie aufweckte, kam ein Wagen herangefahren mit acht weißen Pferden bespannt, die waren mit Federn geschmückt,[38] und giengen in goldenen Ketten, und hinten stand der Diener des Jungen Königs, das war der treue Heinrich. Der treue Heinrich hatte sich so betrübt, als sein Herr war in einen Frosch verwandelt worden, daß er drei eiserne Bande hatte müssen[39] um sein Herz legen lassen, damit es ihm nicht vor Weh und Traurigkeit zerspränge. Der Wagen aber sollte den jungen König in sein Reich abholen; der treue Heinrich hob beide hinein, und stellte sich wieder hinten auf,[40] voller Freude über die Erlösung. Und als sie ein Stück Wegs gefahren waren, hörte der Königssohn hinter sich, daß es krachte,[41] als wär etwas zerbrochen. Da drehte er sich um und rief

"Heinrich, der Wagen bricht."
"Nein, Herr, der Wagen nicht,
es ist ein Band von meinem Herzen,
das da lag in großen Schmerzen,
als ihr in den Brunnen saßt,
als ihr eine Fretsche (Frosch) was't (wart)."

---

expanded, "Als sie aber im Bett lag, kam er gekrochen, und sprach 'ich bin müde, ich will schlafen so gut wie du, heb mich herauf, oder ich sags deinem Vater.' Da ward sie (vi: erst) bitterböse, faßte (vi: holte) ihn und warf ihn . . ."

32. iv and vi: "und sprach" omitted
33. iv: Als aber der Frosch herab fiel, stand da ein Königssohn; vi: Als er aber herab fiel, war er kein Frosch, sondern ein Königssohn
34. vi: "von Recht" omitted
35. vi: nach
36. iv: Da erzählte er ihr, er wäre von einer bösen Hexe verwünscht worden, und hätte nur von ihr aus dem Brunnen erlöst werden können, und morgen wollten sie zusammen in sein Reich gehen; vi: rephrasing, "und Niemand hätte ihn aus dem Brunnen erlösen können als sie allein"
37. iv and vi: Dann schliefen sie ein
38. vi: die hatten weiße Straußfedern auf dem Kopf
39. vi: "müssen" omitted
40. vi: "und war" inserted
41. iv and vi: inversion "daß es henter ihm krachte"

Noch einmal und noch einmal krachte es auf dem Weg, und der Königssohn meinte immer, der Wagen bräche, und es waren doch nur die Bande, die vom Herzen des treuen Heinrich absprangen, weil sein Herr wieder erlöst und glücklich war.

Translations

MANUSCRIPT
*The King's Daughter
and the Enchanted Prince:
Frog King*

The youngest daughter of the king went out into the forest and sat down at a cool well. Then she took a golden ball and was playing with it when it suddenly rolled down into the well. She saw how it fell into the depth and stood by the well and was very sad. All at once a frog stuck his head out of the water and said: why are you lamenting so much? Oh, you horrid frog, she said, you can't help me. My golden ball has fallen into the well. Then the frog said, if you will take me home with you, I will get your golden ball back for you. And when she had promised it, he plunged down and soon came back up to the surface with the ball in his mouth and threw it onto land. Then the king's daughter quickly took her ball again and ran quickly away, and didn't listen to the frog who called after her that she should take him with her as she had promised him. And when she had got home, she sat down at the table with her father, and just as she was about to eat, he knocked at the door and called; king's daughter, youngest, open up for me! And she hurried there and saw who it was, and it was the ugly frog and she hurriedly slammed the door shut again. Her father, however, asked who it was and she told him everything. Again there was a cry:

> King's daughter, youngest
> open up for me
> don't you know what yesterday
> you said to me
> by the cool well water
> king's daughter, youngest
> open up for me.

And the king ordered her to open up for the frog and he hopped in. Then he said to her put me next to you at the table, I want to eat with you. But she didn't want to do it until the king ordered it too. And the frog sat at the side of the king's daughter and ate with her. And when he had had enough, he said to her: take me to your bed I want to sleep beside you. She didn't want to do that at all, because she was very much afraid of the cold frog. But the king ordered it again, then she took the frog and carried him into her room and full of anger she seized him and threw him with all her strength against the wall in her bed. But as he hit the wall, he fell down into the bed and lay there as a handsome young prince, and the king's daughter lay down with him.

The next morning a fine coach came with the faithful servant of the prince, who had suffered so much over his transformation, that he had had to put three iron hoops around his heart. And the prince and the king's daughter got into the coach, and the faithful servant climbed up behind, and they meant to travel to his realm. And when they have gone part of the way, the prince hears behind him a loud crack. Then he calls out

> Henry, the coach is breaking!
> No sir not the coach,
> It is a hoop around my heart,
> which was in great pain
> when you were in the well
> when you were a frog.

FIRST EDITION

There was once a king's daughter, who went out into the forest and sat down at a cool well. She had a golden ball, which was her favorite toy, she threw it up high and caught it again in the air and it was her delight. Once the ball had gone very high, she had already stretched out her hand and cupped her fingers in order to catch it again when it went past her and hit the ground nearby and rolled and rolled right into the water. The king's daughter looked after it and was alarmed, but the well was so deep, that she could not see the bottom. Then she began to weep and lament pitifully: "Oh! If I had my ball again, I would give everything for it, my clothes, my jewels, my pearls, and anything in the world." As she was lamenting in this way, a frog stuck his head out of the water and said: "King's daughter, why are you lamenting so pitifully?"—"Oh," she said, you horrid frog, what can you do to help me! my golden ball has fallen into the well."—The frog said: "your pearls, your jewels and your clothes, I don't ask for them, but if you will take me as your companion, and I shall sit near you and eat from your little golden plate and sleep in your bed and if you will esteem and love me, I will bring you back your ball." The king's daughter thought, what is the silly frog talking about, he will surely have to remain in his water, but perhaps he can get me my ball back, and so I'll just say yes. And she said: "Well, all right then, just get me my golden ball back and I'll promise you everything." The frog stuck his head under the water and plunged down, and it was not long before he came back up again to the surface, had the ball in his mouth and threw it onto land. As the king's daughter saw her ball again, she ran quickly up to it, pcked it up and was so happy to hold it in her hand again that she thought of nothing else, but hurried home with it. The frog called after her: "wait, king's daughter, and take me with you as you promised"; but she didn't listen.

The next day the king's daughter sat at the table, when she heard something coming up the marble staircase, plitch, platch! plitch, platch! soon after there was a knock on the door and a cry, "king's daughter, youngest, open up for me!" She ran and opened the door, it was the frog, of whom she had not thought any more; completely startled, she slammed the door quickly and sat down again at the table. But the king saw that her heart was pounding, and said: "why are you afraid"—"Out there is a horrid frog, she said, who fetched my golden ball out of the water for me, I promised him for that that he should be my companion, but I never believed that he could leave his water, now he is outside the door and wants to come in. Meanwhile, there was a second knock and a cry,

> "King's daughter, youngest,
> open up for me
> don't you know what yesterday
> you said to me
> by the cool well water?
> king's daughter, youngest,
> open up for me."

The king said, "What you have promised, you must do, go and open up the door for the frog." She obeyed and the frog hopped in, and followed her footsteps up to her chair, and when she had sat down again, he cried: "Pick me up and put me onto a chair next to you." The king's daughter didn't want to, but the king ordered her to. When the frog was up, he spoke: "Now push your little golden plate nearer, I want to eat from it with you." She had to do that too. When he had eaten himself full, he said: "Now I'm tired and want to sleep, take me up to your little bedroom, make your little bed ready, and we will lie down in it." The king's daughter was alarmed when she heard that, she was afraid of the cold frog, she didn't think she could touch him and now he was to lie beside her in her bed, she began to cry and didn't want to do it at all. Then the king became angry and ordered her on pain of his displeasure, to do what she had promised. It was no use, she had to do as her father wished, but she was bitterly angry in her heart. She seized the frog with two fingers and carried him up into her room, got into bed and instead of laying him next to her threw him crash! against the wall; "Now you'll leave me in peace, you horrid frog!"

Yet the frog did not fall down dead, but as he fell onto the bed, there was a beautiful young prince. He now became her dear companion, and she cherished him as she had promised and they went to sleep contentedly together. The next morning, however, a resplendent coach with eight horses came decked with feathers and shimmering with gold, and with it was the prince's faithful Henry, who had been so saddened by the transformation of the prince, that he had had to put three iron hoops around his heart, so that it should not burst with sadness. The prince sat down with the king's daughter in the coach, the faithful servant however stood up behind and they meant to travel to his realm. And when they had gone part of the way, the prince heard behind him a loud cracking, and he turned around and cried:

> "Henry, the coach is breaking!"
> "No, Lord, not the coach,
> it is a hoop around my heart,
> which was in great pain,
> when you were in the well,
> when you were a frog."

Once more and still again the prince heard a cracking and thought: the coach was breaking, but it was only the hoops which fell away from the heart of the faithful Henry, because his lord was released and happy.

SECOND EDITION

There was once a king's daughter who was so bored that she did not know what to do. Then she took a golden ball with which she had often played and went out into the forest. In the middle of the forest however was a pure cool well, she sat herself down by it, threw the ball into the air, caught it again and it was a plaything for her. But it happened that once when the ball had flown very high and the king's daughter was reaching upward with her arm and stretching out her little fingers to catch it, that it went past her and hit the ground nearby and rolled right into the water.

Alarmed, the king's daughter looked after it; but the ball sank down and the well was so deep that no bottom could be seen. As it now completely disappeared the girl began to weep most pitifully and cried: "Oh! my golden ball! if I had it again I would give everything for it: my clothes, my jewels, my pearls, even my golden crown as well." When she had said that, a frog emerged from the water with its thick head and said: "King's daughter, why are you lamenting so pitifully?" "Oh," she said, "You horrid frog, what can you do to help me? My golden ball has fallen into the well." The frog continued: "Your clothes, your jewels, your pearls, even your golden crown I don't want; but if you will accept me as your friend and companion, if I shall sit at your table at your right hand side, eat with you off your little golden plate, drink from your little goblet and sleep in your little bed then I will fetch your ball up again for you." The king's daughter thought in her heart: what nonsense the silly frog talks! A frog is not a companion for a human being, and has to remain in the water with his own kind, but perhaps he can get my ball out for me; and she said to him: "Well, all right then, just get my golden ball for me and I'll promise you everything."

When she had said that the frog plunged his head under the water again, sank down, and a little while later came swimming up to the surface again, had the ball in his mouth, and threw it out into the grass. Then the king's child was pleased to hold her toy again in her hands. The frog cried: "Now wait, king's daughter, and take me with you." But he spoke in vain, she didn't listen, ran home with her golden ball and thought no more of the frog.

The next day, when she was sitting at the table with the king and all the courtiers and was eating off her little golden plate, something came plitch, platch! plitch, platch! crawling up the marble staircase and when it was at the top, it knocked on the door and cried: "King's daughter, youngest, open up for me!" She ran and wanted to see who was out there, but when she opened the door the frog was sitting in front of it. She slammed the door quickly and sat down again at the table, very alarmed. The king saw that her heart was pounding strongly and said: "Why, what are you afraid of, is there a giant at the door waiting to get you?" "Oh, no," said the child, "it's not a giant but a horrid frog who fetched my golden ball out of the water for me yesterday in the forest; because of that I promised him that he should be my companion, but I didn't ever think that he could leave his water, now he is outside and wants to come in to me." Meanwhile there was a second knock and a cry outside:

> "King's daughter, youngest,
> open up for me!
> don't you know what yesterday
> you said to me
> by the cool well water?
> king's daughter, youngest,
> open up for me!"

Then the king said: "if you've promised it, you must keep your promise, go and open up for him." She went and opened the door, then the frog hopped in, following her steps right to her chair. Then he sat and cried: "lift me up beside you!" She didn't want to, until the king ordered it. When the frog was now sitting up on a chair next to her, he said to her: "now push your little golden plate nearer, so that we can eat together." Full of annoyance she did this too, and the frog enjoyed it very much, but every mouthful stuck in her throat. Then he said: "now I have eaten enough, and I'm tired, carry me up into your little room, and make your little silken bed ready, then we shall lie down to sleep." Then the king's daughter began to cry most bitterly and was afraid of the cold frog, she did not think she could touch him and now he was to sleep in her beautiful clean little bed.

The king however looked angrily at her and said, "what you have promised, you must do, and the frog is your companion." It was no use, whether she wanted to or not, she had to take the frog with her. But she was bitterly angry in her heart, seized him with two fingers and carried him up and when she lay in her bed, instead of lifting him into it, she threw him with all her strength at the wall; "now you will have rest, you horrid frog!"

But what fell down was not a dead frog but a living, young king's son with handsome and friendly eyes. He now became rightfully and with her father's approval, her dear companion and husband. They now fell asleep contentedly together and on the next morning, when the sun woke them, a coach arrived with eight white horses which were adorned with feathers and harnessed with golden chains, and behind stood the servant of the young king, faithful Henry. Faithful Henry had been so unhappy when his lord had been transformed into a frog that he had had to put three iron hoops around his heart so that it should not burst with pain and sadness. The coach was to take the young king to his realm, faithful Henry lifted both of them into it and sat himself up behind again, full of joy at this release. And when they had gone part of the way, the king's son heard something crack behind him, as if something was broken. So he turned around and cried:

> "Henry, the coach is breaking!"—
> "No, Lord, not the coach,
> it is a hoop around my heart,
> which was in great pain,
> when you were in the well,
> when you were a frog."

Once again and still again there was a crack on the way, and the king's son thought each time that the coach was breaking but it was only the hoops which fell away from the heart of the faithful Henry because his lord was once more released and happy.

THIRD EDITION

In olden times, when wishing still counted for something, there lived a king whose daughters were all beautiful, but the youngest was so beautiful that the sun itself who had after all seen so much was amazed whenever it looked at her face. Nearby the castle of the king lay a large, dark forest and in the forest under an old lime tree was a well: when it was a very hot day, the king's child went out into the forest and sat down at the edge of the well, and when she was bored she took a golden ball, threw it into the air and caught it again and that was her favorite toy.

Now it happened once, that the golden ball of the king's daughter fell not into the little hand which she had stretched out, but past it nearby on the ground and rolled right into the water. The king's daughter followed it with her eyes, but the ball disappeared, and the well was deep and no bottom could be seen. Then she began to weep, and wept louder and louder and was inconsolable. And as she lamented so, someone cried to her, "What are you doing, king's daughter, you're crying so much that a stone would take pity." She looked around her to see where the voice came from and saw a frog who stretched his fat ugly head out of the water, "Oh, it's you, old water splasher," she said, "I'm crying over my golden ball which has fallen down into the well." "Never mind," answered the frog, "I can help you, but what will you give me if I bring your toy back up for you?" "Whatever you want, dear frog," she said, "my clothes, my pearls, my jewels, my golden crown which I am wearing as well." The frog answered, "your clothes, your pearls and jewels, your golden crown, I don't want them: but if you will love me and I can be your companion and playmate, sit near you at your little table, eat off your little golden plate, drink out of your little goblet, sleep in your little bed: if you promise me that, then I will fetch your golden ball again from the deep." "Oh,yes," she said, "I promise you everything if only you bring me back the ball." But she thought, "What nonsense the silly frog talks, he stays in the water with his own kind, and croaks, and cannot be the companion of a human being." When the frog had received her agreement, he plunged his head under, sank down, and a little while later came swimming back up, had the ball in his mouth, and threw it into the grass. The king's daughter was full of joy when she saw her beautiful toy again, picked it up and ran off with it. "Wait, wait," cried the frog, "take me with you. I cannot run like you can." But what did it help him that he cried out his croak, croak as loud as he could after her. She did not listen to it, hurried home and had soon forgotten the poor frog who had to climb back into the deep well.

The next day, when she sat at the table with the king and all the courtiers and was eating off her little golden plate, there came "plitch platch, plitch platch" something crawling up the marble steps. And when it had got to the top it knocked at the door and cried, "King's daughter, youngest, open up for me." She ran and wanted to see who was outside, but when she opened up, the frog was sitting there. She slammed the door quickly, sat down at the table again and was quite afraid. The king saw that her heart was pounding strongly and said, "Why, what are you afraid of, is there a giant at the door waiting to get you?" "Oh, no," answered the child, "it is not a giant but a horrid frog, who fetched my golden ball out of the water for me yesterday in the forest, because of that I promised him that he should be my companion, but I didn't ever think that he could leave his water: now he is outside and wants to come in to me." Meanwhile there was a second knock and a cry

> "King's daughter, youngest,
> open up for me,
> don't you know what yesterday
> you said to me
> by the cool well water?
> king's daughter, youngest,
> open up for me!"

Then the king said, "if you've promised it, you must keep your promise; go and open up for him." She went and opened the door, then the frog hopped in following her right to her chair. There he sat and cried, "lift me up beside you." She didn't want to, until the king ordered it. When the frog had got onto the chair, he said "now push your little golden plate nearer to me so that we can eat together." She did that too, but you could see that she didn't want to. The frog enjoyed it well, but every mouthful stuck in her throat. At last he said, "now I have eaten enough, I'm tired, carry me up into your little room, and make your little silk bed ready and we shall lie down to sleep." Then the king's daughter began to cry and was afraid of the cold frog whom she didn't dare to touch and who was now to sleep in her beautiful, clean little bed. The king however looked angrily at her, and said, "what you have promised, you must do, and the frog is your companion." It was no use, whether she wanted to or not, she had to take the frog with her. Then she seized him, bitterly angry, with two fingers and carried him up and as she lay in bed instead of lifting him into it, she threw him with all her strength at the wall, and said "now you'll have peace, you horrid frog."

But what fell down was not a dead frog but a living young king's son with handsome and friendly eyes. He now became rightfully and with her father's approval her dear companion and husband. Then they fell asleep contentedly together, and on the next morning when the sun woke them, a coach arrived with eight white horses which were adorned with feathers and harnessed with golden chains, and behind stood the servant of the young king, faithful Henry. Faithful Henry had been so unhappy when his lord was transformed into a frog, that he had had to set three iron hoops around his heart so that it should not burst with pain and sadness. The coach, however, was to take the young king to his realm; faithful Henry lifted both of them into it and sat himself up behind again, full of joy at this release. And when they had gone part of the way, the king's son heard something behind him crack, as if something was broken. So he turned around and cried

> "Henry, the coach is breaking."
> "No, Lord, not the coach,
> it is a hoop around my heart,
> which was in great pain,
> when you were in the well,
> when you were a frog."

Once again and still again there was a crack on the way, and the king's son thought each time that the coach was breaking, but it was only the hoop which fell away from the heart of the faithful Henry because his lord was once more released and happy.

2. Dornröschen (Sleeping Beauty)

The four most important texts of *Dornröschen* are the manuscript and the first, second and sixth editions. There is a very great difference between the first two of these, but also significant rewriting for the last two. In addition, a noticeable amount of rephrasing was introduced in the texts of the third and fourth editions. Once more, editions five and seven are virtual reprints of their predecessors. The variant readings of the third and fourth editions are given as footnotes to the second.

MANUSCRIPT

ein König u. eine Königin kriegten gar keine Kinder. Eines Tags war die Königin im Bad, da kroch ein Krebs aus dem Waßer ans Land u. sprach: du wirst bald eine Tochter bekommen. Und so geschah es auch und der König in der Freude hielt ein großes Fest u. im Lande waren dreizehn Feen, er hatte aber nur zwölf goldne Teller und konnte also die dreizehnte nicht einladen. Die Feen begabten sie mit allen Tugenden und Schönheiten. Wie nun das Fest zu Ende ging, so kam die dreizehnte Fee u. sprach: ihr habt mich nicht gebeten u. ich verkündige euch, daß eure Tochter in ihrem funfzehnten Jahr sich an einer Spindel in den Finger stechen u. daran sterben wird. Die andern Feen wollten dies so gut noch machen, als sie konnten u. sagten: sie sollte nur hundert Jahre in Schlaf fallen.

Der König ließ aber den Befehl ausgehen, daß alle Spindeln im ganzen Reich abgeschafft werden sollten, welches geschah, u. als die Königstochter nun funfzehnjährig war u. eines Tags die Eltern ausgegangen waren, so ging sie im Schloß herum u. gelangte endlich an einen alten Thurn. In den Thurn führte eine enge Treppe, da kam sie zu einer kleinen Thür, worin ein gelber Schlüßel steckte, den drehte sie um u. kam in ein Stübchen worin eine alte Frau ihren Flachs spann. Und sie scherzte mit der Frau u. wollte auch spinnen. Da stach sie sich in die Spindel u. fiel alsbald in einen tiefen Schlaf. Da auch in dem Augenblick der König u. der Hofstaat zurückgekommen war, so fing alles im Schloß an zu schlafen, bis auf die Fliegen an den Wänden. Und um das ganze Schloß zog sich eine Dornhecke, daß man nichts davon sah.

Nach langer langer Zeit kam ein Königssohn in das Land, dem erzählte ein alter Mann die Geschichte, die er sich erinnerte von seinem Großvater gehört zu haben, u. daß schon viele versucht hätten durch die Dornen zu gehen, aber alle hängen geblieben wären. Als sich aber dieser Prinz der Dornhecke näherte, so thaten sich alle Dornen vor ihm auf u. vor ihm schienen sie Blumen zu seyn, u. hinter ihm wurden sie wieder zu Dörnern. Wie er nun in das Schloß kam, küßte er die schlafende Princeßin und alles erwachte von dem Schlaf u. die zwei heiratheten sich und wenn sie nicht gestorben sind, so leben sie noch.

FIRST EDITION

Ein König und eine Königin kriegten gar keine Kinder, und hätten so gern eins gehabt. Einmal saß die Königin im Bade, da kroch ein Krebs aus dem Wasser ans Land und sprach: "dein Wunsch wird bald erfüllt werden und du wirst eine Tochter zur Welt bringen." Das traf auch ein, und der König war so erfreut über die Geburt der Prinzessin, daß er ein großes Fest anstellen ließ, und dazu lud er auch die Feen ein, die im Lande waren; weil er nur zwölf goldene Teller hatte, konnte er eine nicht einladen: es waren ihrer nemlich dreizehn. Die Feen kamen zu dem Fest, und beschenkten das Kind am Ende desselben: die eine mit Tugend, die zweite mit Schönheit und so die andern mit allem, was nur auf der Welt herrlich und zu wünschen war, wie aber eben die elfte ihr Geschenk gesagt hatte, trat die dreizehnte herein, recht zornig, daß sie nicht war eingeladen worden und rief: "weil ihr mich nicht gebeten, so sage ich euch, daß eure Tochter in ihrem funfzehnten Jahre an einer Spindel sich stechen und todt hinfallen wird." Die Eltern erschracken, aber die zwölfte Fee hatte noch einen Wunsch zu thun, da sprach sie: "es soll aber kein Tod seyn, sie soll nur hundert Jahr in einen tiefen Schlaf fallen."

Der König hoffte immer noch sein liebes Kind zu erretten, und ließ den Befehl ausgehen, daß alle Spindeln im ganzen Königreich sollten abgeschafft werden. Die Prinzessin aber wuchs heran, und war ein Wunder von Schönheit. Eines Tags, als sie ihr funfzehntes Jahr eben erreicht hatte, war der König und die Königin ausgegangen, und sie ganz allein im Schloß, da ging sie aller Orten herum nach ihrer Lust, endlich kam sie auch an einen alten Thurm. Eine enge Treppe führte dazu, und da sie neugierig war, stieg sie hinauf und gelangte zu einer kleinen Thüre, darin steckte ein gelber Schlüssel, den drehte sie um, da sprang die Thüre auf und sie war in einem kleinen Stübchen, darin saß eine alte Frau und spann ihren Flachs. Die alte Frau gefiel ihr wohl, und sie machte Scherz mit ihr und sagte, sie wollte auch einmal spinnen, und nahm ihr die Spindel aus der Hand. Kaum aber hatte sie die Spindel angerührt, so stach sie sich damit, und alsbald fiel sie nieder in einen tiefen Schlaf. In dem Augenblick kam der König mit dem ganzen Hofstaat zurück, und da fing alles an einzuschlafen, die Pferde in den Ställen, die Tauben auf dem Dach, die Hunde im Hof, die Fliegen an den Wänden, ja das Feuer, das auf dem Heerde flackerte, ward still und schlief ein, und der Braten hörte auf zu brutzeln, und der Koch ließ den Küchenjungen los, den er an den Haaren ziehen wollte, und die Magd ließ das Huhn fallen, das sie rupfte, und schlief, und um das ganze Schloß zog sich eine Dornhecke hoch und immer höher, so daß man gar nichts mehr davon sah.

Prinzen, die von dem schönen Dornröschen gehört hatten, kamen und wollten es befreien, aber sie konnten durch die Hecke nicht hindurch dringen, es war als hielten sich die Dornen fest wie an Händen zusammen, und sie blieben darin hängen und kamen jämmerlich um. So währte das lange, lange Jahre: da zog einmal ein Königssohn durch das Land, dem erzählte ein alter Mann davon, man glaube, daß hinter der Dornhecke ein Schloß

stehe, und eine wunderschöne Prinzessin schlafe darin mit ihrem
ganzen Hofstaat; sein Großvater habe ihm gesagt, daß sonst viele
Prinzen gekommen wären und hätten hindurchdringen wollen,,
sie wären aber in den Dornen hängen geblieben und todtgestochen worden. "Das soll mich nicht schrecken, sagte der Königssohn, ich will durch die Hecke dringen und das schöne
Dornröschen befreien;" da ging er fort, und wie er zu der Dornhecke kam, waren es lauter Blumen, die thaten sich von einander, und er ging hindurch, und hinter ihm wurden es wieder
Dornen. Da kam er ins Schloß, und in dem Hof lagen die Pferde
und schliefen, und die bunten Jagdhunde, und auf dem Dach
saßen die Tauben und hatten ihre Köpfchen in den Flügel gesteckt, und wie er hineinkam, schliefen die Fliegen an den Wänden, und das Feuer in der Küche, der Koch und die Magd, da
ging er weiter, da lag der ganze Hofstaat und schlief, und noch
weiter, der König und die Königin; und es war so still, daß einer
seinen Athem hörte, da kam er endlich in den alten Thurm, da
lag Dornröschen und schlief. Da war der Königssohn so erstaunt
über ihre Schönheit, daß er sich bückte und sie küßte, und in
dem Augenblick wachte sie auf, und der König und die Königin,
und der ganze Hofstaat, und die Pferde und die Hunde, und
die Tauben auf dem Dach, und die Fliegen an den Wänden,
und das Feuer stand auf und flackerte und kochte das Essen
fertig, und der Braten brutzelte fort, und der Koch gab dem
Küchenjungen eine Ohrfeige, und die Magd rupfte das Huhn
fertig. Da ward die Hochzeit von dem Königssohn mit Dornröschen gefeiert, und sie lebten vergnügt bis an ihr Ende.

SECOND EDITION

Vor Zeiten war ein König und eine Königin, die sprachen jeden
Tag: "ach, wenn wir doch ein Kind hätten!" und kriegten immer
keins. Da trug sich zu, als die Königin einmal im Bade saß, daß
ein Krebs[1] aus dem Wasser ans Land kroch und zu ihr sprach:
"dein Wunsch wird erfüllt[2] und du wirst eine Tochter zur Welt
bringen." Was der Krebs[3] vorausgesagt hatte, das geschah und

1. iii and iv: Frosch
2. iii and iv: "werden" inserted
3. iii and iv: Frosch

die Königin gebar ein so schönes Mädchen,[4] daß der König vor
Freuden sich nicht zu lassen wußte und ein großes Fest anstellte.
Er lud nicht blos seine Verwandte, Freunde und Bekannte sondern auch die weisen Frauen dazu ein, damit sie dem Kind hold
und gewogen würden. Es waren ihrer dreizehn in seinem Reich,
weil er aber nur zwölf goldene Teller hatte, von welchen sie essen
sollten, konnte er eine nicht einladen. Die geladen waren, kamen
und nachdem das Fest gehalten war,[5] beschenkten sie das Kind
mit ihren Wundergaben; die eine mit Tugend, die andere mit
Schönheit, die dritte mit Reichthum und so mit allem, was Herr-
liches auf der Welt ist. Als zehn[6] ihre Wünsche eben gethan
hatten, kam[7] die dreizehnte herein, die nicht eingeladen war
und sich dafür rächen wollte.[8] Sie rief: "die Königstochter soll
sich in ihrem fünfzehnten Jahr an einer Spindel stechen und
todt hinfallen."[9] Da trat die zwölfte hervor, die noch einen Wunsch
übrig hatte; zwar konnte sie den bösen Ausspruch nicht aufheben, aber sie konnte ihn doch mildern und sprach:[10] "es soll aber
kein Tod seyn, sondern ein hundertjähriger tiefer Schlaf, in
den[11] die Königstochter fällt."

Der König hoffte sein liebes Kind noch vor dem Ausspruch
zu bewahren[12] und ließ den Befehl ausgehen, daß alle Spindeln
im ganzen Königreich sollten abgeschafft werden. An dem
Mädchen aber wurden alle[13] die Gaben der weisen Frauen[14] erfüllt, denn es war so schön, sittsam, freundlich und verständig,
daß es jedermann, der es ansah, lieb haben mußte. Es geschah,
daß an dem Tage, wo es gerade funfzehn Jahr alt ward, der

4. iii and iv: ein Mädchen, das war so schön
5. iii and iv: als das Fest vorbei war
6. iv: elfe
7. iv: trat plötzlich
8. iv: rearranged to "Sie wollte sich dafür rächen daß sie nicht eingeladen war";
   and expanded with "und ohne jemand zu grüßen und anzusehen, rief mit
   lauter Stimme"
9. iv: the next sentence begins with the insertion: "Nach diesen Worten kehrte
   sie sich um, und verließ den Saal, und alle standen erschrocken,"
10. iv: recast as "und weil sie den bösen Ausspruch nicht aufheben, sondern ihn
    nur mildern konnte, so sprach sie"
11. iii and iv: welchen
12. iii and iv: Der König, der sein liebes Kind vor dem Unglück gern bewahren
    wollte,
13. iii and iv: "alle" omitted
14. iii and iv: "sämmtlich" inserted

König und die Königin nicht zu Haus waren und das Fräulein[15] ganz allein im Schloß zurückblieb. Da ging es aller Orten herum, besah Stuben und Kammern, wie es Lust hatte und kam endlich auch an einen alten Thurm. Es stieg eine enge Treppe hinauf und gelangte zu einer kleinen Thüre. In dem Schloß steckte ein gelber[16] Schlüssel und als es umdrehte, sprang die Thüre auf und saß da in einem kleinen Stübchen eine alte Frau und spann emsig ihren Flachs. "Ei du altes Mütterchen, sprach die Königstochter, was machst du da?" "Ich spinne" sagte die Alte und nickte mit dem Kopf." "Wie das Ding[17] herumspringt!" sprach das Fräulein[18] und nahm die Spindel und wollte auch spinnen. Kaum hatte sie die[19] Spindel angerührt, so ging die Verwünschung des Zauberweibes[20] in Erfüllung und sie stach sich damit.

In dem Augenblick aber, wo sie sich gestochen hatte,[21] fiel sie auch nieder in einen tiefen Schlaf. Und[22] der König und die Königin, die eben zurückgekommen[23] waren, fingen an mit dem ganzen Hofstaat einzuschlafen.[24] Da schliefen auch die Pferde im Stall ein, die Hunde im Hof, die Tauben auf dem Dach, die Fliegen an der Wand, ja, das Feuer, das auf dem Herde flackerte, ward still und schlief ein und der Bratern hörte auf zu brutzeln und der Koch, der den Küchenjungen, weil er etwas versehen hatte, in den Haaren ziehen wollte, ließ ihn los und schlief[25] und alles was lebendigen Athem hat, ward still und schlief.

Um[26] das Schloß aber begann eine Dornenhecke zu wachsen, die jedes Jahr höher ward und endlich das ganze Schloß so[27] umzog und drüber hinaus wuchs, daß gar nichts mehr, selbst nicht die Fahnen auf den Dächern, zu sehen war. Es ging aber

15. iv: Mädchen
16. iii and iv: verrosteter
17. iii and iv: "so lustig" inserted
18. iii and iv: Mädchen; "und" omitted
19. iii and iv: "aber" inserted
20. iii and iv: so ging der Zauberspruch
21. iii and iv: wo sie den Stich empfand
22. iv: "dieser Schlaf verbreitete sich über das ganze Schloß" inserted
23. iv: "heim" replaces "zurück"
24. iv: fiengen an einzuschlafen, und die ganze Hofstaat mit ihnen
25. iv: remainder of sentence omitted; following sentence inserted: "Und der Wind legte sich, und auf dem Baum vor dem Schloß regte sich kein Blättchen mehr."
26. iii and iv: Rings um
27. iii and iv: "so" omitted

die Sage in dem Land von dem schönen, schlafenden Dornröschen, denn so wurde die Königstochter genannt, also daß von
Zeit zu Zeit Königssöhne kamen und durch die Hecke in das
Schloß dringen wollten. Es war ihnen aber nicht möglich, denn
die Dornen[28] hielten sich gleichsam wie an Händen[29] zusammen
und sie blieben darin hängen[30] und starben jämmerlich. Nach
langen, langen Jahren kam wieder ein Königssohn durch das
Land, dem erzählte ein alter Mann von der Dornhecke, es solle
ein Schloß dahinter stehen, in welchem ein wunderschönes Kön-
igsfräulein,[31] Dornröschen genannt, schlafe[32] mit dem ganzen
Hofstaat. Er erzählte auch, daß er von seinem Großvater gehört,
wie viele Königssöhne gekommen wären,[33] um durch die
Dornenhecke zu dringen, aber darin hängen geblieben und eines
traurigen Todes gestorben.[34] Da sprach der Jüngling: "das soll
mich nicht abschrecken, ich will hindurch und das schöne Dornröschen sehen." Der Alte mogte ihm abraten, wie er wollte, er
hörte gar nicht darauf.

Nun waren aber gerade an dem Tag, wo der Königssohn kam,
die hundert Jahre verflossen. Und als er sich der Dornhecke
näherte, waren es lauter große, schöne Blumen, die thaten sich
von selbst aus einander, daß er unbeschädigt hindurch ging; hinter ihm aber[35] thaten sie sich wieder als eine Hecke zusammen.
Er kam ins Schloß, da lagen im Hof die Pferde und scheckigen
Jagdhunde und schliefen, auf dem Dache saßen die Tauben und
hatten das Köpfchen unter den Flügel gesteckt. Und als er ins
Haus kam, schliefen die Fliegen an der Wand, der Koch in der
Küche hielt noch die Hand, als wollte er den Jungen anpacken
und die Magd saß vor dem schwarzen Huhn, das sollte gerupft
werden. Da ging er weiter und sah[36] den ganzen Hofstaat da
liegen und schlafen und oben drüber[37] den König und die Kön-

28. iii and iv: Aeste
29. iii and iv: als hätten sie Hände
30. iii and iv: und die Jünglinge blieben in den Dornen hängen
31. iii and iv: Königstochter
32. iii: schlafe, und mit ihm schlafe der ganze Hofstaat; iv: schliefe, und mit ihr
    schliefe der ganze Hofstaat.
33. iv: Er wußte auch von seinem Großvater daß viele Königssöhne schon ver-
    sucht hatten durch . . .
34. iii and iv: "wären" inserted
35. iii and iv: "aber" omitted
36. iii and iv: "im Saale" inserted
37. iii and iv: und oben bei dem Throne lag

igin. Da ging er noch weiter und alles war so still, daß einer seinen Athem hören konnte, und endlich kam er zu dem Thurm und öffnete die Thüre zu der kleinen Stube, in welcher Dornröschen schlief. Da lag es und war so schön, daß er die Augen nicht abwenden konnte und er bückte sich und gab ihm einen Kuß. Wie er ihm den Kuß gegeben,[38] schlug Dornröschen die Augen auf, erwachte und sah ihn[39] freundlich an. Da gingen sie zusammen herab und der König erwachte und die Königin und der ganze Hofstaat und sahen einander mit großen Augen an. Und die Pferde im Hof standen auf und rüttelten sich, die Jagdhunde sprangen und wedelten; die Tauben auf dem Dach zogen das Köpfchen unterm Flügel hervor, sahen umher und flogen ins Feld; die Fliegen an den Wänden krochen weiter; das Feuer in der Küche erhob sich, flackerte und kochte das Essen und[40] der Braten brutzelte fort;[41] der Koch gab dem Jungen eine Ohrfeige, daß er schrie und die Magd rupfte das Huhn fertig. Und da wurde die Hochzeit des Königssohns mit dem Dornröschen in aller Pracht gefeiert und sie lebten vergnügt bis an ihr Ende.

SIXTH EDITION

Vor Zeiten war ein König und eine Königin, die sprachen jeden Tag "ach, wenn wir doch ein Kind hätten!" und kriegten immer keins. Da trug sich zu, als die Königin einmal im Bade saß, daß ein Frosch aus dem Wasser ans Land kroch und zu ihr sprach, "dein Wunsch wird erfüllt werden, ehe ein Jahr vergeht, wirst du eine Tochter zur Welt bringen." Was der Frosch gesagt hatte, das geschah, und die Königin gebar ein Mädchen, das war so schön, daß der König vor Freude sich nicht zu lassen wußte und ein großes Fest anstellte. Er ladete nicht blos seine Verwandte, Freunde und Bekannte, sondern auch die weisen Frauen dazu ein, damit sie dem Kind hold und gewogen wären. Es waren ihrer dreizehn in seinem Reiche, weil er aber nur zwölf goldene Teller hatte, von welchen sie essen sollten, so mußte eine von ihnen daheim bleiben. Das Fest ward mit aller Pracht gefeiert, und als es zu Ende war, beschenkten die weisen Frauen das Kind

---

38. iii and iv: wie er es mit dem Kuß berührt hatte
39. iii and iv: und blickte ihn ganz
40. iv: "und" replaced by semicolon
41. iii and iv: "und" inserted; iv: "fort" replaced by "weiter"

mit ihren Wundergaben: die eine mit Tugend, die andere mit
Schönheit, die dritte mit Reichthum, und so mit allem, was auf
der Welt zu wünschen ist. Als elfe ihre Sprüche eben gethan
hatten, trat plötzlich die dreizehnte herein. Sie wollte sich dafür
rächen daß sie nicht eingeladen war, und ohne jemand zu grüßen
oder nur anzusehen, rief sie mit lauter Stimme "die Königstochter soll sich in ihrem funfzehnten Jahr an einer Spindel stechen
und todt hinfallen." Und ohne ein Wort weiter zu sprechen kehrte
sie sich um und verließ den Saal. Alle waren erschrocken, da
trat die zwölfte hervor, die ihren Wunsch noch übrig hatte und
weil sie den bösen Spruch nicht aufheben, sondern nur ihn mildern konnte, so sagte sie "es soll aber kein Todt sein, sondern ein
hundertjähriger tiefer Schlaf, in welchen die Königstochter fällt."

Der König, der sein liebes Kind vor dem Unglück gern bewahren wollte, ließ den Befehl ausgehen, daß alle Spindeln im
ganzen Königreiche sollten verbrannt werden. An dem Mädchen
aber wurden die Gaben der weisen Frauen sämmtlich erfüllt,
denn es war so schön, sittsam, freundlich und verständig, daß
es jedermann, der es ansah, lieb haben mußte. Es geschah, daß
an dem Tage, wo es gerade funfzehn Jahr alt ward, der König
und die Königin nicht zu Haus waren, und das Mädchen ganz
allein im Schloß zurückblieb. Da gieng es aller Orten herum,
besah Stuben und Kammern, wie es Lust hatte, und kam endlich
auch an einen alten Thurm. Es stieg die enge Wendeltreppe
hinauf, und gelangte zu einer kleinen Thüre. In dem Schloß
steckte ein verrosteter Schlüssel, und als es umdrehte, sprang
die Thüre auf, und saß da in einem kleinen Stübchen eine alte
Frau mit einer Spindel und spann emsig ihren Flachs. "Guten
Tag, du altes Mütterchen," sprach die Königstochter, "was machst
du da?" "Ich spinne," sagte die Alte und nickte mit dem Kopf.
"Was ist das für ein Ding, das so lustig herumspringt?" sprach
das Mädchen, nahm die Spindel und wollte auch spinnen. Kaum
hatte sie aber die Spindel angerührt, so gieng der Zauberspruch
in Erfüllung, und sie stach sich damit in den Finger.

In dem Augenblick aber, wo sie den Stich empfand, fiel sie
auf das Bett nieder, das da stand, und lag in einem tiefen Schlaf.
Und dieser Schlaf verbreitete sich über das ganze Schloß: der
König und die Königin, die eben heim gekommen waren und
in den Saal getreten waren, fiengen an einzuschlafen, und der
ganze Hofstaat mit ihnen. Da schliefen auch die Pferde im Stall,
die Hunde im Hofe, die Tauben auf dem Dache, die Fliegen an

der Wand, ja, das Feuer, das auf dem Herde flackerte, ward still und schlief ein, und der Braten hörte auf zu brutzeln, und der Koch, der den Küchenjungen, weil er etwas versehen hatte, in den Haaren ziehen wollte, ließ ihn los und schlief. Und der Wind legte sich, und auf den Bäumen vor dem Schloß regte sich kein Blättchen mehr.

Rings um das Schloß aber begann eine Dornenhecke zu wachsen, die jedes Jahr höher ward, und endlich das ganze Schloß umzog, und darüber hinaus wuchs, daß gar nichts mehr davon zu sehen war, selbst nicht die Fahne auf dem Dach. Es gieng aber die Sage in dem Land von dem schönen schlafenden Dornröschen, denn so ward die Königstochter genannt, also daß von Zeit zu Zeit Königssöhne kamen und durch die Hecke in das Schloß dringen wollten. Es war ihnen aber nicht möglich, denn die Dornen, als hätten sie Hände, hielten fest zusammen, und die Jünglinge blieben darin hängen, konnten sich nicht wieder los machen und starben eines jämmerlichen Todes. Nach langen langen Jahren kam wieder einmal ein Königssohn in das Land, und hörte wie ein alter Mann von der Dornhecke erzählte, es sollte ein Schloß dahinter stehen, in welchem eine wunderschöne Königstochter, Dornröschen genannt, schon seit hundert Jahren schliefe, und mit ihr schliefe der König und die Königin und der ganze Hofstaat. Er wußte auch von seinem Großvater daß schon viele Königssöhne gekommen wären und versucht hätten durch die Dornenhecke zu dringen, aber sie wären darin hängen geblieben und eines traurigen Todes gestorben. Da sprach der Jüngling "ich fürchte mich nicht, ich will hinaus und das schöne Dornröschen sehen." Der gute Alte mochte ihm abrathen, wie er wollte, er hörte nicht auf seine Worte.

Nun waren aber gerade die hundert Jahre verflossen, und der Tag war gekommen, wo Dornröschen wieder erwachen sollte. Als der Königssohn sich der Dornenhecke näherte, waren es lauter große schöne Blumen, die thaten sich von selbst auseinander und ließen ihn unbeschädigt hindurch, und hinter ihm thaten sie sich wieder als eine Hecke zusammen. Im Schloßhof sah er die Pferde und scheckigen Jagdhunde liegen und schlafen, auf dem Dache saßen die Tauben und hatten das Köpfchen unter den Flügel gesteckt. Und als er ins Haus kam, schliefen die Fliegen an der Wand, der Koch in der Küche hielt noch die Hand, als wollte er den Jungen anpacken, und die Magd saß vor dem schwarzen Huhn, das sollte gerupft werden. Da gieng er weiter, und sah im Saale den ganzen Hofstaat liegen und schlafen, und oben bei dem Throne lag der König und die Königin. Da gieng er noch weiter, und alles war so still, daß einer seinen Athem hören konnte, und endlich kam er zu dem Thurm und öffnete die Thüre zu der kleinen Stube, in welcher Dornröschen schlief. Da lag es und war so schön, daß er die Augen nicht abwenden konnte, und er bückte sich und gab ihm einen Kuß. Wie er es mit dem Kuß berührt hatte, schlug Dornröschen die Augen auf, erwachte, und blickte ihn ganz freundlich an. Da giengen sie zusammen herab, und der König erwachte und die Königin, und der ganze Hofstaat, und sahen einander mit großen Augen an. Und die Pferde im Hof standen auf und rüttelten sich: die Jagdhunde sprangen und wedelten: die Tauben auf dem Dache zogen das Köpfchen unterm Flügel hervor, sahen umher und flogen ins Feld: die Fliegen an den Wänden krochen weiter: das Feuer in der Küche erhob sich, flackerte: und kochte das Essen: der Braten fieng wieder an zu brutzeln: und der Koch gab dem Jungen eine Ohrfeige daß er schrie: und die Magd rupfte das Huhn fertig. Und da wurde die Hochzeit des Königssohns mit dem Dornröschen in aller Pracht gefeiert, und sie lebten vergnügt bis an ihr Ende.

Translations

MANUSCRIPT   *Sleeping Beauty*

A King and queen had no children at all. One day the queen was bathing, when a crab crawled out of the water onto the land and said: you will soon get a daughter. And so it happened also, and the king in his joy held a great celebration and there were thirteen fairies in the land, but he had only twelve golden plates, and so could not invite the thirteenth. The fairies endowed her with every virtue and beauty. As the celebration was coming to an end, the thirteenth fairy came and said: you did not ask me and I prophesy that your daughter in her fifteenth year will prick her finger with a spindle and will die of it. The other fairies wanted to make this as good as they could and said: she should only fall asleep for a hundred years.

The king however issued the order that all spindles in the whole realm should be destroyed, which happened, and when the king's daughter was fifteen years old, and the parents had one day gone out, she went around in the castle and at last reached an old tower. A narrow staircase led into the tower, then she came to a little door, in which there was a yellow key, which she turned, and came into a little room in which an old woman was spinning her flax. And she joked with the woman and wanted to spin also. Then she pricked herself with the spindle, and fell immediately into a deep sleep. Because in that moment the king and his court had returned, everything in the castle began to sleep, even the flies on the walls. And around the whole castle grew a thorn hedge, so that nothing of it could be seen.

After a long, long time a king's son came into the land, he was told the story by an old man who remembered hearing it from his grandfather and that already many had tried to get through the thorns, but all had remained hanging in them. But when this prince went up to the thorn hedge, all the thorns parted in front of him and seemed to be flowers, and behind him they turned into thorns again. As he now entered the castle, he kissed the sleeping princess, and everything awoke from its sleep and the two married and if they are not dead, they are still living.

FIRST EDITION

A king and queen had no children at all, and dearly wished to have had one. Once the queen was bathing, when a crab crawled out of the water onto the land and said: "your wish will soon be fulfilled and you will bring a daughter into the world." This also occurred, and the king was so delighted over the birth of the princess, that he arranged a great celebration, and to it he also invited the fairies who were in the land; because he only had twelve golden plates, he could not invite one: that is to say, there were thirteen of them. The fairies came to the celebration, and at the end of it endowed the child: one with virtue, the second with beauty and similarly the others with everything that is wonderful in the world and to be wished for, but just as the eleventh had said her gift, the thirteenth entered, very angry that she had not been invited, and cried: "because you did not ask me,

I tell you that your daughter in her fifteenth year will prick her finger with a spindle and fall down dead." The parents were shocked, but the twelfth fairy still had a wish to make, and she said: "it shall not be death, however, she shall only fall into a deep sleep for a hundred years."

The king still hoped to save his dear child, and issued the order that all spindles in the whole kingdom should be destroyed. The princess however grew up, and was a marvel of beauty. One day, when she had reached her fifteenth year, the king and the queen had gone out, and she was quite alone in the castle, and went around everywhere she pleased, and at last she came to an old tower. A narrow staircase led to it, and because she was curious, she climbed it and came to a little door in which there was a yellow key which she turned, then the door sprang open, and she was in a little room, in which an old woman sat and was spinning her flax. She liked the old woman well, and she joked with her, and said that she too just wanted to spin, and took the spindle in her hand. Scarcely had she touched the spindle, however, when she pricked herself with it, and immediately fell down into a deep sleep. At that moment the king returned with all his court, and then everything began to fall asleep, the horses in the stables, the doves on the roof, the dogs in the courtyard, the flies on the walls, even the fire which was flaming on the hearth became still and fell asleep, and the roast meat stopped sizzling, and the cook let go of the cook's boy whose hair he was just about to pull, and the maid let the chicken fall which she was plucking, and slept, and around the whole castle a thorn hedge began to grow high and ever higher, so that nothing more of it could be seen at all.

Princes, who had heard of the beautiful Thorn-rose, came and wanted to free her, but could not penetrate through the hedge, it was as if the thorns held fast together like clasped hands, and they remained hanging in them, and died pitifully. That went on for many long years: then once a king's son travelled through the land, an old man told him of the fact that people believed that behind the thorn hedge stood a castle, and a wondrously beautiful princess was sleeping in it with her whole court; his grandfather had told him that many other princes had come and wanted to penetrate, but had remained hanging in the thorns and had been pierced to death. "That shall not frighten me," said the king's son, "I will penetrate through the hedge and free the beautiful Thorn-rose;" then he went off, and as he came to the thorn hedge they were nothing but flowers which moved apart, and he went through, and behind him they became thorns again. Then he entered the castle, and in the courtyard the horses lay asleep, and the spotted hunting dogs, and on the roof sat the doves with their heads tucked into their wings, and as he entered the flies were asleep on the wall, and the fire in the kitchen, the cook and the maid, then he went further, the whole court lay asleep, and still further, the king and queen; and it was so still, that anyone could hear his own breath, then he came at last into the old tower where lay Thorn-rose asleep. Then the king's son was so amazed by her beauty, that he bent over and kissed her, and at that moment she woke up, and the king and queen and the whole court, and the horses and the dogs, and the doves on the roof, and the flies on the walls, and the fire got up and flamed and finished cooking the meal, and the roast meat sizzled on, and the cook boxed the cook's boy's ear, and the maid finished plucking the chicken. Then the wedding of the king's son and Thorn-rose was celebrated, and they lived happily till their end.

SECOND EDITION

A long time ago there lived a king and a queen who said every day: "oh, if only we had a child!" and never had one. Then it happened that once when the queen was bathing, a crab crawled out of the water and onto the land and said to her: "your wish is fulfilled, and you will bring a daughter into the world." What the crab had prophesied happened and the queen gave birth to such a beautiful girl, that the king could not contain himself for joy, and arranged a great celebration. He invited not only his relatives, friends and acquaintances but also the wise women, so that they would be kind and well disposed toward the child. There were thirteen of them in his kingdom, but because he had only twelve golden plates from which they were to eat, he could not invite one of them. Those that were invited came, and after the celebration was over they made presents to the child of their magical gifts: one gave virtue, the other beauty, the third riches and so was given everything in the world that is splendid. When ten had made their wishes, the thirteenth, who had not been invited, came in and wanted to get her revenge for this. She cried: "the king's daughter shall prick herself with a spindle in her fifteenth year, and fall down dead." Then the twelfth stepped forward, who still had a wish left; to be sure, she could not lift the evil pronouncement, but she could nevertheless soften it, and said: "it shall not be death, however, but a hundred-year-long deep sleep, into which the king's daughter falls." The king still hoped to preserve his dear child from the pronouncement and issued the order that all spindles in the whole kingdom should be destroyed. But all the gifts of the wise women were fulfilled in the girl, for she was so beautiful, well-behaved, friendly and intelligent, that everyone who saw her had to like her. It happened that on the day when she became just fifteen years old, the king and the queen were not at home and the young lady remained quite alone in the castle. She went around everywhere, looked at rooms and chambers as she pleased and came at last to an old tower. She climbed a narrow staircase and came to a little door. In the lock was a yellow key, and when it turned, the door sprang open, and an old woman sat in the little room and was busily spinning her flax. "Why, old mother, said the king's daughter, what are you doing there?" "I am spinning" said the old woman, and nodded her head. "How the thing jumps round and around" said the young lady and took the spindle in her hand, and wanted to spin as well. Scarcely had she touched the spindle, when the curse of the witch was fulfilled, and she pricked herself with it.

But at the moment when she had pricked herself, she also fell down in a deep sleep. And the king and the queen, who had just come back, began to fall asleep with all of their court. Then the horse in the stable fell asleep, the dogs in the courtyard, the doves on the roof, and flies on the wall, and the fire which was flaming on the hearth became still and fell asleep and the roast meat stopped sizzling and the cook, who wanted to pull the hair of the cook's boy, because he had neglected to do something, let go of him, and slept and everything that breathed became still and slept.

Around the castle, however, a thorn hedge began to grow, which grew higher each year, and finally so surrounded the castle and grew all over it, that nothing could be seen any longer, not even the flags on the roofs. There was a story in the land, however, of the beautiful sleeping Thorn-rose, for so the king's daughter was called, so that from time to time king's sons came and wanted to penetrate through the hedge into the castle. But it was not possible for them, for the thorns held fast together like clasped hands and they remained hanging in them and died pitifully. After many long years a king's son came again through the land, an old man told him of the thorn hedge, that a castle was supposed to be behind it, in which a wondrously beautiful royal girl, called Thorn-rose, was sleeping with her whole court. He told also that he had heard from his grandfather how many king's sons had come to penetrate the thorn hedge but had remained hanging there and died a sad death. Then the young man said: "that shall not frighten me off, I will get through and see the beautiful Thorn-rose." No matter how the old man warned him, he did not listen to it.

Now on exactly the day on which the king's son came, the hundred years were up. And when he went up to the thorn-hedge, they were nothing but large beautiful flowers, which parted by themselves, so that he went through unharmed; behind him, however, they closed again as a hedge. He entered the castle, there lay in the courtyard asleep the horses and dappled hunting dogs, on the roof sat the doves with their heads tucked under their wings. And as he entered the house, the flies were asleep on the wall, the cook in the kitchen still held his hand as if he meant to grab the boy, and the maid sat in front of the black hen that was to be plucked. Then he went further and saw the whole court lying there asleep and up opposite him the king and queen. Then he went still further and everything was so still, that one could hear his own breath, and at last he came to the tower, and opened the door to the little room, in which Thorn-rose slept. She lay there and was so beautiful that he could not take his eyes from her, and bent over, and gave her a kiss. As he gave her the kiss, Thorn-rose opened her eyes, woke up and looked at him cheerfully. Then they went down together and the king awoke and the queen and the whole court and they looked at one another astonished. And the horses stood up in the courtyard and shook themselves, and the hunting dogs jumped and wagged their tails; the doves on the roof took their heads from under their wings, looked around and flew off into the fields; the flies on the walls crept forward; the fire in the kitchen rose, flamed and cooked the meal, and the roast meat sizzled on; the cook boxed the boy's ears, so that he cried out, and the maid finished plucking the hen. And then the marriage of the king's son with Thorn-rose was celebrated in magnificent fashion and they lived happily up to their end.

SIXTH EDITION

A long time ago there lived a king and a queen who said every day, "oh, if only we had a child!" and never had one. Then it happened that once when the queen was bathing, a frog crawled out of the water onto the land and said to her: "your wish will be fulfilled, before a year has passed you will bring a daughter into the world." What the frog had said happened, and the queen gave birth to a girl, who was so beautiful that the king could not contain himself and arranged a great celebration. He invited not only his relatives, friends and acquaintances, but also the wise women, so that they might be kind and well disposed toward the child. There were thirteen of them in his kingdom, but because he had only twelve golden plates, from which they were to eat, one of them had to stay at home. The celebration was held with all manner of splendor, and when it was at an end, the wise women made presents to the child of their magical gifts: one gave virtue, the other beauty, the third riches, and thus was given everything in the world that could be wished. When eleven had made their pronouncements, the thirteenth suddenly entered. She wanted to avenge herself for not having been invited, and without greeting or even looking at anyone she cried in a loud voice: "the king's daughter shall prick herself with a spindle in her fifteenth year and fall down dead." And without saying another word, she turned around and left the hall. All were shocked, then the twelfth stepped forward, who still had her wish left, and because she could not lift the evil sentence, but only soften it, she said: "it shall not be death, however, but a hundred-year-long deep sleep, into which the king's daughter falls." The king, who wanted to preserve his dear child from misfortune, issued the order that all spindles in the whole kingdom should be burned. But the gifts of the wise women were all fulfilled in the girl, because she was so beautiful, well behaved, friendly and intelligent, that everyone who saw her had to like her. It happened that on the day when she became just fifteen years old, the king and the queen were not at home, and the girl remained quite alone in the castle. She went around everywhere, looked at rooms and chambers as she pleased, and at last came to an old tower. She climbed up the narrow spiral staircase and came to small door. In the lock was a rusty key, and when it turned, the door sprang open, and an old woman sat in the little room with a spindle, and was busily spinning flax. "Good-day, old mother" said the king's daughter, "what are you doing there?" "I am spinning" said the old woman, and nodded her head. "What kind of thing is that, that jumps around so merrily?" said the girl, took the spindle and wanted to spin as well. But scarcely had she touched the spindle, when the spell was fulfilled and she pricked herself in the finger with it.

But the moment that she felt the prick, she fell down onto the bed that stood there, and lay in a deep sleep. And this sleep spread over the whole castle: the king and queen, who had just come home and had entered the hall, began to fall asleep, and the whole court with them. Then the horses in the stable slept, the dogs in the courtyard, the doves on the roof, the flies on the wall, even the fire which was flaming on the hearth became still and fell asleep, and the roast meat stopped sizzling, and the cook, who wanted to pull the hair of the cook's boy, because he had neglected to do something, let go of him and slept. And the wind died down, and in the trees in front of the castle not a small leaf moved any more.

Around the castle, however, a thorn hedge began to grow, which grew higher each year and finally surrounded the whole castle and grew all over it, so that nothing more could be seen of it, not even the flag on the roof. There was a story in the land, however, of the beautiful sleeping Thorn-rose, for so the king's daughter was called, so that from time to time king's sons came and wanted to penetrate through the hedge into the castle. But it was not possible for them, for the thorns held fast together, as if they had hands, and the young men remained hanging in them, could not get themselves free again, and died a pitiful death. After many long years a king's son came once again into the land and heard that an old man told of a thorn hedge, that a castle was supposed to be behind it, in which a wondrously beautiful king's daughter, called Thorn-rose, had been sleeping for a hundred years and with her was sleeping the king and the queen and the whole court. He knew also from his grandfather that many king's sons had come and had tried to penetrate through the thorn hedge, but had remained hanging in them and died a sad death. Then the young man said "I am not afraid, I will go out and see the beautiful Thorn-rose." No matter how the good old man tried to warn him, he did not listen to his words.

Now however the hundred years were just up, and the day had come, when Thorn-rose was to wake up. When the king's son went up to the thorn hedge, they were nothing but large beautiful flowers, which parted by themselves and let him pass through unharmed, and behind him they closed again as a hedge. In the castle yard he saw the horses and dappled hunting dogs lying asleep, on the roof the doves sat and had their heads tucked under their wings. And as he entered the house, the flies slept on the wall, the cook in the kitchen held his hand as if he meant to grab the boy, and the maid sat in front of the black hen that was to be plucked. Then he went on, and saw in the hall the whole court lying asleep, and up by the throne lay the king and queen. Then he went still further, and everything was so still that one could hear his own breath, and at last he came to the tower and opened the door to the little room in which Thorn-rose slept. She lay there and was so beautiful that he could not take his eyes from her, and bent over, and gave her a kiss. But when he had touched her with the kiss, Thorn-rose opened her eyes, woke up, and looked at him quite cheerfully. Then they went down together, and the king awoke and the queen, and the whole court, and they looked at one another astonished. And the horses in the courtyard stood up and shook themselves: the hunting dogs jumped and wagged their tails: the doves on the roof took their heads from under their wings, looked around and flew off into the fields: the flies on the walls crept forward: the fire in the kitchen rose up, flamed, and cooked the meal: the roast meat began to sizzle again: and the cook boxed the boy's ears so that he cried out: and the maid finished plucking the hen. And then the marriage of the king's son with Thorn-rose was celebrated in magnificent fashion and they lived happily up to their end.

3. Hänsel und Gretel
(Hansel and Gretel)

The four basic texts of the story given below are the manuscript and the first, second and fifth editions. There are considerable differences between the four in phraseology and in the development of plot and character. The texts of editions three and four are for the most part similar to that of the second, with a certain amount of rephrasing, although one very significant change is introduced in the fourth edition: the children's mother becomes a stepmother. The sixth edition varies from the fifth only in some altered phraseology. As before, changes introduced in the third and fourth editions are given as notes to the second, and changes in the sixth as notes to the fifth.

MANUSCRIPT: *Das Brüderchen und*
                das Schwesterchen

Es war einmal ein armer Holzhacker, der wohnte vor einem großen Wald. Es ging ihm gar jämmerlich, daß er kaum seine Frau, und seine zwei Kinder ernähren konnte. Einsmals hatte er auch kein Brod mehr und war in großer Angst, da sprach seine Frau Abends im Bett zu ihm: nimm die beiden Kinder morgen früh und führ sie in den großen Wald, gib ihnen das noch übrige Brod, und mach' ihnen ein groß Feuer an und darnach geh weg und laß sie allein. Der Mann wollte lang nicht, aber die Frau ließ ihm keine Ruh, bis er endlich einwilligte.

Aber die Kinder hatten alles gehört, was die Mutter gesagt hatte das Schwesterchen fing an gar sehr zu weinen, das Brüderchen sagte ihm es solle still seyn und tröstete es. Dann stand er leis auf und ging hinaus vor die Thüre, da wars Mondenschein und die weißen Kieselsteine glänzten vor dem Haus. Der Knabe las sie sorgfältig auf und füllte sein Rocktäschlein damit, soviel er nur hineinbringen konnte. Darauf ging er wieder zu seinem Schwesterchen ins Bett, und schlief ein.

Des Morgens früh, ehe die Sonne aufgegangen war, kam der Vater und die Mutter und weckten die Kinder auf, die mit in den großen Wald sollten. Sie gaben jedem ein Stücklein Brod, die nahm das Schwesterchen unter das Schürzchen, denn das Brüderchen hatte die Tasche voll von den Kieselsteinen. Darauf machten sie sich fort auf den Weg zu dem großen Wald. Wie sie nun so gingen, da stand das Brüderchen oft still, und guckte nach ihrem Haüschen zurück. Der Vater sagte: was bleibst du immer stehn und guckst zurück; ach antwortete das Brüderchen, ich seh nach meinem weißen Kätzchen, das sitzt auf dem Dach und will mir Ade sagen heimlich ließ es aber immer einen von den weißen Kieselsteinchen fallen. Die Mutter sprach: geh nur fort, es ist dein Kätzchen nicht, es ist das Morgenroth, das auf den Schornstein scheint. Aber der Knabe blickte immer noch zurück, und immer ließ er wieder ein Steinchen fallen.

So gingen sie lang and kamen endlich mitten in den großen Wald. Da machte der Vater ein großes Feuer an, und die Mutter sagt: schlaft dieweil ihr Kinder, wir wollen in den Wald gehn und Holz suchen, wartet bis wir wieder kommen. Die Kinder setzten sich an das Feuer, und jedes aß sein Stücklein Brot. Sie warten lang bis es Nacht ward, aber die Eltern kamen nicht wieder. Da fing das Schwesterchen an gar zu weinen, das Brüderchen tröstete es aber und nahm es an die Hand. Da schien der Mond, und weißen Kieselsteinchen glänzten, und zeigten ihnen den Weg. Und das Brüderchen führte das Schwesterchen die ganze Nacht durch, und sie kamen des Morgens wieder vor das Haus. Der Vater war gar froh, denn er hatte es nicht gern gethan; aber die Mutter was bös.

Bald darnach hatten sie wieder kein Brod und das Brüderchen hörte wieder Abends im Bett, wie die Mutter zu dem Vater sagte, er solle die Kinder hinaus in den großen Wald bringen. Da fing das Schwesterchen wieder an heftig zu weinen, und das Brüderchen stand wieder auf, und wollte Steinchen suchen. Wie es aber as die Thür kam, war sie verschloßen von der Mutter, da fing das Brüderchen an traurig zu werden, und konnte das Schwesterchen nicht trösten.

Vor Tag standen sie wieder auf, jedes erhielt wieder ein Stücklein Brot. Wie sie auf dem Weg waren, guckt das Brüderchen oft zurück der Vater sagte: mein Kind was bleibst du immer stehn, und guckst zurück nach dem Haüschen? Ach! antwortete das Brüderchen, ich seh nach meinem Taübchen, das sitzt auf dem Dach, und will mir Ade sagen, heimlich aber zerbrößelte es sein Stückchen Brot, und ließ immer ein Krümchen fallen. Die Mutter sprach: geh nur fort, es ist dein Taübchen nicht, es ist das Morgenroth, das auf den Schornstein scheint. Aber das Brüderchen blickte immer noch zurück, und immer ließ es ein Krümchen fallen.

Als sie mitten in den großen Wald gekommen, machte der Vater wieder ein großes Feuer an, die Mutter sprach wieder dieselbigen Worte, und beide gingen fort. Das Schwesterchen gab dem Brüderchen die Hälfte von seinem Stücklein Brot, denn das Brüderchen hatte seins auf den Weg geworfen. und sie warteten bis zum Abend, da wollte das Brüderchen das Schwesterchen beim Mondschein wieder zurückführen. Aber die Vöglein hatten die Brodkrümchen aufgefreßen und sie konnten den Weg nicht finden. Sie gingen immer fort, und verirrten sich in dem großen Wald. Am dritten Tag kamen sie an ein Haüschen, das war aus Brod gemacht, das Dach war mit Kuchen gedeckt und die Fenster von Zucker. Die Kinder waren gar froh, wie sie das sahen und das Brüderchen aß von dem Dach und das Schwesterchen von dem Fenster. Wie sie so standen und sichs gut schmecken ließen, da rief eine feine Stimme heraus:

> Knuper, knuper, Kneischen!
> wer knupert an meim Haüschen?

Die Kinder erschracken sehr; bald darauf kam eine kleine alte Frau heraus, die nahm die Kinder freundlich bei der Hand, führte sie in das Haus, und gab ihnen gutes eßen, und legte sie in ein schönes Bett. Am andern Morgen aber steckte sie das Brüderchen in ein Ställchen, das sollte ein Schweinchen seyn, und das Schwesterchen mußte ihm Waßer bringen, und gutes Essen. Alle Tag kam sie herzu da mußte das Brüderchen den

Finger herausstrecken, und sie fühlte ob es bald fett wäre. Es streckte aber immer dafür ein Knöchelchen heraus, da meinte sie es wäre noch nicht fett u. es dauerte länger. Dem Schwesterchen gab sie nichts zu eßen, als Krebsschalen, weil es nicht fett werden sollte. Nach vier Wochen sagte sie am Abend zu dem Schwesterchen, geh hin und hole Waßer, und mache es morgen früh heis, wir wollen dein Brüderchen schlachten und sieden, ich will dieweil den Teich zurecht machen, daß wir auch backen können dazu. Am andern Morgen, wie das Wasser heis war, rief sie das Schwesterchen vor den Backofen, und sprach zu ihm: setz dich auf das Brett, ich will dich in den Ofen schieben, sieh, ob das Brot bald fertig ist; sie wollte aber das Schwesterchen darin laßen und braten. Das merkt das Schwesterchen und sprach zu ihr: ich versteh das nicht, setz dich zuerst darauf, ich will dich hineinschieben. Die Alte setzte sich darauf, und das Schwesterchen schob sie hinein, machte die Thüre zu, und die Hexe verbrannte. Darauf ging es zum Brüderchen u. macht ihm sein Ställchen auf. Sie fanden das ganze Haüschen voll Edelgestein, damit füllten sie alle Taschen und brachten sie ihrem Vater, der ward ein reicher Mann; die Mutter aber war gestorben.

FIRST EDITION

Vor einem großen Walde wohnte ein armer Holzhacker, der hatte nichts zu beißen und zu brechen, und kaum das tägliche Brod für seine Frau und seine zwei Kinder, Hänsel und Gretel. Einmal konnte er auch das nicht mehr schaffen, und wußte sich nicht zu helfen in seiner Noth. Wie er Abends vor Sorge sich im Bett herumwälzte, da sagte seine Frau zu ihm: "höre Mann, morgen früh nimm die beiden Kinder, gieb jedem noch ein Stückchen Brod, dann führ sie hinaus in den Wald, mitten inne, wo er am dicksten ist, da mach ihnen ein Feuer an, und dann geh weg und laß sie dort, wir können sie nicht länger ernähren." "Nein Frau, sagte der Mann, das kann ich nicht über mein Herz bringen, meine eigenen lieben Kinder zu den wilden Thieren zu führen, die sie bald in dem Wald zerreißen würden." "Wenn du das nicht thust, sprach die Frau, so müssen wir alle miteinander Hungers sterben;" da ließ sie ihm keine Ruhe, bis er Ja sagte.

Die zwei Kinder waren auch noch wach von Hunger, und hatten alles gehört, was die Mutter zum Vater gesagt hatte. Gretel dachte, nun ist es um mich geschehen und fing erbärmlich an zu weinen, Hänsel aber sprach: "sey still, Gretel, und gräm dich nicht, ich will uns helfen." Damit stieg er auf, zog sein Röcklein an, machte die Unterthüre auf und schlich hinaus. Da schien der Mond hell und die weißen Kieselsteine glänzten wie lauter Batzen. Hänsel bückte sich und machte sich sein ganz Rocktäschlein voll davon, so viel nur hinein wollten, dann ging er zurück ins Haus: "tröste dich, Gretel, und schlaf nur ruhig," legte sich wieder ins Bett und schlief ein.

Morgens früh, ehe die Sonne noch aufgegangen war, kam die Mutter und weckte sie alle beide: "steht auf, ihr Kinder, wir wollen in den Wald gehen, da habt ihr jedes ein Stücklein Brod, aber haltets zu Rathe und hebts euch für den Mittag auf." Gretel nahm das Brod unter die Schürze, weil Hänsel die Steine in der Tasche hatte, dann machten sie sich auf den Weg in den Wald hinein. Wie sie ein Weilchen gegangen waren, stand Hänsel still und guckte nach dem Haus zurück, bald darauf wieder und immer wieder. Der Vater sprach: "Hänsel, was guckst du zurück und hältst dich auf, hab Acht und marschir zu."—"Ach, Vater, ich sehe nach meinem weißen Kätzchen, das sitzt oben auf dem Dach und will mir Ade sagen." Die Mutter sprach: "ei Narr, das ist dein Kätzchen nicht, das ist die Morgensonne, die auf den Schornstein scheint." Hänsel aber hatte nicht nach dem Kätzchen gesehen, sondern immer einen von den blanken Kieselsteinen aus seiner Tasche auf den Weg geworfen.

Wie sie mitten in den Wald gekommen waren, sprach der Vater, "nun sammelt Holz, ihr Kinder, ich will ein Feuer anmachen, daß wir nicht frieren." Hänsel und Gretel trugen Reisig zusammen, einen kleinen Berg hoch. Da steckten sie es an, und wie die Flamme recht groß brannte, sagte die Mutter: "nun legt euch ans Feuer und schlaft, wir wollen in dem Wald das Holz fällen, wartet, bis wir wieder kommen, und euch abholen.

Hänsel und Gretel saßen an dem Feuer, bis Mittag, da aß jedes sein Stücklein Brod, und dann wieder bis an den Abend; aber Vater und Mutter blieben aus, und niemand wollte kommen und sie abholen. Wie es nun finstere Nacht wurde, fing Gretel an zu weinen, Hänsel aber sprach: "wart nur ein Weilchen, bis der Mond aufgegangen ist. Und als der Mond aufgegangen war, faßte er die Gretel bei der Hand, da lagen die Kieselsteine wie neugeschlagene Batzen und schimmerten und zeigten ihnen den Weg. Da gingen sie die ganze Nacht durch, und wie es Morgen war, kamen sie wieder bei ihres Vaters Haus an. Der Vater freute sich von Herzen, als er seine Kinder wieder sah, denn er hatte sie ungern allein gelassen, die Mutter stellte sich auch, als wenn sie sich freute, heimlich aber war sie bös.

Nicht lange darnach, war wieder kein Brod im Hause und Hänsel und Gretel hörten wie Abends die Mutter zum Vater sagte: "einmal haben die Kinder den Weg zurückgefunden, und da habe ichs gut seyn lassen, aber jetzt ist wieder nichts, als nur noch ein halber Laib Brod im Haus, du mußt sie morgen tiefer in den Wald führen, daß sie nicht wieder heim kommen können, es ist sonst keine Hülfe für uns mehr." Dem Mann fiels schwer aufs Herz, und er gedachte, es wäre doch besser, wenn du den letzten Bissen mit deinen Kindern theiltest, weil er es aber einmal gethan hatte, so durfte er nicht nein sagen. Hänsel und Gretel hörten das Gespräch der Eltern; Hänsel stand auf und wollte wieder Kieselsteine auflesen, wie er aber an die Thüre kam, da hatte sie die Mutter zugeschlossen. Doch tröstete er die Gretel und sprach: "schlaf nur, lieb Gretel, der liebe Gott wird uns schon helfen."

Morgens früh erhielten sie ihr Stücklein Brod, noch kleiner als das vorigemal. Auf dem Wege bröckelte es Hänsel in der Tasche, stand oft still, und warf ein Bröcklein an die Erde. Was bleibst du immer stehen, Hänsel, und guckst dich um, sagte der Vater, geh deiner Wege."—"Ach! ich seh nach meinem Täubchen, das sitzt auf dem Dach und will mir Ade sagen"—"du Narr, sagte die Mutter, das ist dein Täubchen nicht, das ist die Morgensonne, die auf den Schornstein oben scheint." Hänsel aber zerbröckelte all sein Brod und warf die Bröcklein auf den Weg.

Die Mutter aber führte sie noch tiefer in den Wald hinein, wo sie ihr Lebtag nicht gewesen waren, da sollten sie wieder einschlafen bei einem großen Feuer, und Abends wollten die Eltern kommen und sie abholen. Zu Mittag theilte Gretel ihr Brod mit Hänsel, weil der seins all auf den Weg gestreut; der Mittag verging und der Abend verging, aber niemand kam zu den armen Kindern. Hänsel tröstete die Gretel und sagte: "wart, wenn der Mond aufgeht, dann seh ich die Bröcklein Brod, die ich ausgestreut habe, die zeigen uns den Weg nach Haus." Der Mond ging auf, wie aber Hänsel nach den Bröcklein sah, da waren sie weg, die viel tausend Vöglein in dem Wald, die hatten sie gefunden und aufgepickt. Hänsel meinte doch den Weg nach Haus zu finden und zog die Gretel mit sich, aber sie verirrten sich bald in der großen Wildniß und gingen die Nacht und den ganzen Tag, da schliefen sie vor Müdigkeit ein; und gingen noch einen Tag, aber sie kamen nicht aus den Wald heraus, und waren so hungrig, denn sie hatten nichts zu essen, als ein paar kleine Beerlein, die auf der Erde standen.

Am dritten Tage gingen sie wieder bis zu Mittag, da kamen sie an ein Häuslein, das war ganz aus Brod gebaut und war mit Kuchen gedeckt, und die Fenster waren von hellem Zucker. "Da wollen wir uns niedersetzen und uns satt essen, sagte Hänsel; ich will vom Dach essen, iß du vom Fenster, Gretel, das ist fein süß für dich." Hänsel hatte schon ein gut Stück vom Dach und Gretel schon ein paar runde Fensterscheiben gegessen, und brach sich eben eine neue aus, da hörten sie eine feine Stimme, die von innen herausrief:

"knuper, knuper, Kneischen!
"wer knupert an meinem Häuschen!"

Hänsel und Gretel erschracken so gewaltig, daß sie fallen ließen, was sie in der Hand hielten, und gleich darauf sahen sie aus der Thüre eine kleine steinalte Frau schleichen. Sie wackelte mit dem Kopf und sagte: "ei, ihr lieben Kinder, wo seyd ihr denn hergelaufen, kommt herein mit mir, ihr sollts gut haben," faßte beide an der Hand und führte sie in ihr Häuschen. Da ward gutes Essen aufgetragen, Milch und Pfannkuchen mit Zucker, Aepfel und Nüsse, und dann wurden zwei schöne Bettlein bereitet, da legten sich Hänsel und Gretel hinein, und meinten sie wären wie im Himmel.

Die Alte aber war eine böse Hexe, die lauerte den Kindern auf, und hatte um sie zu locken ihr Brodhäuslein gebaut und wenn eins in ihre Gewalt kam, da machte sie es todt, kochte es und aß es, und das war ihr ein Festtag. Da war sie nun recht froh, wie Hänsel und Gretel ihr zugelaufen kamen. Früh, ehe sie noch erwacht waren, stand sie schon auf, ging an ihre Bettlein und wie sie die zwei so lieblich ruhen sah, freute sie sich und gedachte, das wird ein guter Bissen für dich seyn. Sie packte Hänsel und steckte ihn in einen kleinen Stall, und wie er da aufwachte, war er von einem Gitter umschlossen, wie man junge Hühnlein einsperrt, und konnte nur ein paar Schritte gehen. Das Gretel aber schüttelte sie und rief: "steh auf, du Faullenzerin,

hol Wasser und geh in die Küche und koch gut zu essen, dort
steckt dein Bruder in einem Stall, den will ich erst fett machen,
und wann er fett ist, dann will ich ihn essen, jetzt sollst du ihn
füttern." Gretel erschrack und weinte, mußte aber thun, was die
Hexe verlangte. Da ward nun alle Tage dem Hänsel das beste
Essen gekocht, daß er fett werden sollte, Gretel aber bekam
nichts, als die Krebsschalen, und alle Tage kam die Alte und
sagte: "Hänsel, streck deine Finger heraus, daß ich fühle, ob du
bald fett genug bist." Hänsel streckte ihr aber immer ein Knöchlein heraus, da verwunderte sie sich, daß er gar nicht zunehmen
wolle.

Nach vier Wochen sagte sie eines Abends zu Gretel: "sey flink,
geh und trag Wasser herbei, dein Brüderchen mag nun fett
genug seyn oder nicht, morgen will ich es schlachten und sieden,
ich will derweile den Teig anmachen, daß wir auch dazu backen
können." Da ging Gretel mit traurigem Herzen und trug das
Wasser, worin Hänsel sollte gesotten werden. Früh Morgens
mußte Gretel aufstehen, Feuer anmachen und den Kessel mit
Wasser aufhängen. "Gieb nun Acht, bis es siedet, sagte die Hexe,
ich will Feuer in den Backofen machen und das Brod hineinschieben;" Gretel stand in der Küche und weinte blutige Thränen,
und dachte, hätten uns lieber die wilden Thiere im Walde gefressen, so wären wir zusammen gestorben und müßten nun
nicht das Herzeleid tragen, und ich müßte nicht selber das Wasser zu dem Tod meines lieben Bruders sieden, du lieber Gott,
hilf uns armen Kindern aus der Noth.

Da rief die Alte: "Gretel komm gleich einmal hierher zu dem
Backofen," wie Gretel kam, sagte sie: guck hinein, ob das Brod
schon hübsch braun und gar ist, meine Augen sind schwach, ich
kann nicht so weit sehen, und wenn du auch nicht kannst, so
setz dich auf das Brett, so will ich dich hineinschieben, da kannst
du darin herumgehen und nachsehen." Wenn aber Gretel darin
war, da wollte sie zumachen und Gretel sollte in dem heißen
Ofen backen, und sie wollte es auch aufessen: das dachte die
böse Hexe, und darum hatte sie das Gretel gerufen. Gott gab
es aber Gretel ein und sie sagte: "ich weiß nicht, wie ich das
anfangen soll, zeigs mirs erst, setz dich drauf, ich will dich hineinschieben." Und die Alte setzte sich auf das Brett, und weil sie
leicht war, schob sie Gretel hinein so weit sie konnte, und dann
machte sie geschwind die Thüre zu, und steckte den eisernen
Riegel vor. Da fing die Alte an in dem heißen Backofen zu schreien

und zu jammern, Gretel aber lief fort, und sie mußte elendiglich verbrennen.

Und Gretel lief zum Hänsel, machte ihm sein Thürchen auf und Hänsel sprang heraus, und sie küßten sich einander und waren froh. Das ganze Häuschen war voll von Edelgesteinen und Perlen, davon füllten sie ihre Taschen, gingen fort und fanden den Weg nach Haus. Der Vater freute sich als er sie wieder sah, er hatte keinen vergnügten Tag gehabt, seit seine Kinder fort waren, und ward nun ein reicher Mann. Die Mutter aber war gestorben.

SECOND EDITION

Vor einem großen Walde wohnte ein armer Holzhacker, der hatte nichts[1] zu beißen und zu brechen und kaum das tägliche Brot für seine Frau und seine zwei Kinder, Hänsel und Grethel. Endlich kam die Zeit, da konnte er auch das nicht schaffen, und wußte keine Hülfe mehr für seine Noth. Wie er sich nun Abends vor Sorge im Bett herumwälzte, sprach seine Frau zu ihm: "höre Mann, morgen früh[2] nimm die beiden Kinder, gieb jedem noch ein Stückchen Brot, dann[3] führ sie hinaus in den Wald, mitten inne, wo er am dicksten ist, da mach ihnen ein Feuer an, und dann geh weg und laß sie dort allein, wir können sie nicht länger ernähren." "Nein Frau, sagte der Mann, das kann ich nicht über mein[4] Herz bringen, meine eigenen lieben Kinder den wilden Thieren im Wald zu bringen,[5] die sie bald würden[6] zerrißen haben." "Nun,[7] wenn du das nicht thust, sprach die Frau, so müssen wir alle miteinander Hungers sterben;" und ließ ihm keine Ruhe, bis er einwilligte.

Die zwei Kinder waren auch noch vor Hunger wach gewesen, und hatten mit angehört, was die Mutter[8] zum Vater gesagt hatte. Grethel dachte, nun ist es um mich geschehen und fing erbärm-

1. iv: wenig
2. iv: in aller Frühe
3. iv: "dann" replaced by "und"
4. iii and iv: "das kann ich nicht über" replaced by "wie soll ich übers"
5. iii and iv: zu überliefern
6. iii and iv: "würden" placed before "sie"
7. iii and iv: "nun" omitted
8. iv: Stiefmutter

lich an zu weinen, Hänsel aber sprach: "sey still, Grethel, und
gräm dich nicht, ich will uns[9] helfen." Damit stieg er auf, zog sein
Röcklein an, machte die Unterthüre auf und schlich hinaus. Da
schien der Mond hell und die weißen Kieselsteine glänzten wie
lauter Batzen. Hänsel bückte sich und steckte so viel in sein
Rocktäschlein als nur hinein wollten, dann ging er zurück ins
Haus. "Tröste dich, Grethel, und schlaf nur ruhig," sprach er,
legte sich wieder ins Bett und schlief ein.

Morgens früh, ehe die Sonne noch aufgegangen war, kam die
Mutter[10] und weckte sie all beide:[11] "steht auf, ihr Kinder, wir
wollen in den Wald gehen; da hat jedes von euch ein Stücklein
Brot, aber haltets zu Rathe und hebts euch für den Mittag auf."
Grethel nahm das Brot unter die Schürze, weil Hänsel die Steine
in der Tasche hatte, dann machten sie sich auf den Weg zum
Wald hinein. Wie sie ein Weilchen gegangen waren, stand Hänsel
still und guckte nach dem Haus zurück, bald darauf wieder und
immer wieder. Der Vater sprach: "Hänsel, was guckst du zurück
und hältst dich auf,[12] hab Acht und heb deine Beine auf."[13]—
"Ach, Vater, ich seh nach meinem weißen Kätzchen, das sitzt
oben auf dem Dach und will mir Ade sagen." Die Mutter[14] sprach:
"ei[15] Narr, das ist dein Kätzchen nicht, das ist die Morgensonne,
die auf den Schornstein scheint." Hänsel aber hatte nicht nach
dem Kätzchen gesehen, sondern immer einen von den blanken
Kieselsteinen aus seiner Tasche auf den Weg geworfen.

Wie sie mitten in den Wald gekommen waren, sprach der
Vater, "nun sammelt Holz, ihr Kinder, ich will ein Feuer anmachen, daß wir nicht frieren." Hänsel und Grethel trugen Reisig
zusammen, einen kleinen Berg hoch. Da steckten sie es an, und
wie die Flamme recht groß brannte, sagte die Mutter:[16] "nun
legt euch ans Feuer und schlaft, wir wollen in dem Wald das
Holz fällen, wartet, bis wir wieder kommen, und euch abholen.

Hänsel und Grethel saßen an dem Feuer, bis Mittag, da aß
jedes sein Stücklein Brot; sie glaubten, der Vater wär noch im

9. iii and iv: "schon" inserted
10. iv: Frau
11. iii and iv: weckte die beiden Kinder; "ihr Kinder" omitted from next phrase
12. iii and iv: was guckst du da und bleibst zurück
13. iv: und vergiß deine Beine nicht
14. iv: Frau
15. iii and iv: "ei" omitted
16. iv: Frau

Wald, weil sie die Schläge seiner Axt hörten, aber das war ein Ast, den er an einen Baum gebunden hatte und den der Wind hin und her schlug. Nun warteten sie bis zum Abend, aber Vater und Mutter[17] blieben aus, und niemand wollte kommen und sie abholen. Wie es nun finstere Nacht wurde, fing Grethel an zu weinen, Hänsel aber sprach: "wart nur ein Weilchen, bis der Mond aufgegangen ist. Und als der Mond aufgegangen war, faßte er die[18] Grethel bei der Hand, da lagen die Kieselsteine, und schimmerten wie neugeschlagene Batzen und zeigten ihnen den Weg. Da giengen sie die ganze Nacht durch, und wie es Morgen war, kamen sie wieder bei ihres Vaters Haus an. Der Vater freute sich von Herzen, als er seine Kinder wieder sah, denn es hatte ihm weh gethan, wie er sie allein gelassen,[19] die Mutter[20] stellte sich auch, als wenn sie sich freute, heimlich aber war sie bös.

Nicht lange darnach, war wieder kein Brot im Hause und Hänsel und Grethel hörten, wie Abends die Mutter[21] zum Vater sagte: "einmal haben die Kinder den Weg zurückgefunden und da habe ichs gut seyn lassen; aber jetzt ist wieder nichts, als nur noch ein halber Laib Brot im Haus, du mußt sie morgen tiefer in den Wald führen, daß sie den Weg nicht zurück finden, es ist sonst keine Hülfe für uns mehr."[22] Dem Manne fiels schwer aufs Herz, und er gedachte,[23] es wäre doch besser, wenn du den letzten Bissen mit deinen Kindern theiltest, weil er es aber einmal gethan hatte,[24] so dürfte er nicht nein sagen. Als die Kinder das Gespräch gehört hatten, stand Hänsel auf und wollte wieder Kieselsteine auflesen, wie er aber an die Thüre kam, da hatte sie die Mutter[25] zugeschlossen. Doch tröstete er die Grethel und sprach: "schlaf nur, lieb[26] Grethel, der liebe Gott wird uns schon helfen."

17. "Mutter" stands unchanged in fourth edition
18. iii and iv: "die" omitted
19. iii and iv: denn es war ihm zu Herzen gegangen, wie er sie so allein gelassen; previous "von Herzen" omitted
20. iv: Stiefmutter
21. "Mutter" stands unchanged in fourth edition
22. iii and iv: "mehr" placed before "für"
23. iii and iv: dachte
24. iii and iv: weil er aber einmal eingewilligt hatte,
25. iv: Frau
26. iii and iv: "lieb" omitted

Morgens früh erhielten sie ihr Stücklein Brot, noch kleiner als das vorigemal. Auf dem Wege bröckelte es Hänsel in der Tasche, stand oft still, und warf ein Bröcklein an die Erde. "Was bleibst du immer stehen, Hänsel, und guckst dich um, sagte der Vater, geh deiner Wege."—"Ach![27] ich seh nach meinem Täubchen, das sitzt auf dem Dach und will mir Ade sagen."— "du Narr, sagte die Mutter,[28] das ist dein Täubchen nicht, das ist die Morgensonne, die auf den Schornstein oben scheint." Hänsel aber zerbröckelte all sein Brot, und warf die Bröcklein auf den Weg.

Die Mutter[29] führte sie noch tiefer in den Wald hinein, wo sie ihr Lebtag nicht gewesen waren, da sollten sie wieder bei einem großen Feuer sitzen und schlafen, und Abends wollten die Eltern kommen und sie abholen. Zu Mittag theilte Grethel ihr Brot mit Hänsel, weil der seins all auf den Weg gestreut hatte, aber der Mittag verging und der Abend verging, und niemand kam zu den armen Kindern. Hänsel tröstete die Grethel und sagte: "wart, wenn der Mond aufgeht, dann seh ich die Bröcklein Brot, die ich ausgestreut habe, die zeigen uns den Weg nach Haus." Der Mond ging auf, wie aber Hänsel nach den Bröcklein sah, da waren sie weg, die viel tausend Vöglein in dem Wald, die hatten sie gefunden und aufgepickt. Hänsel meinte doch den Weg nach Haus zu finden und zog die Grethel mit sich, aber sie verirrten sich bald[30] in der großen Wildniß und gingen die Nacht und den ganzen Tag, da schliefen sie vor Müdigkeit ein.[31] Dann gingen sie noch einen Tag, aber kamen nicht aus den[32] Wald heraus, und waren so hungrig, denn sie hatten nichts zu essen, als ein paar kleine Beerlein,[33] die auf der Erde standen.

Als sie am dritten Tag wieder bis zu Mittag gegangen waren, da kamen sie an ein Häuslein, das war ganz aus Brod gebaut und war mit Kuchen gedeckt, und die Fenster waren von hellem Zucker. "Da wollen wir uns niedersetzen und uns satt essen, sagte Hänsel; ich will vom Dach essen, iß du vom Fenster, Grethel, das

27. iii and iv: "Ach!" omitted
28. iv: Stiefmutter
29. iv: Frau
30. iv: "bald" omitted
31. iv: und schliefen endlich vor Müdigkeit ein; "Dann" omitted from next phrase
32. iii and iv: dem
33. iii and iv: Beeren

ist fein süß für dich." Wie nun Grethel an dem Zucker knuperte, rief drinnen eine feine Stimme:

"knuper, knuper, Kneischen!
"wer knupert an meinem Häuschen!"

Die Kinder antworteten:

"der Wind! der Wind!
"das himmlische Kind!"

Und aßen weiter. Grethel brach sich eine ganze runde Fensterscheibe heraus und Hänsel riß sich ein gewaltig[34] Stück Kuchen vom Dach ab. Da ging die Thüre auf und eine steinalte Frau kam herausgeschlichen. Hänsel und Grethel erschracken so gewaltig, daß sie fallen ließen, was sie in Händen hatten. Die Alte aber wackelte mit dem Kopf und sagte: "ei, ihr lieben Kinder, wo seyd ihr denn hergelaufen, kommt herein mit mir, ihr sollts gut haben," faßte beide an der Hand und führte sie in ihr Häuschen. Da ward gutes Essen aufgetragen, Milch und Pfannkuchen mit Zucker, Aepfel und Nüsse, und dann wurden zwei schöne Bettlein bereitet, da legten sich Hänsel und Grethel hinein, und meinten sie wären wie im Himmel.

Die Alte aber war eine böse Hexe, die lauerte den Kindern auf, und hatte[35] um sie[36] zu locken ihr Brodhäuslein gebaut, und wenn eins in ihre Gewalt kam, da machte sie es todt, kochte es und aß es, und das war ihr ein Festtag. Da war sie nun recht froh,[37] wie Hänsel und Grethel ihr zugelaufen kamen. Früh, ehe sie noch erwacht waren, stand sie[38] schon auf, ging an ihre Bettlein und wie sie die zwei so lieblich ruhen sah, freute sie sich und murmelte:[39] "das wird ein guter Bissen für mich seyn."[40] Darauf packte sie den[41] Hänsel und steckte ihn in einen kleinen Stall, wie er nun aufwachte, war er von einem Gitter umschlossen, wie man junge Hühnlein einsperrt,[42] und konnte nur ein

34. iii and iv: großes
35. iii and iv: "bloß" inserted
36. iv: "herbei" inserted
37. iv: Da lachte sie boshaft als Hänsel . . .
38. iv: die Alte
39. iv: "freute sie sich und murmelte" replaced by "da murmelte sie vor sich hin"
40. iv: ein guter Bissen werden
41. iii and iv: "den" omitted
42. iv: "wie man junge Hühnlein einsperrt" placed before "Stall"

paar Schritte gehen. Das Grethel aber schüttelte sie[43] und rief:
"steh auf, du Faullenzerin, hol Wasser und geh in die Küche
und koch was gutes zu essen, dort steckt dein Bruder in einem
Stall, den will ich erst fett machen, und wenn er fett ist, dann
will ich ihn essen, jetzt sollst du ihn füttern. Grethel erschrak
und weinte, mußte aber thun, was die[44] Hexe verlangte. Da ward
nun alle Tage dem Hänsel das beste Essen gekocht, daß er fett
werden sollte, Grethel aber bekam nichts, als die Krebsschalen,
und[45] alle Tage kam die Alte und sagte:[46] "Hänsel, streck deine
Finger heraus, daß ich fühle, ob du bald fett genug bist." Hänsel
streckte ihr aber immer[47] ein Knöchlein heraus, da verwunderte
sie sich, daß er[48] gar nicht zunehmen wolle.

Nach vier Wochen sagte sie eines Abends zu Grethel: "sey flink,
geh und trag Wasser herbei, dein Brüderchen mag nun fett seyn
oder nicht, morgen will ich es schlachten und sieden, ich will
derweile den Teig anmachen, daß wir auch dazu backen können." Da ging Grethel mit traurigem Herzen und trug das Wasser, worin Hänsel sollte gesotten werden. Früh Morgens mußte
Grethel aufstehen, Feuer anmachen[49] und den Kessel mit Wasser
aufhängen. "Gieb nun Acht, sagte die Hexe, ich will Feuer in
den Backofen machen und das Brod hineinschieben;" Grethel
stand in der Küche und weinte blutige Thränen, und dachte,
hätten uns lieber die wilden Thiere im Walde gefressen, so wären
wir zusammen gestorben und müßten nun nicht das Herzeleid
tragen, und ich müßte nicht selber das Wasser[50] zu dem Tod
meines lieben Bruders sieden: "du lieber[51] Gott, hilf uns armen
Kindern aus der Noth!"

Da rief die Alte: "Grethel, komm gleich hierher[52] zu dem
Backofen," wie Grethel kam, sagte sie: "guck hinein, ob das Brot
schon hübsch braun und gar ist, meine Augen sind schwach,

43. iii: Gretel aber schüttelte sie wach, und rief; iv: Dann aber rüttelte sie die
Grethel aus dem Schlaf und rief
44. iii and iv: "böse" inserted
45. iii and iv: "und" omitted; new sentence
46. iv: Jeden Morgen schlich die Alte herbei und sagte
47. iii and iv: "statt des Fingers" inserted
48. iii and iv: "so mager blieb, und" inserted
49. iv: anzünden
50. iii: "sieden" moved up from the end of the sentence; iv: "heiß machen"
replaces "sieden" of third edition
51. iii and iv: "du lieber" replaced by "barmherziger"
52. iii and iv: "gleich einmal hierher" reduced to "her"

ich kann nicht so weit sehen, und wenn du[53] auch nicht kannst, so setz dich auf das Brett, so will ich dich hineinschieben, da kannst du darin herumgehen und nachsehen." Wenn[54] aber Grethel darin war, da[55] wollte sie zumachen und Grethel sollte in dem heißen Ofen backen, und[56] sie wollte es auch aufessen: das dachte die böse Hexe, und darum hatte sie Grethel gerufen.[57] Gott gab es aber dem Mädchen ein, daß es sprach:[58] "ich weiß nicht, wie ich das anfangen soll, zeige mirs erst, und setz dich auf, ich will dich hineinschieben." Da setzte sich die Alte auf das Brett, und weil sie leicht war, schob Grethel sie hinein so weit es konnte,[59] und dann machte es geschwind die Thüre zu und steckte den eisernen Riegel vor. Nun fing die Alte an in dem heißen Backofen zu schreien und zu jammern,[60] Grethel aber lief fort und sie[61] mußte elendiglich verbrennen.

Da lief Grethel zum Hänsel, machte ihm sein Thürchen auf und rief: "spring heraus, Hänsel, wir sind erlöst!" Da sprang Hänsel heraus, wie ein eingesperrtes Vöglein aus dem Bauer.[62] Und sie weinten vor Freude und küßten sich einander.[63] Das ganze Häuschen aber war voll von Edelgesteinen und Perlen, damit füllten sie ihre Taschen, gingen fort und suchten den Weg nach Haus. Sie kamen aber vor ein großes Wasser und konnten nicht hinüber. Da sah das Schwesterchen ein weißes Entchen hin und her schwimmen, dem rief es zu:[64] "ach, liebes Entchen nimm uns auf deinen Rücken" als das Entchen das hörte, kam es geschwommen und trug das Grethel hinüber und hernach[65] holte es auch das Hänsel. Darnach fanden sie bald ihre Heimath, der Vater freute sich herzlich als er sie wieder sah, denn er hatte keinen vergnügten Tag gehabt, seit seine Kinder fort waren. Die

53. iv: du's
54. iii and iv: "Wenn" replaced by "Sobald"
55. iii and iv: "da" omitted
56. iii and iv: und dann wollte sie es
57. iii and iv: "das dachte die böse Hexe . . . gerufen" omitted
58. iii: Gott gab es aber dem Mädchen in dem Sinn, daß es sprach; iv: Da merkte das Mädchen, was sie im Sinn hatte, und sprach
59. iii and iv: "es konnte" replaced by "der Stiel an dem Brett reichte"
60. iv: zu heulen
61. iii and iv: die gottlose Hexe
62. iii and iv: "Bauer" replaced by "Käfig springt, wenn ihm das Thürchen geöffnet wird"
63. iii and iv: küßten einander herzlich
64. iii and iv: "zu" omitted
65. iii and iv: "hernach" replaced by "dann"

Mutter[66] aber war gestorben. Nun brachten die Kinder Reich-
thümer genug mit und sie brauchten für Essen und Trinken
nicht mehr zu sorgen.

FIFTH EDITION

Vor einem großen Walde wohnte ein armer Holzhacker mit seiner
Frau und seinen zwei Kindern; das Bübchen hieß Hänsel und
das Mädchen Grethel. Er hatte wenig zu beißen und zu brechen,
und einmal als große Theuerung ins Land kam, konnte er auch
das tägliche Brot nicht mehr schaffen. Wie er sich nun Abends
im Bett Gedanken machte, und sich vor Sorgen herumwälzte,
seufzte er und sprach zu seiner Frau "was soll aus uns werden?
wie können wir unsere armen Kinder ernähren, da wir für uns
selbst nichts mehr haben?" "Weißt du was, Mann," antwortete
die Frau, "wir wollen Morgen in aller Frühe die Kinder hinaus
in den Wald führen, wo er am dicksten ist, da machen wir ihnen
ein Feuer an, und geben jedem noch ein Stückchen Brot, dann
gehen wir an unsere Arbeit, und lassen sie allein. Sie finden den
Weg nicht wieder nach Haus, und wir sind sie los." "Nein, Frau,"
sagte der Mann, "das thue ich nicht; wie sollt ichs übers Herz
bringen meine Kinder im Walde allein zu lassen, die wilden
Thiere würden bald kommen und sie zerreißen." "O du Narr,"
sagte sie, "dann müssen wir alle viere Hungers sterben, du kannst
nur die Bretter für die Särge hobeln," und ließ ihm keine Ruhe
bis er einwilligte. "Aber die armen Kinder dauern mich doch"
sagte der Mann.

Die zwei Kinder hatten aber[1] auch vor Hunger nicht einschlafen können, und hatten gehört was die Stiefmutter zum
Vater gesagt hatte. Grethel weinte bittere Thränen, und sprach
zu Hänsel "nun ists um uns geschehen." "Still, Grethel," sprach
Hänsel, "gräme dich nicht, ich will uns schon helfen." Und als
die Alten eingeschlafen waren, stand er auf, zog sein Röcklein
an, machte die Unterthüre auf, und schlich sich hinaus. Da schien
der Mond ganz helle, und die weißen Kieselsteine, die vor dem
Haus lagen, glänzten wie lauter Batzen. Hänsel bückte sich, und
steckte so viel in sein Rocktäschlein, als nur hinein wollten. Dann

66. iv: Stiefmutter
1. vi: "aber" omitted

gieng er wieder zurück, sprach zu Grethel "sei getrost, liebes Schwesterchen, und schlaf nur ruhig ein, Gott wird uns nicht verlassen, und legte sich wieder in sein Bett.

Als der Tag anbrach, noch ehe die Sonne aufgegangen war, kam schon die Frau, und weckte die beiden Kinder, "steht auf, ihr Faullenzer, wir wollen in den Wald gehen und Holz holen." Dann gab sie jedem ein Stückchen Brot, und sprach "da habt ihr etwas für den Mittag, aber eßts nicht vorher auf, weiter kriegt ihr nichts." Grethel nahm das Brot unter die Schürze, weil Hänsel die Steine in der Tasche hatte. Darnach[2] machten sie sich alle zusammen auf den Weg nach dem Wald. Als sie ein Weilchen gegangen waren, stand Hänsel still, und guckte nach dem Haus zurück, und that das wieder und immer wieder. Der Vater sprach "Hänsel, was guckst du da, und bleibst zurück, hab Acht und vergiß deine Beine nicht." "Ach, Vater," sagte Hänsel, "ich sehe nach meinem weißen Kätzchen, das sitzt oben auf dem Dach und will mir Ade sagen." Die Frau sprach "Narr, das ist dein Kätzchen nicht, das ist die Morgensonne, die auf den Schornstein scheint." Hänsel aber hatte nicht nach dem Kätzchen gesehen, sondern immer einen von den blanken Kieselsteinen aus seiner Tasche auf den Weg geworfen.

Als sie mitten in den Wald gekommen waren, sprach der Vater "nun sammelt Holz, ihr Kinder, ich will ein Feuer anmachen damit ihr nicht friert. Hänsel und Grethel trugen Reisig zusammen, einen kleinen Berg hoch. Das[3] ward angezündet, und als die Flamme recht hoch brannte, sagte die Frau "nun legt euch ans Feuer, ihr Kinder, und ruht euch aus, wir gehen in den Wald und hauen Holz. Wenn wir fertig sind, kommen wir wieder, und holen euch ab.

Hänsel und Grethel saßen am Feuer, und als der Mittag kam, aß jedes sein Stücklein Brot. Und weil sie die Schläge der Holzaxt hörten, so glaubten sie ihr Vater wäre in der Nähe. Es war aber nicht die Holzaxt, es war ein Ast, den er an einen dürren Baum gebunden hatte, und den der Wind hin und her schlug. Und als sie so lange gesessen hatten, fielen ihnen die Augen vor Müdigkeit zu, und schliefen fest ein, als sie[4] erwachten, war es schon finstere Nacht. Grethel fieng an zu weinen, und sprach 'wie sollen wir nun aus dem Wald kommen!" Hänsel aber tröstete sie, "wart

2. vi: danach
3. vi: "Reisig" inserted
4. vi: "endlich" inserted; new sentence after "fest ein"

nur ein Weilchen, bis der Mond aufgegangen ist, dann wollen
wir den Weg schon finden." Und als der volle Mond aufgestiegen
war, so nahm Hänsel sein Schwesterchen an der Hand, und gieng
den Kieselsteinen nach, die schimmerten wie neu geschlagene
Batzen, und zeigten ihnen den Weg. Sie giengen die ganze Nacht
hindurch; und kamen bei anbrechendem Tag wieder zu ihres
Vaters Haus. Sie klopften an die Thür, und als die Frau aufmachte, und sah daß es Hänsel und Grethel war, sprach sie "ihr
bösen Kinder, was habt ihr so lange im Walde geschlafen, wir
haben geglaubt ihr wolltet gar nicht wieder kommen." Der Vater
aber freute sich, denn es war ihm zu Herzen gegangen daß er
sie so allein zurück gelassen hatte.

Nicht lange darnach[5] war wieder Noth in allen Ecken, und
die Kinder hörten wie die Mutter Nachts im Bette zu dem Vater
sprach "alles ist wieder aufgezehrt, wir haben noch einen halben
Laib Brot, hernach hat das Lied ein Ende. Die Kinder müssen
fort, wir wollen sie tiefer in den Wald hineinführen, damit sie
den Weg nicht wieder heraus finden; es ist sonst keine Rettung
für uns." Dem Mann fiels schwer aufs Herz, und er dachte "es
wäre besser, daß du den letzten Bissen mit deinen Kindern theiltest." Aber die Frau hörte auf nichts, was er sagte, schalt ihn und
machte ihm Vorwürfe. Wer A sagt muß auch B sagen, und weil
es das erste Mal nachgegeben hatte, so mußte er es auch zum
zweiten Mal.

Die Kinder waren aber noch wach gewesen, und hatten das
Gespräch mit angehört. Und als die Alten schliefen, stand Hänsel wieder auf, wollte hinaus und Kieselsteine auflesen, wie das
vorigemal, aber die Frau hatte die Thür verschlossen, und Hänsel konnte nicht heraus. Aber er tröstete sein Schwesterchen,
und sprach "weine nicht, Grethel, und schlaf nur ruhig, der
liebe Gott wird uns schon helfen."

Am frühen Morgen kam die Frau, und holte die Kinder aus
dem Bette. Sie erhielten ihr Stückchen Brot, das war aber noch
kleiner, als das vorigemal. Auf dem Wege nach dem Wald bröckelte es Hänsel in der Tasche, stand oft still, und warf ein Bröcklein auf die Erde. "Hansel, was stehst du, und guckst dich um,"
sagte der Vater, "geh deiner Wege." "Ich sehe nach meinem
Täubchen, das sitzt auf dem Dache, und will mir Ade sagen,"
antwortete Hänsel. "Narr," sagte die Frau, "das ist dein Täubchen

5. vi: danach

nicht, das ist die Morgensonne, die auf den Schornstein oben scheint." Hänsel aber warf nach und nach alle Bröcklein auf den Weg.

Die Frau führte die Kinder noch tiefer in den Wald, wo sie ihr Lebtag noch nicht gewesen waren. Da ward wieder ein großes Feuer angemacht, und die Mutter sagte "bleibt nur da sitzen, ihr Kinder, und wenn ihr müd seid, könnt ihr ein wenig schlafen, wir gehen in den Wald und hauen Holz, und Abends, wenn wir fertig sind, kommen wir, und holen euch ab." Als es Mittag war, theilte Grethel ihr Brot mit Hänsel, der sein Stück auf den Weg gestreut hatte. Dann schliefen sie ein, und der Abend vergieng, aber neimand kam zu den armen Kindern. Sie erwachten erst in der finstern Nacht, und Hänsel tröstete sein Schwesterchen und sagte, "wart nur, Grethel, bis der Mond aufgeht, dann werden wir die Brotbröcklein sehen, die ich ausgestreut habe, die zeigen uns den Weg nach Haus." Als der Mond kam, machten sie sich auf, aber sie fanden kein Bröcklein mehr, denn die viel tausend Vögel, die im Walde und im Felde herumfliegen,[6] die hatten sie weggepickt. Hänsel sagte zu Grethel "wir werden den Weg schon finden," aber sie fanden ihn nicht. Sie giengen die ganze Nacht und noch einen Tag von Morgen bis Abend, aber sie kamen aus dem Wald nicht heraus, und waren so hungrig, denn sie hatten nichts als die paar Beeren, die auf der Erde standen. Und weil sie so müd waren daß die Beine sie nicht mehr tragen wollten, so legten sie sich unter einen Baum, und schliefen ein.

Nun wars schon der dritte Morgen, daß sie ihres Vaters Haus verlassen hatten. Sie fiengen wieder an zu gehen, aber sie kamen nur immer tiefer in den Wald hinein.[7] Als es Mittag war, sahen sie ein schönes schneeweißes Vöglein auf einem Ast sitzen, das sang so schön, daß sie stehen blieben, und ihm zuhörten. Dann[8] schwang es seine Flügel, und flog vor ihnen her, und sie giengen ihm nach,[9] da sahen sie daß es sich auf ein Häuslein setzte, und als sie herankamen, so sahen sie daß das Haüslein ganz aus Brot und mit Kuchen gedeckt war, aber die Fenster waren von hellem

6. vi: umher fliegen
7. vi: recast and expanded to "aber sie geriethen immer tiefer in den Wald und wenn nicht bald Hilfe kam, so mußten sie verschmachten."
8. vi: Und als es fertig war, schwang
9. vi: bis sie zu einem Häuschen gelangten, auf dessen Dach es sich setzte, und als sie ganz nah heran kamen, so sahen sie daß das Häuslein aus Brot gebaut war, und mit Kuchen gedeckt . . .

Zucker. "Da wollen wir uns dran machen," sprach Hänsel, "und eine gute Mahlzeit halten. Ich will ein Stück vom Dach essen, Grethel, iß du vom Fenster, das ist süß."[10] Hänsel reichte in die Höhe und brach sich ein wenig vom Dach ab, um zu versuchen wie es schmeckte, und Grethel stellte sich an die Scheiben und knuperte daran. Da rief eine feine Stimme aus der Stube heraus

"knuper, knuper, kneischen,
wer knupert an meinem Haüschen?"

die Kinder antworteten

"der Wind, der Wind,
das himmlische Kind,"

und aßen weiter, ohne sich irre machen zu lassen. Hänsel, dem das Dach sehr gut schmeckte, riß sich ein großes Stück davon herunter, und Grethel stieß eine ganze runde Fensterscheibe heraus, setzte sich damit, und ließ es sich schmecken.[11] Da gieng auf einmal die Thüre auf, und eine steinalte Frau, die sich auf eine Krücke stützte, kam herausgeschlichen. Hänsel und Grethel erschraken so gewaltig, daß sie fallen ließen was sie in den Händen hielten. Die Alte aber wackelte mit dem Kopfe, und sprach "ei, ihr lieben Kinder, wer hat euch hierher gebracht? kommt nur herein und bleibt bei mir, ihr sollts gut haben."[12] Sie faßte beide an der Hand und führte sie in ihr Häuschen. Da ward gutes Essen aufgetragen, Milch und Pfannekuchen mit Zucker, Äpfel und Nüsse. Darnach[13] wurden zwei schöne Bettlein weiß gedeckt, und Hänsel und Grethel legten sich hinein, und meinten sie wären im Himmel.

Die Alte hatte sich nur so freundlich angestellt, sie war eine böse Hexe, die den Kindern auflauerte, und sie hatte das Brothäuslein bloß gebaut um sie herbeizulocken. Wenn eins in ihre Gewalt kam, so machte sie es todt, kochte es und aß es, und das war ihr ein Festtag.[14] Als Hänsel und Grethel sich dem Haus genähert hatten, da hatte sie boshaft gelacht und höhnisch aus-

10. vi: Grethel, du kannst vom Fenster essen, das schmeckt süß.
11. vi: setzte sich nieder, und that sich wohl damit.
12. vi: geschieht euch kein Leid.
13. vi: Hernach
14. vi: inserted: "Die Hexen haben rothe Augen und können nicht weit sehen, aber sie haben ein feine Witterung, wie die Thiere, und merkens wenn Menschen heran kommen."

gerufen "die sollen mir nicht entwischen."[15] Früh Morgens, ehe die Kinder erwacht waren, stand sie schon auf, und als sie beide so lieblich ruhen sah, mit den vollen rothen Backen, so murmelte sie vor sich hin "das wird ein guter Bissen werden." Da packte sie Hänsel mit ihrer dürren Hand, und trug ihn in einen kleinen Stall.[16] Er mochte schreien wie er wollte, es half ihm nichts; sie sperrte ihn mit einer Gitterthüre ein, und gieng dann[17] zu Grethel, rüttelte sie wach, und rief "willst du aufstehen, Faullenzerin, du sollst Wasser holen, und deinem Bruder etwas gutes kochen, der sitzt im Stall,[18] und soll fett werden. Und wenn er fett ist, so will ich ihn essen." Grethel fieng an bitterlich zu weinen, aber es war alles vergeblich, sie mußte thun was die böse Hexe verlangte.

Nun ward dem armen Hänsel das beste Essen gekocht, aber Grethel bekam nichts als Krebsschalen. Jeden Morgen schlich die Alte zu dem Ställchen und rief "Hänsel, streck deine Finger heraus, damit ich fühle ob du bald fett bist." Hänsel streckte ihr aber ein Knöchlein heraus, und die Alte, die trübe Augen hatte, konnte es nicht sehen, und meinte es wären Hänsels Finger, und verwunderte sich daß er gar nicht fett werden wollte. Als vier Wochen herum waren, und Hänsel immer mager blieb, da übernahm sie die Ungeduld und sie wollte nicht länger warten. "Heda, Grethel," rief sie dem Mädchen zu, "sei flink und trag Wasser: Hänsel mag fett oder mager sein, morgen will ich ihn schlachten und sieden."[19] Ach, wie jammerte das arme Schwesterchen, als es das Wasser tragen mußte, und wie flossen ihm die Thränen über die Backen herunter! "Lieber Gott, hilf uns doch," rief sie aus, "hätten uns nur die wilden Thiere im Wald gefressen, so wären wir doch zusammen gestorben." "Spar nur dein Geblärre," sagte die Alte, "es hilft dir alles nichts."

Früh Morgens mußte Grethel heraus, den Kessel mit Wasser aufhängen und Feuer anzünden. "Erst wollen wir backen" sagte die Alte, "ich habe den Backofen schon eingeheizt und den Teig geknätet." Sie stieß das arme Grethel hinaus zu dem Backofen,

15. vi: previous sentence recast: "Als Hänsel und Grethel in ihre Nähe kamen, da lachte sie boshaft und sprach höhnisch 'die habe ich, die sollen mir nicht wieder entwischen.' "
16. vi: this sentence is extended with a phrase displaced from two lines below: "und sperrte ihn mit einer Gitterthüre ein;"
17. vi: Dann gieng sie zur Grethel
18. vi: steh auf, Faullenzerin, trag Wasser und koch deinem Bruder etwas gutes, der sitzt draußen im Stall . . .
19. vi: kochen

aus dem die Feuerflammen schon heraus schlugen. "Kriech hinein," sagte die Hexe, "und sieh zu ob recht eingeheizt ist, damit wir das Brot hineinschießen können." Und wenn Grethel darin war, wollte sie den Ofen zumachen, und Grethel sollte darin braten, und dann wollte sies auch aufessen. Aber Grethel merkte was sie im Sinn hatte und sprach "ich weiß nicht wie ichs machen soll; wie komm ich da hinein?" "Dumme Gans," sagte die Alte, "die Öffnung ist groß genug, siehst du wohl, ich könnte selbst hinein," krappelte heran, und steckte den Kopf in den Backofen. Da gab ihr Grethel einen Stoß daß sie weit hinein fuhr, machte die eiserne Thür zu und schob den Riegel vor. Hu! da fieng sie an zu heulen, ganz grauselich; aber Grethel lief fort, und die gottlose Hexe mußte elendiglich verbrennen.

Grethel aber lief schnurstracks zu Hänsel, öffnete sein Ställchen, und rief "Hänsel, wir sind erlöst, die alte Hexe ist todt." Da sprang Hänsel heraus, wie ein Vogel aus dem Käfig, dem man die Thüre aufmacht.[20] Wie haben sie sich gefreut,[21] sind herumgesprungen und haben sich geküßt! Und weil sie sich nicht mehr zu fürchten brauchten, so giengen sie in das Haus der Hexe hinein, da standen in allen Ecken Kasten mit Perlen und Edelsteinen. "Die sind noch besser als Kieselsteine" sagte Hänsel, und steckte in seine Taschen was hinein wollte, und Grethel sagte "ich will auch etwas mit nach Haus bringen" und füllte sich sein Schürzchen voll. "Aber jetzt wollen wir fort," sagte Hänsel, "damit wir aus dem Hexenwald herauskommen." Als sie aber ein paar Stunden gegangen waren, kamen[22] sie an ein großes Wasser. "Wir können nicht hinüber," sprach Hänsel, "ich sehe keinen Steg und keine Brücke." "Es kommt auch kein Schiffchen," antwortete Grethel, "aber da schwimmt eine weiße Ente, wenn ich die bitte, so hilft sie uns hinüber." Da reif sie

"Entchen, Entchen,
da steht Grethel und Hänsel.
Kein Steg und keine Brücke,
nimm uns auf deinem weißen Rückchen."

Das Entchen kam auch heran, und Hänsel setzte sich auf, und bat sein Schwesterchen sich zu ihm zu setzen. "Nein," antwortete

20. vi: wenn ihm die Thüre aufgemacht wird
21. vi: "sind sich um den Hals gefallen," inserted
22. vi: gelangten

Grethel, "es wird dem Entchen zu schwer, es soll uns nach einander hinüber bringen." Das that das gute Thierchen, und als sie glücklich drüben waren, und ein Weilchen fortgiengen, da kam ihnen der Wald immer bekannter und immer bekannter vor, und endlich erblickten sie von weitem ihres Vaters Haus. Da fiengen sie an zu laufen, stürzten in die Stube hinein, und fielen ihrem Vater um den Hals. Der Mann hatte keine frohe Stunde gehabt, seitdem er die Kinder im Walde gelassen hatte, die Frau aber war gestorben. Grethel schüttete sein Schürzchen aus daß die Perlen und Edelsteine in der Stube herumsprangen, und Hänsel warf eine Handvoll nach der andern aus seiner Tasche dazu. Da hatten alle Sorgen ein Ende, und sie lebten in lauter Freude zusammen. Mein Märchen ist aus, dort lauft eine Maus, wer sie fängt, darf sich eine große große Pelzkappe daraus machen.

Translations

MANUSCRIPT   *The Little Brother and*
the Little Sister

There was once a poor woodcutter, who lived in front of a great forest. He fared so miserably, that he could scarcely feed his wife and his two children. Once he had no bread any longer, and suffered great anxiety, then his wife said to him in the evening in bed: take the two children tomorrow morning and take them into the great forest, give them the bread we have left, and make a large fire for them and after that go away and leave them alone. The husband did not want to for a long time, but the wife left him no peace, until he finally agreed.

But the children had heard everything that the mother had said the little sister began to weep a lot, the little brother said to her she should be quiet and comforted her. Then he quietly got up and went outside in front of the door, the moon shone there and the white pebbles shone in front of the house. The boy picked them up carefully and filled his little coat pocket with them, as many as he could put there. Then he went back to his little sister into bed, and went to sleep.

Early next morning, before the sun had risen, the father and mother came and woke the children up, who were to go with them into the great forest. They gave each a little piece of bread, little sister took it under her little apron, for the little brother had his pocket full of pebbles. Then they set off on their way to the great forest. As they were walking like this, the little brother often stood still, and looked back at their little house. The father said: why are you always standing and looking back; oh, answered the little brother, I am looking at my little white cat, it is sitting on the roof and wants to say goodbye to me but secretly he kept letting one of the little white pebbles drop. The mother spoke: just keep going, it's not your little cat, it is the morning glow which is shining on the chimney. But the boy kept looking back and kept letting another little stone drop.

They walked like this for a long time and at last came to the middle of the great forest. Then the father made a great fire, and the mother says: sleep a while children, we will go into the forest and look for wood, wait until we come back. The children sat down by the fire, and they both ate their little piece of bread. They wait a long time until it was night, but the parents did not come back. Then the little sister began to weep, but the little brother comforted her and took her by the hand. Then the moon shone, and the little white pebbles shone, and showed them the way. And the little brother led the little sister through the whole night. And in the morning they came again in front of the house. The father was glad, for he had not done it willingly; but the mother was angry.

Soon after they had no bread again, and the little brother heard again in the evening in bed, how the mother said to the father, he should take the children out into the great forest again. Then the little sister began again to sob her heart out, and the little brother got up again, and wanted to look for little stones. When he got to the door, however, it was bolted by the mother, then the little brother began to feel sad, and could not comfort the little sister.

They got up again before daybreak, each received a little piece of bread again. When they were on their way, the little brother looks back often the father said: my child why are you always standing still and looking back towards the little house? Oh! answered the little brother, I am looking at my little dove, it is sitting on the roof, and wants to say goodbye to me, but secretly he crumbled his little piece of bread, and kept letting a crumb fall. The mother spoke: just keep going, it's not your little dove, it's the morning glow shining on the chimney. But the little brother still kept looking back, and kept letting another little crumb drop.

When they had come to the middle of the great forest, the father again made a great fire, the mother again said the same words and both went away. The little sister gave the little brother a half of her little piece of bread, for the little brother had thrown his onto the path. And they waited until evening, then the little brother wanted to lead the little sister back by the moonshine. But the little birds had eaten up the little crumbs of bread and they could not find the way. They walked further and further and got lost in the great forest. On the third day they came to a little house that was made of bread, the roof was covered with cake and the windows of sugar. The children were glad when they saw it and the little brother ate some of the roof and the little sister some of the window. As they stood like this and enjoyed it, a delicate voice cried out:

> nibble, nibble, gnaw!
> who is nibbling at my little house?

The children were badly startled; soon after a small old woman came out, she took the children by the hand in a kindly way, took them into the house, and gave them something good to eat, and put them in a nice bed. But the next morning she put the little brother in a little stable, he was to be a little pig, and the little sister had to bring him water and good food. Every day she went to it then the little brother had to stick out his finger, and she felt if it was already fat. He always stuck out in place of it a little bone, then she thought that he was still not fat, and this went on for a long time. She gave to the little sister nothing to eat but crab-shells, because she was not to be fattened. After four weeks she said in the evening to the little sister, go and fetch water, and heat it tomorrow morning, we will slaughter and boil your little brother, meanwhile I'll make the dough, so that we can also bake as well. The next morning, when the water was hot, she called the little sister to the oven, and said to her: sit on the board, I will push you into the oven, see if the bread is already done; but she wanted to leave the little sister in there and roast her. The little sister notices this and said to her: I don't understand that, sit there first yourself, I will push you in. The old woman sat on it, and the little sister pushed her in, shut the door, and the witch burned to death. Then she went to the little brother and opens his little stable for him. They found the whole little house full of jewels, filled all their pockets with them, and took them to their father, who became a rich man; but the mother was dead.

FIRST EDITION

In front of a large forest lived a poor woodcutter who had nothing to eat and scarcely daily bread for his wife and his two children, Hansel and Gretel. Once he could not even get that any more, and could not see how to make his plight any better. As he was tossing and turning in bed in the evening because of his worries, his wife said to him: "listen husband, tomorrow morning take both the children, give each one a little piece of bread, then take them out into the forest, right in, where it is thickest, make them a fire, and then go away and leave them there, we cannot feed them any longer." "No, wife, said the husband, I cannot find it in my heart to take my own dear children to the wild animals, who would soon tear them apart in the forest." "If you don't do it, said the wife, we shall all have to die of hunger together," then she left him no peace, until he said yes.

The two children were also still awake through hunger, and had heard everything which the mother had said to the father. Gretel thought, now it's all up with me and began to weep pitifully, but Hansel said: "be quiet Gretel, and don't grieve, I will help us." With that he got up, put on his little coat, opened the door below, and slipped out. The moon was shining brightly, and the white pebbles shone like silver pennies. Hansel bent down and got his whole little coat pocket full of them, as many as would go in, then he went back into the house: "Console yourself, Gretel, and just sleep peacefully," got into bed again and went to sleep.

Early next morning, still before the sun had risen, the mother came and woke them both: "get up, you children, we will go into the forest, there is a little piece of bread for each of you, but save it and keep it for lunch. Gretel took the bread under her apron, because Hansel had the stones his pocket, then they set out to go into the forest. When they had walked for a little while, Hansel stood still and looked back at the house, soon after that once more and again and again. The father said: "Hansel, why are you looking back and stopping, pay attention and march on."—"Oh, father, I am looking at my little white cat, which is sitting up on the roof and wants to say goodbye to me." The mother said: "oh, fool, that is not your little cat, that is the morning sun which is shining on the chimney." But Hansel had not been looking at the little cat, but had every time thrown one of the shiny pebbles from his pocket onto the path.

When they had come to the middle of the forest, the father said, "now collect wood, children, I will start a fire, so that we don't freeze." Hansel and Gretel gathered firewood together, as high as a little mountain. Then they lit it, and when the flames burned very high the mother said: "now lie down by the fire and sleep, we will cut wood in the forest, wait until we come back and fetch you."

Hansel and Gretel sat by the fire until noon, when they both ate their little piece of bread, and then still till evening; but father and mother were not there, and no one would come and fetch them. As the night became black dark Gretel began to weep, but Hansel said: "wait a little while until the moon has risen." And when the moon had risen, he grasped Gretel by the hand, there were the pebbles like newly minted silver pennies, shining and showing him the way. Then they walked the whole night and when it was morning arrived back at their father's house. The father was heartily glad, when he saw his children again, because he had not wanted to leave them alone, the mother also pretended that she was glad, but secretly she was angry.

Not long afterward, there was again no bread in the house, and Hansel and Gretel heard the mother saying to the father: "the children found their way back once, and I let it be so; but now there is nothing but a half a loaf of bread in the house, tomorrow you must take them deeper into the forest, so that they don't come home again, otherwise there is no longer any help for us." The husband felt sad about it, and he thought, yet it would be better if you shared your last mouthful with your children, but because he had done it once, he could not say no. Hansel and Gretel heard the conversation of their parents; Hansel got up and wanted to collect pebbles again, but when he got to the door, the mother had bolted it. He still comforted Gretel and said: "just sleep, dear Gretel, the good lord will help us."

The next morning they got their little piece of bread, still smaller than the last time. On the way Hansel crumbled it in his pocket, often stood still, and threw a crumb onto the ground. "Why are you always standing, Hansel, and looking round you, said the father, come along." "Oh, I am looking at my little dove, it is sitting on the roof and wants to say goodbye to me."—"You fool, said the mother, that is not your little dove, that is the morning sun that is shining up above on the roof." But Hansel crumbled all his bread and threw the crumbs onto the path.

But the mother took them even deeper into the forest, where they had not been in all their days, there they were to go to sleep again by a great fire, and in the evening the parents would come and fetch them. At noon Gretel shared her bread with Hansel because he had strewn all of his on the path; noon and then the evening passed, but no one came to the poor children. Hansel comforted Gretel and said: "wait, when the moon rises, I'll see the crumbs of bread which I have scattered, they will show us the way home." The moon rose, but when Hansel looked for the crumbs, they had gone, the many thousand little birds in the forest had found them and pecked them up. Hansel still thought he could find the way home and pulled Gretel along with him, but they soon got lost in the great wilderness and walked the night and the whole day, then they fell asleep from weariness; and walked another day, but they did not get out of the forest, and were so hungry, because they had nothing to eat but a few little berries which were on the ground.

On the third day they walked again until midday, then they came to a little house, which was built completely of bread and covered with cake, and the windows were of pure sugar. "We'll sit down there and eat our fill, said Hansel; I'll eat some of the roof, you eat some of the window, Gretel, that is deliciously sweet for you." Hansel had already eaten a good piece of the roof and Gretel a few round windowpanes, and was just breaking out another, when they heard a delicate voice calling out from inside:

> "nibble, nibble, gnaw,
> who is nibbling at my little house?"

Hansel and Gretel were so frightened, that they let fall what they held in their hands, and imediately afterwards they saw a small, very old woman creep out of the door. She shook her head and said: "well, you dear children, where have you come from, come in with me, you'll be alright," took both of them by the hand and led them into her little house. Then a good meal was prepared, milk and pancakes with sugar, apples and nuts, and then two nice little beds were made, then Hansel and Gretel put themselves into them, and thought they were in heaven.

The old woman, however, was a wicked witch, who lay in wait for children and had built her little house of bread to tempt them, and whenever one of them got into her power, she killed it, cooked it, and ate it, and that was for her a day to celebrate. And so she was very happy when Hansel and Gretel came in her direction. Early, before they had yet awoken, she got up, went to their little beds, and when she saw the two resting so sweetly, she was glad and thought, that will be a nice morsel for you. She seized Hansel and put him in a little stable, and when he awoke there, he was surrounded by iron bars, just as young chickens are penned in, and could only walk a few steps. But she shook Gretel and cried: "get up, you lazy-bones, fetch water and go into the kitchen, and cook good food,—your brother is there in a stable, I'll make him fat first, and when he is fat, I will eat him, now you shall feed him." Gretel was frightened and wept, but had to do what the witch demanded. Every day the best food was cooked for Hansel, so that he should get fat, but Gretel got nothing but crab-shells and every day the old woman came and said: "Hansel, stick your finger out so that I can feel if you are already fat enough." But Hansel always stuck out a little bone for her, then she was puzzled that he would not put on weight.

After four weeks she said one evening to Gretel: "be lively, go and carry water here, whether your little brother is now fat enough or not, tomorrow I will slaughter and boil him, meanwhile I will prepare the dough, so that we can also bake as well." Then Gretel went sad at heart and carried the water, in which Hansel was to be boiled. Early next morning Gretel had to get up, make a fire, and hang the cauldron full of water. "Pay attention until it boils, said the witch, I will light the fire in the oven and push the bread inside;" Gretel stood in the kitchen and wept bloody tears and thought, rather the wild animals in the forest should have eaten us, then we should have died together and would not have to suffer this sorrow, and I should not have to boil the water for the death of my dear brother, dear God, help us poor children out of this distress.

Then the old woman cried: "Gretel, come here at once to the oven," when Gretel came, she said: "look inside, see if the bread is already nicely brown and done, my eyes are weak, I can't see very far, and if you can't either, sit on the board, and I will push you in, then you can move around inside and look." But when Gretel was inside, she wanted to shut it and Gretel was to bake in the hot oven, and she wanted to eat her up too: that was what the wicked witch was thinking, and that was why she had called Gretel. But God inspired Gretel and she said: "I don't know how I should begin to do that, show me first, sit on it yourself, I will push you in." And the old woman sat on the board, and because she was light, Gretel pushed her in as far as she could, and then she quickly shut the door, and bolted it with the iron bolt. Then the old woman began to scream and wail in the hot oven, but Gretel ran off, and she had to burn to death wretchedly.

And Gretel ran to Hansel, opened his little door for him and Hansel jumped out, and they kissed each other and were happy. The whole little house was full of jewels and pearls, they filled their pockets of them, went off and found the way home. The father was joyful to see them again, he had not had one happy day since his children had gone, and now became a rich man. But the mother was dead.

SECOND EDITION

In front of a large forest lived a poor woodcutter who had nothing to eat and scarcely daily bread for his wife and his two children, Hansel and Gretel. Finally there came a time when he could not even get that, and could no longer see any help for his plight. As he was tossing and turning in bed in the evening because of his worries, his wife said to him: "listen husband, tomorrow morning take both the children, give each one a little piece of bread, then take them out into the forest, right in, where it is thickest, make them a fire, and then go away and leave them alone there, we cannot feed them any longer." "No, wife, said the husband, I cannot find it in my heart to bring my own dear children to the wild animals in the forest, who would soon have torn them apart." "Well, if you don't do it, said the wife, we shall

all have to die of hunger together;" and left him no peace, until he agreed.

The two children had also still been awake through hunger, and had listened to what the mother had said to the father. Gretel thought, now it's all up with us, and began to weep pitifully but Hansel said: "be quiet, Gretel, and don't grieve, I will help us." With that he got up, put on his little coat, opened the door below, and slipped out. The moon was shining brightly and the white pebbles shone like silver pennies. Hansel bent down and put as many in his little coat pocket as would go in, then he went back into the house. "Console yourself, Gretel, and just sleep peacefully," he said, got into bed again and went to sleep.

Early next morning, still before the sun had risen, the mother came and woke them both: "get up, you children, we will go into the forest; there is a little piece of bread for each of you, but save it and keep it for lunch. Gretel took the bread under her apron, because Hansel had the stones in his pocket, then they set out to go into the forest. When they had walked for a little while, Hansel stood still and looked back at the house, soon after that once more, and again and again. The father said: "Hansel, why are you looking back and stopping, pay attention and pick up your feet."—"Oh, father, I am looking at my little white cat, it is sitting up on the roof and wants to say goodbye to me." The mother said "oh, fool, that's not your little cat, that is the morning sun which is shining on the chimney." But Hansel had not been looking at the little cat, but had every time thrown one of the white pebbles from his pocket onto the path.

When they had come to the middle of the forest, the father said, "now collect wood, children, I will start a fire so that we don't freeze." Hansel and Gretel gathered firewood together, as high as a little mountain. Then they lit it, and when the flames burned very high, the mother said: "now lie down by the fire and sleep, we will cut wood in the forest, wait, until we come back and fetch you."

Hansel and Gretel sat by the fire until noon when both ate their little piece of bread; they believed that the father was still in the forest, because they heard the blows of his axe, but it was only a bough that he had tied to a tree and that the wind blew back and forth. Now they waited until evening, but father and mother were not there, and no one would come and fetch them. As the night became black dark Gretel began to weep, but Hansel said: "wait a little while until the moon has risen. And when the moon had risen, he grasped Gretel by the hand, there were the pebbles, shining like newly minted silver pennies and showing them the way. Then they walked the whole night and when it was morning they arrived back at their father's house. The father was heartily glad when he saw his children again, because it had pained him to leave them alone, the mother also pretended that she was glad, but secretly she was angry.

Not long afterward, there was again no bread in the house, and Hansel and Gretel heard the mother saying to the father: "the children found their way back once, and I let it be so; but now there is again nothing but a half a loaf of bread in the house, tomorrow you must take them deeper into the forest so that they don't find their way back, otherwise there is no longer any help for us." The husband felt sad about it, and he thought, yet it would be better if you shared your last mouthful with your children, but because he had done it once, he could not say no. When the children had heard the conversation, Hansel got up and wanted to collect pebbles again, but when he got to the door, the mother had bolted it. He still comforted Gretel and said: "just sleep, dear Gretel, the good Lord will help us."

The next morning they got their little piece of bread, still smaller than the last time. On the way Hansel crumbled it in his pocket, often stood still, and threw a crumb on the ground. "Why are you always standing, Hansel, and looking round you, said the father, come along."—"Oh, I am looking at my little dove, it is sitting on the roof and wants to say goodbye to me."—"You fool, said the mother, that is not your little dove, that is the morning sun that is shining up above on the roof." But Hansel crumbled all his bread and threw the crumbs onto the path.

The mother took them even deeper into the forest, where they had not been in all their days, there they were again to sit and sleep by a great fire, and the parents were to come and fetch them in the evening. At noon Gretel shared her bread with Hansel because he had strewn all of his on the path, but noon and then the evening passed, and no one came to the poor children. Hansel comforted Gretel and said: "wait, when the moon rises, I'll see the crumbs of bread which I have scattered, they will show us the way home." The moon rose, but when Hansel looked for the crumbs, they had gone, the many thousand little birds in the forest had found them and pecked them up. Hansel still thought he could find the way home and pulled Gretel along with him, but they soon got lost in the great wilderness and walked the night and the whole day, then they fell asleep from weariness. Then they walked another day, but they did not get out of the forest, and were so hungry, because they had nothing to eat but a few little berries which were on the ground.

When they had walked until midday on the third day, they came to a little house, which was built completely of bread and covered with cake, and the windows were of pure sugar. "We'll sit down and eat our fill, said Hansel: I'll eat some of the roof, you eat some of the window, Gretel, that is deliciously sweet for you." As Gretel nibbled at the sugar, there called inside a delicate voice:

> "nibble, nibble, gnaw
> who is nibbling at my little house?"

The children answered:

> "the wind! the wind!
> the heavenly child!"

And continued eating. Gretel broke out a whole round window-pane for herself, and Hansel tore off a mighty piece of cake from the roof for himself. Then the door opened, and a very old woman came creeping out. Hansel and Gretel were startled so badly, that they let fall what they had in their hands. The old woman, however, shook her head and said: "well, you dear children, where have you come from, come in with me, you'll be all right," took both of them by the hand and led them into her little house. Then a good meal was served, milk and pancakes with sugar, apples and nuts, and then two nice little beds were made, then Hansel and Gretel put themselves into them, and thought they were in heaven.

The old woman, however, was a wicked witch, who lay in wait for children and had built her little house of bread to tempt them, and whenever one of them got into her power, she killed it, cooked it, and ate it, and that was for her a day to celebrate. And so she was very happy, when Hansel and Gretel came in her direction. Early, before they had yet awoken, she got up, went to their little beds, and when she saw the two resting so sweetly, she was glad and murmured: "that will be a nice morsel for me." Then she seized Hansel and put him in a little stable, when he now awoke, he was surrounded by iron bars, just as young chickens are penned in, and could only walk a few steps. But she shook Gretel and cried: "get up, you lazy-bones, fetch water and go into the kitchen and cook something good to eat, your brother is there in a stable, I'll make him fat first, and when he is fat, I will eat him, now you shall feed him. Gretel was frightened and wept, but had to do what the witch demanded. Every day the best food was now cooked for Hansel, so that he should get fat, but Gretel got nothing but the crab-shells and every day the old woman came and said: "Hansel, stick your finger out, so that I can feel if you are already fat enough." But Hansel always stuck out a little bone for her, then she was puzzled that he would not put on weight.

After four weeks she said one evening to Gretel: "be lively, go and carry water here, whether your little brother is now fat or not, to-morrow I will slaughter and boil him, meanwhile I will prepare the dough, so that we can also bake as well." Then Gretel went sad at heart and carried the water in which Hansel was to be boiled. Early next morning Gretel had to get up, make a fire, and hang the cauldron full of water. "Pay attention, said the witch, I will light the fire in the oven and push the bread inside;" Gretel stood in the kitchen and wept bloody tears and thought, rather the wild animals in the forest should have eaten us, then we should have died together and would not have to suffer this sorrow, and I should not have had to boil the water for the death of my dear brother; "dear God, help us poor children out of this distress."

Then the old woman cried: "Gretel, come here at once to the oven," when Gretel came, she said: "look inside, see if the bread is already nicely brown and done, my eyes are weak, I can't see very far, and if you can't either, sit on the board, and I will push you in, then you can move around inside and look." But when Gretel was inside, she wanted to shut it and Gretel was to bake in the hot oven, and she wanted to eat her up too; that was what the wicked witch was thinking, and that was why she had called Gretel. But God inspired the girl to say: "I don't know how I should begin to do that, show me first, and sit on it yourself and I will push you in." Then the old woman sat on the board, and because she was light, Gretel pushed her in as far as she could, and then quickly shut the door and bolted it with the iron bolt. Now the old woman began to scream and wail in the hot oven, but Gretel ran off, and she had to burn to death wretchedly.

Then Gretel ran to Hansel, opened his little door for him and cried: "jump out, Hansel, we are saved!" Then Hansel jumped out like a little caged bird out of his cage. And they wept for joy and kissed each other. But the whole little house was full of jewels and pearls, they filled their pockets with them, went off and looked for the way home. They came to a great stretch of water, however, and could not get across. Then the little sister saw a little white duck swimming to and fro, and cried to it: "oh, dear little duck, take us on your back." When the little duck heard that it came swimming and carried Gretel over and after that it fetched Hansel as well. After that they soon found their home country, the father was heartily glad when he saw them again, for he had not had one happy day, since his children had gone. The mother, however, was dead. Now the children brought an abundance of riches with them, and they no longer needed to worry about their food and drink.

FIFTH EDITION

In front of a large forest lived a poor woodcutter with his wife and his two children; the little boy was called Hansel and the little girl Gretel. He had little to eat, and once when great need arose in the land, he could no longer even get his daily bread. As he was thinking about things in the evening in bed, and was tossing and turning because of his worries, he sighed and said to his wife "what will become of us? how can we feed our poor children, when we have no more for ourselves?" "Do you know what, husband," answered the wife, "we shall take the children out into the forest tomorrow very early, to where it is at its most dense, we'll make a fire for them there and give each one a little piece of bread, then we'll go to our work, and leave them alone. They will not find their way back home again, and we shall be rid of them." "No, wife," said the husband, "I won't do that; how could I find it in my heart to leave my children alone in the forest, the wild animals would soon come and tear them apart." "Oh, you fool," she said, "then we shall all four have to die of hunger, you can just smooth the boards for the coffins," and gave him no peace until he agreed. "But I still feel sorry for the poor children," said the husband.

The two children, however, had not been able to go to sleep for hunger, and had heard what the stepmother had said to the father. Gretel wept bitter tears, and said to Hansel "now it's all up with us." "Quiet, Gretel," said Hansel, "don't grieve, I will help us." And when the grown-ups had gone to sleep, he got up, put on his little coat, opened the door below, and crept out. The moon was shining quite brightly, and the white pebbles which were in front of the house shone like silver pennies. Hansel bent down and put as many in his little coat pocket as would go in. Then he went back again, said to Gretel "be comforted, dear little sister, and go to sleep in peace, God will not forsake us," and got into his bed again.

When the day broke, still before the sun had risen, the wife came and woke both the children, "get up, you lazy-bones, we will go into the forest and fetch wood." Then she gave each one a little piece of bread, and said "there is something for lunch, but don't eat it up before that, you will get nothing more." Gretel took the bread under her apron, because Hansel had the stones in his pocket. Then they all set out together for the forest. After they had walked for a little while, Hansel stood still, and looked back at the house, and did it again and again. The father said "Hansel, why are you looking there, and lagging behind, pay attention and don't forget to use your legs." "Oh, father," said Hansel, "I'm looking at my little white cat, it is sitting up on the roof and wants to say goodbye to me." The wife said "fool, that is not your little cat, that is the morning sun shining on the chimney." But Hansel had not been looking at the little cat, but had every time thrown one of the white pebbles from his pocket onto the path.

When they had come to the middle of the forest, the father said "now collect wood, you children, I will start a fire so that you don't freeze." Hansel and Gretel gathered firewood together, as high as a little mountain. This was lit, and when the fire burned very high, the wife said "now lie down by the fire, you children, and rest, we are going into the forest to cut wood. When we are finished, we will come back again and fetch you.

Hansel and Gretel sat by the fire, and when noon came, they both ate their little pieces of bread. And because they heard the blows of the axe, they believed that their father was nearby. But it was not the axe, it was a bough which he had tied to a dead tree and which the wind blew back and forth. And when they had sat in this way for a very long time, their eyes fell shut in tiredness, and they fell asleep, when they woke up it was already black night. Gretel began to weep and said "how are we to get out of the forest." Hansel however comforted her, "just wait a little while until the moon has risen, then we'll find the way." And when the full moon had risen, Hansel took his little sister by the hand, and went towards the pebbles, which shone like newly minted silver pennies, and showed them the way. They walked through the whole night; and came again to their father's house as day was breaking. They knocked at the door, and as the wife opened it, and saw that it was Hansel and Gretel, she said: "You wicked children, why have you slept so long in the forest, we thought you would not come back at all." The father, however, was pleased because he had been sad that he had left them behind so alone.

Not long afterward, there was distress everywhere, and the children heard how the mother said to the father in bed at night "everything has been eaten up again, we still have a half loaf of bread, after that the song is over. The children must go, we shall lead them deeper into the forest, so that they don't find their way out again; otherwise there is no escape for us." The husband felt sad about it, and he thought "it would be better that you shared your last mouthful with your children." But the wife did not listen to anything that he said, chided him and reproached him. If someone begins something, they have to continue, and because he had given in once, he had to do it again.

The children, however, had still been awake, and had listened to the conversation. And when the grown-ups had gone to sleep, Hansel got up, wanted to go out and pick up pebbles, like the last time, but the wife had bolted the door and Hansel could not get out. But he comforted his little sister, and said "don't weep, Gretel, and sleep peacefully, the good Lord will help us."

Early the next day the wife came and fetched the children from their bed. They received their little piece of bread, which was however even smaller than the last time. On the way to the forest Hansel crumbled it in his pocket, often stood still, and threw a crumb onto the ground. "Hansel, why are you standing there, and looking round you," said the father, "come along." "I am looking for my little dove, it is sitting on the roof and wants to say goodbye to me," answered Hansel. "Fool," said the wife, "that is not your little dove, that is the morning sun that is shining up above on the chimney." But gradually Hansel threw all the little pieces onto the path.

The wife led the children even deeper into the forest, where they had not been in all their days. Then a great fire was made again, and the mother said "just stay sitting there children, and when you are tired, you can sleep a little, we are going into the forest to cut wood, and in the evening when we are finished we'll come and fetch you." When it was noon, Gretel shared her bread with Hansel, who had strewn his piece on the path. Then they fell asleep, and the evening passed, but no one came to the poor children. They did not awake until it was black night, and Hansel comforted his little sister and said, "just wait, Gretel, until the moon rises, then we'll see the crumbs of bread which I have scattered, they will show us the way home. When the moon came, they got up, but they didn't find any crumbs left, because the many thousand birds which fly in the forest and the fields had pecked them all away. Hansel said to Gretel "we'll soon find the way," but they didn't find it. They walked the whole night and another day from morning to evening, but they didn't get out of the forest and were very hungry, for they had nothing but the few berries that were on the ground. And because they were so tired that their legs would not carry them any longer, they lay down under a tree, and went to sleep.

It was now the third morning since they had left their father's house. They began to walk again, but they only got deeper and deeper into the forest. When it was noon, they saw a beautiful snow-white little bird sitting on a bough, which sang so beautifully that they stood still and listened to it. Then it flapped its wings, and flew in front of them, and they followed it, then they saw that it alighted on a little house, and as they came up to it, they saw that the little house was completely made out of bread and covered with cake, but the windows were of pure sugar. "We'll start on that," said Hansel, "and have a good meal. I'll eat a piece of the roof, Gretel, you eat some of the window, it's sweet." Hansel reached up high, and broke off a piece of the roof, to see how it tasted, and Gretel went to the panes and nibbled at them. Then a delicate voice called out of the room,

> "nibble, nibble, gnaw
> who is nibbling at my little house?"

the children answered,

> "the wind, the wind,
> the heavenly child,"

and continued eating without letting themselves be put out. Hansel, who liked the taste of the roof, pulled down a large piece of it, and Gretel picked out a whole round window pane, sat down with it, and enjoyed it. Then suddenly the door opened and a very old woman who leaned on a crutch came creeping out. Hansel and Gretel were startled so badly, that they let fall what they had in their hands. The old woman, however, shook her head and said, "well, you dear children, who brought you here? just come in and stay with me, you'll be all right." She took both of them by the hand and led them into her little house. Then a good meal was served, milk and pancakes with sugar, apples and nuts. After that two nice little beds were made with white covers, and Hansel and Gretel put themselves into them, and thought they were in heaven.

The old woman had only pretended to be so kind, she was a wicked witch, who lay in wait for children, and she had only built the little house of bread to lure them there. If one got into her power, she killed it, cooked it, and ate it, and that was for her a day to celebrate. When Hansel and Gretel had come near to the house, she had laughed wickedly, and cried out scornfully "they shall not escape me." Early in the morning, before the children had awoken, she got up, and when she saw both sleep so sweetly, with full red cheeks, she murmured to herself, "that will be a nice morsel." Then she seized Hansel with her thin hand, and carried him into a little stable. No matter how he screamed, it didn't help him; she locked him in with an iron-barred door, and then went to Gretel, jolted her awake, and cried "will you get up, lazy-bones, you shall fetch water and cook something good for your brother, he is in the stable and must get fat. And when he is fat, I'll eat him." Gretel began to weep bitterly, but all was in vain, she had to do what the wicked witch demanded.

Now the best food was cooked for poor Hansel, but Gretel got nothing but crab-shells. Every morning the old woman crept up to the little stable, and cried "Hansel, stick your fingers out, in order that I can feel if you are already fat." But Hansel stuck out a little bone for her, and the old woman, whose eyes were dim, could not see it, and thought it was Hansel's finger, and was puzzled that he wouldn't get fat at all. When four weeks had passed by, and Hansel still stayed thin, she was overtaken by impatience and would not wait any longer. "Hey, Gretel," she cried to the girl, "be lively and carry water: whether Hansel is fat or thin, tomorrow I will slaughter and boil him. Oh, how the poor little sister lamented when she had to carry water, and how the tears flowed down her cheeks! "Dear God, help us," she cried out, "if only the wild animals in the forest had eaten us, we should still have died together." "Just stop your noise," said the old woman, "all that won't help you."

Early next morning Gretel had to go out, hang the cauldron full of water, and light the fire. "First, we'll bake," said the old woman, "I have already heated the oven and kneaded the dough." She pushed Gretel out to the oven, out of which the flames were already coming. "Crawl inside," said the witch, "and see if it is well heated, so that we can shove the bread inside." And when Gretel was inside, she was going to shut the oven, and Gretel was to roast inside, and then she wanted to eat her too. But Gretel saw what she had in mind, and said "I don't know how to do that; how do I get in?" "Silly goose," said the old woman, "the opening is big enough, look now, I could get in myself" scuttled up to it and stuck her head in the oven. Then Gretel gave her a push, so that she went right inside, shut the iron door and bolted it. Whoo! then she began to howl, quite horribly; but Gretel ran off, and the godless witch had to burn to death wretchedly.

Gretel, however, ran straight away to Hansel, opened his little stable, and cried "Hansel, we are saved, the old witch is dead." Then Hansel jumped out, like a bird out of the cage when the door is opened. How they rejoiced, jumped up and down, and kissed each other. And because they did not need to be afraid any more, they went into the witch's house, there stood boxes of pearls and jewels everywhere. "These are much better than pebbles" said Hansel, and put as much in his pockets as would go in and Gretel said "I too want to take something home," and filled her little apron full. "But now we must go," said Hansel, "so that we get out of the witch's forest." When they had walked a few hours, however, they came to a large stretch of water. "We can't get across," said Hansel, "I can't see a footpath or a bridge."

"There won't be any little ship either," said Gretel, "but there is a white duck swimming, if I ask, it will help us across." Then she cried:

> "Little duck, little duck,
> here are Gretel and Hansel.
> No footpath and no bridge,
> take us on your little white back."

The little duck came to them, and Hansel got on it, and told his little sister to sit next him. "No," answered Gretel, "that will be too heavy for the little duck, it shall take us over one after the other." The good little animal did this, and when they were safely across, and had walked a little while, the forest seemed more and more familiar, and at last they saw from afar their father's house. Then they began to run, burst into the room and embraced their father. The husband had not had a joyful moment, since he had left his children in the forest, but the wife had died. Gretel shook out her little apron, so that the pearls and jewels bounced around in the room, and Hansel threw after them one handful after another out of his pockets. Then all their troubles were at an end, and they lived together in pure happiness. My tale is at an end, there runs a mouse, who catches it can make himself a big, big fur cap out of it.

Notes

For bibliographic details, see Works Cited, below.

CHAPTER ONE

1. *Kinder- und Hausmärchen, Gesammelt durch die Brüder Grimm,* 2 vols. (Berlin, 1812 and 1815). The six subsequent editions of the Grimms' collection supervised by them were published in 1819, 1837, 1840, 1843, 1850 and 1857 respectively. The second and third editions (1819 and 1837) contained a third volume in addition to the two volumes of all the other editions; this third volume contains notes to the tales, and the dates of these volumes are 1822 (second edition) and 1856 (third edition) respectively. In the first edition, much briefer notes had been included at the end of each of the two volumes. Because of the long delay in the issue of the third edition's third volume, it became virtually a part of the seventh edition. In the course of this study, I cite the text of the first edition of the *KHM* as reprinted in *Die Kinder- und Hausmärchen der Brüder Grimm. Vollständige Ausgabe in der Urfassung,* edited by Friedrich Panzer (Wiesbaden, 1953), itself virtually a reprint of his earlier edition in two volumes (Munich, 1913), apart from new material in the introduction. A thorough and detailed analysis of the differences in the gross contents of the various editions (stories added or subtracted; different prefaces, etc.) can be found in Crane 1917.

2. Johann Gottfried Herder, "Auszug aus einem Briefwechsel über Ossian und die Lieder alter Völker," in Herder 1773. I cite this essay in the edition by Heinz Kindermann, in the series *Deutsche Literatur: Reihe Irrationalismus,* 6 (Darmstadt, 1968), 149–89.

3. I cite Musäus's *Volksmärchen der Deutschen* in the edition of the Winkler-Verlag (Munich, 1961), here p. 13. This edition erroneously gives the dates of Musäus's *Volksmärchen* as 1782–86, probably because Musäus published the tales in five volumes at the rate of one a year, and that would seem to indicate 1782–

86 as the correct dates. However, Musäus missed a year (1785); the dates of the five volumes were 1782, 1783, 1784, 1786 and 1787.

4. "Über Ossian," Herder 1773, p. 168.

5. Reed 1972, p. 520.

6. From the anonymous preface of the *Grimm's Fairy Tales* (Anon. 1968).

7. Rölleke 1975b. See also Rölleke 1977. See chapters 3 and 4 of the present work for discussion of this material.

8. Michaelis-Jena 1970; Gerstner 1970; Peppard 1971; Denecke 1971. The justification for the summary statements on these works and others made in this introductory chapter will emerge during the rest of my study.

9. Campbell 1944, pp. 834–35. In her original translator's preface to the 1901 edition, Margaret Hunt had written that "they wrote down every story exactly as they heard it."

10. Opie and Opie 1974, p. 26.

11. Ibid., p. 27.

12. Michaelis-Jena 1971, pp. 265, 268.

13. Dégh 1979, p. 87.

14. Ludwig Denecke, "Grimm Brothers," in *The New Encyclopaedia Britannica*, 15th ed., *Macropaedia* 8 (1980): 427–29.

15. Martini 1955, p. 322.

16. Robertson 1953, p. 457.

17. Louis L. Snyder (1951) proceeded to investigate their significance, given this assumption. He found in them "many sentiments typical of German nationalism . . . which . . . existed among the old peasants, nurses, and workers from whom the Grimms obtained their material" (p. 216). This conclusion, too, is based on misconception; in chapter 6 I consider the conclusions Snyder draws from his analysis of the *KHM*.

18. Cocchiara 1981, p. 231.

19. Opie and Opie 1974, p. 26; Michaelis-Jena 1971, p. 266. See also Michaelis-Jena 1970, p. 52: "They wrote down the stories as close to the original as possible, including peculiarities of the teller's turn of phrase and speech."

20. Gerstner 1970, p. 92.

21. Schmidt 1931, p. 81. For a similar view, see Panzer 1953, p. 50. Also Michaelis-Jena 1970, p. 52: they were "purely scientific within the limits of their time."

22. Gerstner 1970, p. 92.

23. The account of the development of German literature given at the beginning of this chapter is unavoidably brief and schematic; the reader should be mindful of the fact that the generalizations offered there, while justified as such, have the limitations of all generalizations. A fuller account would have to deal with exceptions and special cases, but for such a treatment the reader is referred to the standard histories of German literature.

CHAPTER TWO

1. Panzer 1953, p. 61.

2. Ibid., p. 62.

3. Ibid., pp. 341–42.

4. Schumann 1977, p. 138.

5. Rölleke 1980, 3:601. The most that Rölleke can bring himself to acknowledge (p. 599) is that these facts "were until now little known. . . . Not least of
the reasons for this is that the Grimms did not allow any glimpse into their
workshop." This statement glosses over two uncomfortable truths: first, that the
facts had been in print and ignored for a very long time; second, that the Grimms
were *not* silent about their procedures, as Rölleke suggests, but instead had given
a very clear and utterly false account of what happened in their workshop. They
had not simply prevented a look at how they worked in the sense that they
wished to have nothing known on that subject at all; they had instead prevented
anyone from seeing that their published descriptions of what went on in their
workshop were fraudulent misdescriptions of what happened there.

6. I cite the second edition from one of the few remaining copies (in the
Harvard University Library): *Kinder- und Hausmärchen. Gesammelt durch die
Brüder Grimm.* Zweite vermehrte und verbesserte Ausgabe. 2 vols. (Berlin,
1819). The preface is pp. v–xx.

7. Details of these opinions are considered in chapter 4, where their adequacy
is also measured against the actual evidence of the extent of the Grimms' rewriting of their source material.

8. An extreme of unwillingness to see the contradiction between the two prefaces in the case of Gerstner (1970, p. 93), who cites the key parts of the two
different programmatic statements as if they were part of the same statement,
made at the same time, and simply setting out two sides of the same intent.

9. Examples (at random) are Opie and Opie 1974, p. 26; and Panzer 1953, p.
50.

10. Carsch 1968, p. 469.

11. Schoof 1941, p. 191.

12. E.g., Bolte 1915, p. 31: "While Jacob at first asserted the scientific necessity
of reproducing the texts . . . unaltered and uncorrupted, later on Wilhelm's
artistic sense prevailed . . ."; Michaelis-Jena 1971, p. 267; Panzer 1953, p. 47: "If
Jacob had shaped the Tales, they would have looked radically different"; also
Gerstner 1970, pp. 92–93.

13. W. Grimm, *Kleinere Schriften*, 4 vols. (1881–87). Jacob's *Kleinere Schriften*
are a separate publication in 8 vols. (1864–84). Crane (1917, p. 153) even spec-
ulates that it was the preface of the second edition that was the *joint* work of the
brothers, not the first, since the second was not reprinted in the *Kleinere Schriften*
of either brother. This fact, if true, would undermine the theory under discussion
even further, though Crane does not draw this conclusion from his speculation.
But he is very likely incorrect here; the substantial duplication of the two prefaces
(apart from the key passages that were altered) is what probably prevented
republication of the second preface.

14. First in Ginschel 1963; later, in a more elaborate account, in Ginschel 1967.

15. Rölleke (1980, 3:604), for example, is clearly not convinced; he thinks that
Jacob and Wilhelm took different positions regarding the charge made by their
friends that the first edition was unfit for children, and that Wilhelm's editing
of the second and subsequent editions shows this. But in fact (see present volume,
chapter 4) the changes introduced by the brothers into the first edition are very
much the same kind of changes introduced into the later editions. Here Rölleke
expresses an important part of the traditional defense of the integrity of the
first edition—a strange thing for him to do after having reissued the 1810

manuscript material which shows that defense to be untenable. Denecke (1971, p. 71), and Peppard (1971, p. 69), however, picked up and stated the point of Ginschel's work; cf. the latter: "It was not only Wilhelm who felt free to alter his informants' versions, for Jacob agreed with him and cooperated in writing up the account they obtained."

CHAPTER THREE

1. Panzer 1913, p. 59.
2. Details are conveniently and well set out in Rölleke's edition (1975b), but they had been available in print well before this in the revision and updating of the notes to the *KHM* by Bolte and Polivka (1913–32). Wilhelm Schoof, too, had made the main facts available (1959). It is true, however, that in one important respect the information available from these sources became contaminated with the myth of the figure of "die alte Marie," which Herman Grimm created, and which is discussed below.
3. Peppard 1971, p. 51.
4. Schumann 1977, p. 137.
5. Rölleke 1975a, p. 75. After giving his own explanation, however, Rölleke himself seems to acknowledge its incompleteness: "In any case, the Grimms were not prepared to communicate anything more to the public about their sources." Yet in his 1980 edition of the earliest printed version of the *KHM*, Rölleke still repeated his old argument, if anything in an even less convincing form: "Accordingly [i.e. because of stress on the collective tradition] it could not really have mattered to them to display their informant in each case" (p. 579). Now Rölleke tries to make the whole matter of individuals one of indifference to the Grimms, and to see their behavior as rather nonchalant. But people who actually mislead their readers and misdescribe the nature of the informants are not behaving casually—they are showing that something *does* matter to them.
6. Herman Grimm 1895.
7. Michaelis-Jena 1970, p. 48.
8. Peppard 1971, p. 51.
9. Gerstner 1970, p. 87.
10. Ibid., p. 91.
11. Rölleke 1975a.
12. Details in ibid., pp. 78–79. Here Rölleke also (p. 79) marvels at the way in which Herman's identification of Marie has survived for so long without contradiction, but still avoids any attempt to give an explanation for this strange fact other than Herman Grimm's authority as Wilhelm's son.
13. Textor 1955. Oddly enough, Textor published the same material again, exactly ten years later (1965). Yet this time he omitted the passages cited below which repeat the old clichés about Dorothea Viehmann. Perhaps by 1965 he had begun to realize that his material did not allow those clichés to be repeated any longer, and his republication of the material may also indicate that he now saw that it needed more attention than it had so far received.
14. Hagen 1955, p. 410.
15. Gerstner 1970, p. 128.
16. Schoof 1959, pp. 62–64. Schoof had actually published a study (1930) with the same title. His 1959 book is an updated version of this earlier study, and it

seems that the revelation of 1955 was simply inserted into the revised study without having any impact on its argument. This, evidently, is the reason for the contradiction noted in the text.

17. Peppard 1971, p. 65.

18. Textor 1955, pp. 10–19, is the source of the citations in this paragraph.

19. Weber-Kellermann 1970, p. 432.

20. Ibid., p. 434.

21. Cf. Friderici 1969, p. 167: "The Grimms had the Ramus daughters to thank for their acquaintance with Frau Viehmann . . . the daughters of Pastor Charles François Ramus, second preacher of the Oberneustadt French community in Cassel."

22. Schumann 1977, p. 138; Dégh 1979, p. 86: "As Rölleke has pointed out, she came 'directly from a Huguenot family' . . ."; McGlathery 1977, p. 94: "Thus Rölleke notes that Dorothea Viehmann . . . was in reality . . . descended from a French Huguenot family and had grown up speaking French."

CHAPTER FOUR

1. There is one relatively small qualification to be made to this statement: the collection was expanded somewhat in the later editions, so that a few new stories that had been collected after the appearance of the first edition were included in the final *KHM* collection. The "Nachlaß" manuscript collection contains some material relevant to these added stories, though, to judge from Rölleke's published selection (1977), not very much. For example, of 48 items published here by Rölleke, only three (numbers 19, 20 and 21) relate to the stories added in the late *KHM* editions (numbers 171 and 173 from the 1840 fourth edition; number 193 from the 1843 fifth edition). These instances support the conclusions which can be derived from the evidence as to the character of the Grimms' procedure in the first edition, but in what follows I have preferred to concentrate on the first edition evidence, since cases in the later editions arise a quarter of a century later than the main body of the *KHM,* and a conceivable (though, I should argue, not actual) change in the Grimms' procedure over so long a period of time might unnecessarily complicate my argument. The evidence relating to the first edition is by itself sufficient to establish the conclusions that follow in my text.

2. Just how distorted situations can become in the eyes of writers on the Grimms can be seen in the case of Antoine Faivre (1978, p. 9), who first reports the destruction of their manuscript material by the Grimms, but without comment or judgment, and then twice in three sentences attacks the "negligence" of Brentano in not returning his copies to the Grimms. This display of disapproval toward Brentano rather than the Grimms can only seem completely misdirected: Brentano merely failed to return papers which he received in late 1810, and which by 1812, when the *KHM* were published, he could easily consider to be no longer of use to the Grimms; the Grimms themselves destroyed an indispensable set of records to protect their deception.

3. It is, however, fairly clear that the 1810 manuscripts sent to Brentano take precedence over the manuscripts that they kept; that is, the *copies* which the brothers had made of the material that they had collected by 1810 were kept by them, while the material from which those copies were made was sent to

Brentano. This is almost certainly the conclusion that must be drawn from the survival in the Grimms' papers of four tales identical to four in the Brentano material—these being four *not* used by the Grimms in preparing the *KHM* first edition. Obviously the brothers saw no problem in preserving material which could not be compared to *KHM* printed texts—further confirmation that the destruction of the rest of the 1810 material was deliberate, not accidental. The uniformity and quality of the copies of these four tales suggests the work of a professional copyist. Cf. Rölleke 1978.

4. Schulz 1924; Lefftz 1927; Lemmer 1964; Rölleke 1975b. One indicator of the general neglect of the two earliest of these editions is frequent erroneous reference to them; for example, Faivre (1978, p. 10) sets the earliest publication of the 1810 material at 1928, Peppard (1971, pp. 46–47) at 1929, Dégh (1979) at 1927. The correct date is of course 1924.

5. Schumann (1977), p. 139.

6. Lefftz (1927), p. 7.

7. Lemmer (1964), p. 73.

8. Tonnelat 1912, pp. 201–2.

9. Bolte 1915, p. 31.

10. All important questions were, in fact, already decided in Freitag's title *"Die Kinder- und Hausmärchen der Brüder Grimm im ersten Stadium ihrer stilgeschichtlichen Entwicklung* (1929).

11. Freitag 1929, pp. 2–4.

12. Schmidt 1931, pp. 15 and 40; Schmidt did also talk of content changes, but summarized these as "principally a work of completion," that is, of rounding out what is already there (p. 68). He specifically absolved Wilhelm of any lack of respect for the "mythological" facts; everything important was preserved as it was.

13. Schoof 1941, p. 191; of course, the theory of the differences between the two brothers should also have been abandoned long before this.

14. Michaelis-Jena 1970, p. 48.

15. Peppard 1971, pp. 47 and 69.

16. This is Rölleke's conjecture (1975b, p. 15), on the basis of various kinds of evidence, all of it reasonably solid.

17. Many have incautiously proceeded to compare the 1810 and 1812 texts *without* taking this important caveat into account. It is a great irony that Schoof (1959, p. 164) recommends a study of *Sneewittchen* in the 1810 and 1812 versions (the former "sparing with words" the latter "ornamented") in order to get a sense of Wilhelm's stylistic tendencies, for this is a case of incomparable texts.

18. The notes, at this stage very brief, were simply an appendix in each of the two volumes in the first edition; it was the expansion of the notes to form a separate volume of *Anmerkungen* in the second and third editions which brought most of the additional kind of information referred to in my text, information which had been largely absent from the notes in the first edition's appendixes.

19. Both this and the following example occur already in the notes to the first edition: Panzer 1913, pp. 312 and 310.

20. I follow the text of the 1810 manuscripts as given in Rölleke's edition (1975b).

21. Freitag (1929—e.g. pp. 13 and 39) overlooks this point in using this tale to make comparisons of the 1810 and 1812 texts.

22. The same relationship is visible when the manuscripts in the *Nachlaß* are compared to their first printed versions in the later editions; for example, *Der Zaunkönig (The Willow-Wren)* and *Der Trommler (The Drummer)* in the seventh edition of the *KHM* are about twice the length of the manuscript versions in the *Nachlaß* material (*Der Zaunkönig* and *Vom gläsernen Berg* respectively).

23. Lüthi 1973, p. 12. Lüthi's further comments rely heavily on the Grimms' second edition preface.

24. Schoof 1941, p. 190. Schoof tried in this way to see only minor tinkering with the texts (*glätten*, "smoothing," and *feilen*, "polishing"—a decidedly euphemistic way of dealing with wholesale recasting and restructuring of the texts).

25. This is obvious because the story line of the 1812 edition follows closely that of the 1810 manuscript, and the variant readings set out in the *Notes* are all quite different from either of these two texts. Winter (1962, p. 819) asserts that this tale was not among those preserved in the 1810 manuscripts—a surprising error in a separate study devoted specifically to comparing the first and last versions of *Hänsel und Gretel*. Since Winter completely omits any mention of the *real* first version (she takes it to be the 1812 text), her entire study is virtually beside the point. She also mistakenly asserts that the source is Dortchen Wild; in fact, however, there is no note in the brothers' copy to that effect, while other stories are specifically attributed to her. In the absence of such a notation, it seems almost certain that Dortchen was *not* the source.

26. The very great limitations of previous attempts to compare the 1810 manuscripts with the *KHM* first edition, all guided by notions such as "stylization," are vividly shown in Freitag's commentary on this last sentence of the story *Vom Schreiner und Drechsler*. She comments only on the fact that the king's offer is given a separate sentence in the final version: "The king's decree is of great importance for the plot, and is therefore better made in the content of a separate sentence; the subordinate form 'that the father of the princess . . .' detracts from a clear overview, and with this the effect of what is told" (1929, p. 30). This point is trivial at best, and probably not valid at all in any case; I doubt very much that the subordinate form is a barrier to clear awareness of what is happening. But pursuit of it prevents the writer from seeing the very much more important point that the final version is compatible with the more cozy, safe world of the *KHM*, where the original was not. Most of Freitag's comparisons are similarly trivial; cf. for example, her comments (pp. 8–9) on the passage from *Dornröschen* which I discuss earlier in this chapter. What this shows is that once a scholar has allowed the prevalent notions "stylizing" and "stylistic unity" to dominate his thinking, he is in practice blind to the real and serious changes of content introduced by the Grimms into the *KHM*.

27. Another of the least elaborated texts is again an animal story, *Vom treuen Gevatter Sperling*.

28. The 1810 manuscripts even cast more doubt on the Grimms' veracity concerning the identity of their sources. In the first edition *KHM* the brothers had published a brief story (*Armes Mädchen—Poor Girl*) a version of which had already appeared in a novel by Jean Paul. The brothers said in their printed notes that they had set this story down "from a dim memory" and went on to say that Jean Paul too, had remembered it in his novel. But the 1810 manuscript,

which is the source of the 1812 *KHM* text, bears a notation acknowledging Jean Paul as the source, and the manuscript is nearly identical to his version—evidently it was simply copied from the novel and elaborated for the *KHM*. Once more, Rölleke (1975b, p. 353) states frankly that the source was Jean Paul, but is careful not to discuss the discrepancy behind his conclusion and the Grimms' printed claim.

CHAPTER FIVE

1. Winter concludes that it is the *final* version which shows the father in a bad light—in order to demonstrate that the evil stepmother has had a bad effect on him. This serious misreading is obviously in large part a consequence of her not seeing a *Hänsel und Gretel* text among the 1810 texts. But it is also related to the conventional fixation on stylistic development and stylizing as the processes to observe during the progress of the *KHM* through their various editions. For example, Winter takes the substitution of stepmother for mother as part of the search for what is genuinely fairy-tale-like ("Märchen-echt") not as a substantive change in the constellation of the family.

2. Bruno Bettelheim (1976, pp. 66–73), puts forward the theory that fairy tales split the mother into two separate persons (the good mother, the evil stepmother) to deal with the fact—a bewildering one to the child—that the angry mother looks a completely different person from the loving, protecting mother. An interesting theory, but of somewhat limited relevance to the fairy tales of the Grimms, where the malevolent side of mothers was often faced squarely until the Grimms—not the symbolic imagination of children—tried in a mechanical way to cover it up.

3. A fragment of yet another version of the tale included in the 1810 manuscript collection extends the role of the queen's husband even further; there it is *he* who wishes for the beautiful girl, and she appears from nowhere at the side of the couple's coach. This version makes the girl even more explicitly a sexual rival of the queen for the attention of her husband.

4. A striking exception to this general rule is the first tale of the *KHM*, *Der Froschkönig oder der eiserne Heinrich (The Frog-King, or Iron Henry)*. In this tale, a little girl meets a frog who turns into a handsome prince, whom she marries. So far, this might sound like a "beauty and the beast" story, but the little girl here behaves abominably towards the frog, and it is an act of violence (she throws him against the wall in a fit of rage) which turns him back into his real self, not any generosity toward him. How, then, does the little girl deserve her prince, or her tranquil future with him? The Grimms were perhaps more concerned with some kinds of moral questions than with others.

5. Hermand 1975, p. 63, is therefore incorrect in charging that, in the progress of the *KHM* from 1812 to 1857, "Grausames und Erotisches wird degegen mehr und mehr abgedämpft." This is perhaps true of the latter, but *not* of the former. Lüthi also misses this point in stressing, as Hermand does, the way in which the Grimms' revisions show their dependence on the taste of their time: "Romantische Wald- und Blumenpoesie, romantisch spielende Ironie verbinden sich mit der gemütvollen Innigkeit des biedermeierlichen Lebensgefühls" (p. 12). To see no more than this in the *KHM* is to miss a good deal.

6. It is true that some violent details of *KHM* tales not present in Perrault were already present in the 1810 manuscripts. For example, Dornröschen's prince

reaches her after many have already perished in the thicket of thorns which protect her, but *La Belle au bois dormant (Sleeping Beauty)* has no thorn thicket and no deaths in it—only dense trees. But this does not match the obtrusive cruelty of the ugly sisters' fate.

7. Panzer's (1953) introduction contains an excellent, though brief (pp. 44–47) account of some of the stylistic change typical of the progress from the first to seventh edition; he criticizes these changes in a forceful and effective manner. Schmidt (1931) considers the development of the *KHM* through the seven editions in far more detail than Panzer, but his account is nevertheless far less valuable; though covering the changes at length and in meticulous fashion, Schmidt lacks Panzer's ability to cut through a mass of detail to make abstractions and draw general conclusions.

8. For example, in the manuscript tale *Fündling (Foundling)*, a cook persecutes and tries to kill a child; but when the Grimms included this tale in the *KHM* as number 51, *Vom Fundevogel*, they made her a witch. In the *KHM, people* are not evil—only witches are.

9. Damann (1978) has recently attempted to provide a different explanation of the Grimms' dropping some of their first edition *KHM* tales. His suggested explanation lies in the fact that *KHM* stories have a characteristic plot structure different from those that were dropped. But when Damann tries to set out the actual plot difference that he is talking about, the result is not impressive. The typical structure of non-*KHM* plots is said (a) to involve two levels, one in which problems arise in everyday realistic terms, the other in which those problems are solved by supernatural means; and (b) to involve problems or mysteries which the plot proceeds to clear up. The typical structure of *KHM* plots is simply said to be exclusive of such features. Objections to this are too obvious and too many to be worth setting out fully here; for example, (i) these criteria do *not* exclude *KHM* stories, many of which involve *both* a setting recognizable as part of the real world *and* supernatural elements in the development and resolution of its problems; (ii) Damann's attempt to isolate one type of plot structure allegedly (though not actually) absent from the *KHM,* even if true, would say nothing positively about the type or types found in the *KHM;* (iii) his definitions are really too vague to test in any reasonably clear way. Damann's analysis is full of the technical jargon of structural analysis, but this is really a pseudoprecision superimposed on thought that was never initially clarified. But perhaps the most important defect in Damann's study is his assumption that the Grimms simply found and recorded *KHM* tales, which therefore can for him represent a preexisting type that guided the Grimms' actions in accepting into or rejecting from their collection particular tales—those tales being already fully formed in themselves. Had Damann known anything about the nature and sources of the 1810 material (his bibliography makes it clear that he has no familiarity with that material) and therefore about the Grimms' own considerable part in creating those texts, he could not have even begun to think in the way that he does in this study.

CHAPTER SIX

1. Michaelis-Jena 1970, pp. 265–66.
2. Hettner 1928, 4:242–43.
3. Thomson 1951, pp. 80–81.

4. Macpherson's contemporary, Hugh Blair, said as much and he even went on to say, "Nor did he himself seem to disavow it" (quoted by Thomson 1951, p. 83).

5. Thomson 1951, p. 84.

6. Ibid., p. 73.

7. Ibid., p. 74.

8. Cf. Sharp 1896.

9. Peppard 1971, p. 40. W. Emmerich, on the other hand, is highly critical of the Grimms' conservative political attitudes that underlie their romanticizing the German *Volk* and national past, but still ignores the question of the distortions that these attitudes introduced into the *KHM*. (Emmerich 1971, pp. 34–39).

10. Snyder 1951, p. 209.

11. Ibid., pp. 213–14.

12. Ibid., p. 214.

13. Ibid., p. 222.

14. Ibid., p. 219.

15. Ibid., p. 215.

16. Ibid., p. 220.

CONCLUSION

1. Riemen 1977, p. 192.

2. Schumann 1977, p. 138.

3. Rölleke 1980, 3:601.

4. Ibid., p. 602.

5. Dégh 1979, p. 85.

6. See chapter 5.

7. Winter (1962), writing about Wilhelm's continual rewriting of *Hänsel und Gretel,* comes curiously close to seeing what he was doing, and yet at the same time misunderstands it completely, when she says: "What one tale-teller had let slip from his memory another would still know. And so the fairy tale grew from one stage to another. Wilhelm Grimm was particularly concerned with perfecting both the core and the appearance of the fairy tale material, and for this reason attended to its composition again and again" (p. 808). Wilhelm was indeed interested in and continually concerned with perfecting the style of the *KHM*—but it is fanciful to suppose that in so doing he was simply restoring an original folk version by getting a detail here and a detail there from a stream of folk informants over his entire lifetime; the differences between the 1810 and 1812 versions alone show that Wilhelm's additions were his own.

8. Dégh 1979, p. 84.

9. Hamann 1906, p. 2. To be sure, Hamann's not knowing anything about the Grimms' sources prevented his reaching the radically skeptical conclusions about the status of the *KHM* which would later have been possible.

Works Cited

Anon. 1968. Preface to *Grimm's Fairy Tales*. An Airmont Classic. Toronto and Clinton, Mass.

Basile, Gianbattista. 1634–46. *Lo Cunto de li Cunti*. (Reprinted as *Il Pentamerone*). 5 vols. Naples.

Bettelheim, Bruno. 1976. *The Uses of Enchantment*. New York.

Bolte, Johannes. 1915. "Deutsche Märchen aus dem Nachlaß der Brüder Grimm." *Zeitschrift des Vereins für Volkskunde* 25:31–51.

Bolte, Johannes, and Georg Polivka. 1913–32. *Anmerkungen zu den Kinder- und Hausmärchen der Brüder Grimm*. Neu bearbeitet von Johannes Bolte und Georg Polivka. 5 vols. Leipzig.

Campbell, Joseph. 1944. "Folkloristic Commentary" to *The Complete Grimm's Fairy Tales*. Translated by Margaret Hunt; revised, corrected and completed by James Stern. New York.

Carsch, Henry. 1968. "The Role of the Devil in Grimms' Tales: An Exploration of the Content and Function of Popular Tales." *Social Research* 35:466–99.

Cocchiara, Giuseppe. 1981. *The History of Folklore in Europe*. Translated from the Italian by John N. McDaniel. Philadelphia.

Crane, T. F. 1917. "The External History of the *Kinder- und Hausmärchen* of the Brothers Grimm." This appeared in three parts: *Modern Philology* 14 (February): 577–610; 15 (June): 65–77; and 15 (October): 355–83.

Damann, Gunter. 1978. "Über Differenz des Handelns im Märchen." In *Erzählforschung. Theorien, Modellen und Methoden der Narrativik*, ed. Wolfgang Haubrichs. Göttingen. 3:71–106.

Dégh, Linda. 1979. "Grimm's Household Tales and Its Place in the Household: The Social Relevance of a Controversial Classic." *Western Folklore* 38:83–103.

Denecke, Ludwig. 1971. *Jacob Grimm und sein Bruder Wilhelm*. Stuttgart.

Emmerich, Wolfgang. 1968. *Germanistische Volkstumsideologie*. Tübingen.

———. 1971. *Zur Kritik der Volkstumsideologie*. Frankfurt.

Faivre, Antoine. 1978. *Les Contes de Grimm*. Paris. (*Circe*, vols. 10–11).

Freitag, Elisabeth. 1929. *Die Kinder- und Hausmärchen der Brüder Grimm im ersten Stadium ihrer stilgeschichtlichen Entwicklung*. Diss. Frankfurt.

Friderici, Robert. 1969. "Wer entdeckte die Märchenfrau?" *Hessische Blätter für Volkskunde* 60:166–67.

Gerstner, Hermann. 1970. *Die Brüder Grimm*. Gerabronn-Crailsheim.

Ginschel, Gunhild. 1963. "Der Märchenstil Jacob Grimms." *Deutsches Jahrbuch für Volkskunde* 11:131–68.

———. 1967. *Der junge Jacob Grimm, 1805–1819*. Berlin.

Grimm, Herman. 1895. "Die Brüder Grimm. Erinnerungen von Herman Grimm." *Deutsche Rundschau* 82:85–100.

Grimm, Jacob. 1864–84. *Kleinere Schriften*. 8 vols. Berlin.

Grimm, Jacob, and Wilhelm Grimm. 1812, 1815. *Kinder- und Hausmärchen, Gesammelt durch die Brüder Grimm*. 2 vols. Berlin. (Six subsequent editions: 1819, 1837, 1840, 1843, 1850 and 1857.) The second and third editions have a third volume: *Anmerkungen zu den einzelnen Märchen;* the dates of publication being 1822 and 1856 respectively.

Grimm, Wilhelm. 1881–87. *Kleinere Schriften*. 4 vols. Berlin.

Hagen, Rolf. 1954. *Der Einfluss der Perraultschen Contes auf die volkstümliche deutsche Erzählgut und besonders auf die Kinder- und Hausmärchen der Brüder Grimm*, Diss. Göttingen.

———. 1955. "Perraults Märchen und die Brüder Grimm." *Zeitschrift für deutsche Philologie* 74:392–410.

Hamann, Hermann. 1906. *Die literarischen Vorlagen der Kinder- und Hausmärchen und ihre Bearbeitung durch die Brüder Grimm*. Berlin.

Herder, Johann Gottfried. 1773. *Von Deutscher Art und Kunst. Einige fliegende Blätter.* Hamburg.

Hermand, Jost. 1975. "Biedermeier Kids: Eine Mini-Polemik." *Monatshefte* 67:59–66.

Hettner, Hermann. 1928. *Geschichte der deutschen Literatur im achtzehnten Jahrhundert.* Ed. Georg Witkowski. 4 vols. Leipzig.

Lefftz, Joseph, ed. 1927. *Märchen der Brüder Grimm. Urfassung nach der Originalhandschrift der Abtei Ölenberg im Elsaß.* Heidelberg.

Lemmer, Manfred, ed. 1964. *Grimms Märchen in ursprünglicher Gestalt. Nach der Oelenberger Handschrift von 1810.* Frankfurt.

Lüthi, Max. 1973. *Es war Einmal. Vom Wesen des Volksmärchens.* 4th ed. Göttingen. (Originally published 1962.)

Martini, Fritz. 1955. *Deutsche Literaturgeschichte.* 7th ed. Stuttgart.

McGlathery, James. 1977. Review of Heinz Rölleke, ed., *Die älteste Märchensammlung der Brüder Grimm.* In *Journal of English and Germanic Philology* 76:93–96.

Michaelis-Jena, Ruth. 1970. *The Brothers Grimm.* London.

———. 1971. "Oral Tradition and the Brothers Grimm." *Folklore* 82:265–75.

Musäus, Johann Karl August. 1782–87. *Volksmärchen der Deutschen.* 5 vols. Berlin.

Opie, Iona, and Peter Opie, eds. 1974. *The Classic Fairy Tales.* London.

Panzer, Friedrich. 1913a. "Die Kinder- und Hausmärchen der Brüder Grimm." *Zeitschrift für den deutschen Unterricht* 27:481–503.

———, ed. 1913b. *Die Kinder- und Hausmärchen der Brüder Grimm in ihrer Urgestalt.* 2 vols. Munich.

———, ed. 1953. *Die Kinder- und Hausmärchen der Brüder Grimm. Vollständige Ausgabe in der Urfassung.* Wiesbaden.

Peppard, Murray. 1971. *Paths Through the Forest: A Biography of the Brothers Grimm.* New York, Chicago, San Francisco.

Perrault, Charles. 1897. *Histoires ou Contes du temps passé avec des moralités.* Paris.

Reed, T. J. 1972. "The 'Goethezeit.'" In *Germany: A Companion to German Studies.* Edited by Malcolm Pasley. London.

Rieman, Alfred. 1977. Review of Heinz Rölleke, *Die älteste Märchensammlung der Brüder Grimm,* in *Aurora* 37:192–96.

Robertson, J. G. 1953. *A History of German Literature.* New and revised edition. Edinburgh and London.

Rölleke, Heinz. 1974a. "Die Marburger Märchenfrau." *Fabula* 15:87–94.

———. 1974b. "Die Urfassung der Grimmschen Märchensammlung von 1810. Eine Rekonstruktion ihres tatsächlichen Bestandes." *Euphorion* 68:331–36.

———. 1975a. "Die 'stockhessischen' Märchen der 'alten Marie.' " Das Ende eines Mythos um die frühesten KHM-Aufzeichnungen der Brüder Grimm." *Germanisch-Romanische Monatsschrift*, N.F. 25:74–86.

———. 1975b. *Die älteste Märchensammlung der Brüder Grimm. Synopse der handschriftlichen Urfassung von 1810 und der Erstdrucke von 1812*. Herausgegeben und erläutert von Heinz Rölleke. Collogny-Genève.

———, ed. 1977. *Märchen aus dem Nachlaß der Brüder Grimm*. Herausgegeben und erläutert von Heinz Rölleke. Bonn.

———. 1978. "Zur Vorgeschichte der Kinder- und Hausmärchen: Bislang unbekannte Materialien im Nachlaß der Brüder Grimm." *Euphorion* 72:102–5.

———. 1980. *Kinder- und Hausmärchen. Ausgabe letzter Hand mit den Originalanmerkungen der Brüder Grimm*. 3 vols. Stuttgart.

Schmidt, Kurt. 1931. *Die Entwicklung der Grimmschen Kinder- und Hausmärchen seit der Urhandschrift nebst einem kritischen Texte der in die Drucke übergegangenen Stücke*. Dissertation: Halle-Wittenberg.

Schoof, Wilhelm. 1930. "Zur Entstehungsgeschichte der Grimm'schen Märchen." *Hessische Blätter für Volkskunde* 29:1–118.

———. 1941. "Schneewittchen. Ein Beitrag zur deutschen Stilkunde." *Germanisch-Romanische Monatsschrift* 29:190–201.

———. 1953. "Neue Urfassungen Grimmscher Märchen." *Hessische Blätter für Volkskunde* 44:65–88.

———. 1954. "Neue Beiträge zur Entstehungsgeschichte der Grimmschen Märchen." *Zeitschrift für Volkskunde* 51:209–14.

———. 1959. *Zur Entstehungsgeschichte der Grimmschen Märchen*. Bearbeitet unter Benutzung des Nachlaßes der Brüder Grimm. Hamburg.

Schulz, Franz, ed. 1924. *Die Märchen der Brüder Grimm in der Urform nach der Handschrift*. Zweite Jahresgabe Der Frankfurter Bibliophilen-Gesellschaft. Frankfurt a.M.

Schumann, Thomas B. 1977. "Französische Quellen zu den Grimmschen Kinder- und Hausmärchen." *Philobiblon* 21:136–40.

Sharp, William, ed. 1896. *The Poems of Ossian.* Translated by James Macpherson. Edinburgh.

Snyder, Louis L. 1951. "Nationalistic Aspects of the Grimm Brothers' Fairy Tales." *Journal of Social Psychology* 33:209–23.

Textor, Georg. 1955. "Zum 200 Geburtstage der Zwehrener Märchenfrau Dorothea Viehmann, geb. Pierson, 8 November 1755–8 November 1955," in *Märchenfest in Kassel-Niederzwehren. Zur Erinnerung an den 200. Geburtstag der Zwehrener Märchenfrau Dorothea Viehmann. Vom. 4. bis 11. Juli 1955. Veranstaltet vom Schul und Heimatverein Dorothea Viehmann E.V. und der Dorothea Viehmann-Schule.* Kassel. Pp. 10–31.

———. 1965. "Die Märchenfrau von Niederzwehren," *Heimatbrief. Heimatverein Dorothea Viehmann Kassel-Niederzwehren* 9:4–19.

Thomson, Derick S. 1951. *The Gaelic Sources of Macpherson's Ossian.* Edinburgh and London.

Tonnelat, Ernest. 1912a. *Les Contes des Frères Grimm.* Paris.

———. 1912b. *Les Frères Grimm. Leur oeuvre de jeunesse.* Paris.

Weber-Kellermann, Ingeborg. 1970. "Interethnische Gedanken beim Lesen der Grimmschen Märchen." *Acta Ethnographica Academiae Scientarum Hungaricae* 19:425–34.

Winter, Elisabeth. 1962. "Ur- und Endfassung des Grimmschen Märchens 'Hänsel und Gretel.' " *Pädagogische Rundschau* 16:808–19.

Woeller, Waltraud. 1965. "Die Bedeutung der Brüder Grimm für die Märchen- und Sagenforschung." *Wissenschaftliche Zeitschrift der Humboldt-Universität zu Berlin,* 14:507–14.

Index of Names

Index of Tales

Titles given below are those of the particular manuscript or edition referred to in the text; for that reason, any particular entry may not give the full range of references to a given tale. In such cases, the text should be consulted for the variant titles of the tale.